DEC 16 '67

THE
SOCIAL & POLITICAL IDEAS OF SOME REPRESENTATIVE THINKERS OF THE REVOLU-TIONARY ERA

THE
SOCIAL & POLITICAL IDEAS
OF SOME REPRESENTATIVE
THINKERS OF THE REVOLU-
TIONARY ERA

A SERIES OF LECTURES DELIVERED AT KING'S COLLEGE UNIVERSITY OF LONDON DURING THE SESSION 1929-30

EDITED BY

F. J. C. HEARNSHAW M.A. LL.D.

FELLOW OF KING'S COLLEGE AND PROFESSOR OF MEDIÆVAL
HISTORY IN THE UNIVERSITY OF LONDON

BARNES & NOBLE, INC., NEW YORK

PUBLISHERS • BOOKSELLERS • SINCE 1873

First published 1931
by GEORGE G. HARRAP & CO. LTD.
Facsimile reprint 1967
BARNES & NOBLE, INC.
New York, N.Y., 10003

PRINTED IN GREAT BRITAIN
BY PHOTOLITHOGRAPHY
UNWIN BROTHERS LIMITED
WOKING AND LONDON

PREFACE

THE "Revolutionary Era" covered by this series of studies is broadly the sixty years of the reign of George III (1760–1820). This period, we may venture to say, saw greater changes in the European system than any other period of equal length, except that of the sixty years inaugurated by the Franco-Prussian War (1870–1930). Within its compass it included no fewer than three movements so subversive of old institutions and so creative of new ones that each of them has justifiably been termed a 'revolution.' First in order of time came the American Revolution, which shattered the first British Empire, brought Britain herself almost to the verge of destruction, and terminated for ever the dominance of the old colonial system of the administration of dependencies. Next gradually developed the less spectacular but even more transformative Industrial Revolution in England, a movement which slowly but inexorably converted Great Britain from a country primarily agricultural into a country primarily industrial; a movement, too, which by concentrating masses of artisans in factories and factory towns did much to hasten the triumph of democracy. Finally occurred the French Revolution, the most tremendous social and political upheaval between the dissolution of Christendom in the sixteenth-century Reformation and the overthrow of the three Kaiserdoms in the world-crisis of 1914–18.

The three revolutions that came about in the reign of George III were, of course, not unconnected with one another. It was, for example, widely recognised at the time, and it has been even more clearly evident to later generations, that the American colonists in resisting the claims of the Georgian Governments were fighting the battles of English freedom. The political agitations that accompanied the Industrial Revolution were to no small extent inspired by the same idea, and even organised by the same men, as became prominent in the

5

controversies that preluded the war of American Independence. In particular the doctrines of the "natural rights" of man and the sovereignty of the people, which dominated the crucial American Declaration of July 4, 1776, stirred the English radicals to challenge the claims of both the Hanoverian monarchy and the Whig oligarchy to exercise supreme authority over Great Britain. Again, the examples of English rebels and the pronouncements of English constitutionalists exercised a profound influence upon the thinkers who prepared the way for the French Revolution. But more immediately operative were the deeds and words of the American colonists. In three ways at least the disruption of the British Empire in 1783, for which the French Government was primarily responsible, directly hastened and precipitated the overthrow of the old *régime* in France. First, it trained a large number of Frenchmen—among whom the Marquis de la Fayette was the most eminent—in the principles and practice of republicanism; secondly, it flooded France with revolutionary literature, which—because it was evidently anti-British —the injudicious French Government allowed to circulate freely; thirdly, it—by reason of the enormous expense of the aid which France, in her hatred of Britain, rendered to the revolting American colonists—dragged the Bourbon monarchy over the edge of bankruptcy, and made the calling of the States-General inevitable.

The far-reaching changes which these three revolutions involved generated a prodigious number of social and political ideas. In particular the French Revolution of the eighteenth century vied with the Italian Renaissance of the fifteenth, the German Reformation of the sixteenth, and the English Rebellion of the seventeenth as a stimulant of profound and impassioned thought. So many powerful interests were affected, so many venerable institutions were overthrown or menaced, that men were compelled to reconsider problems long regarded as closed, and to defend claims looked upon for ages as firmly established. On the other hand, when politics, society, religion, everything, seemed to be tumbling into the melting-pot the opportunity appeared to present itself to ardent ideologues to make all things new. Hence books poured from the press propounding schemes of demolition and

PREFACE

reconstruction based on such revolutionary conceptions as primitive liberty, social equality, popular sovereignty, and the supremacy over all human enactments of a natural law which each man could interpret according to his inclination. True it may be, as has been asserted, that very few of the ideas enunciated in these Jacobinical works were wholly new. There are, indeed, in the realm of social and political theory remarkably few principles, albeit enunciated in modern times as startling novelties, which were not anticipated in the writings of ancient or mediæval thinkers. Nevertheless, even if the Jacobins borrowed from Rousseau, Rousseau from Locke, Locke from Hooker, Hooker from Aquinas, Aquinas from Augustine and Aristotle, and so on back to the speculations introduced into the Garden of Eden by the devil, yet, all the same, the applications of old ideas to new circumstances in this revolutionary era produced programmes of reformation and proposals for re-edification of the utmost interest and importance.

The majority of the thinkers treated in this volume would be classed among progressives: Paine was a republican, Godwin an anarchist of the amiable type; Bentham a utilitarian reformer, Babeuf a communist. Burke alone stands out as a conservative, a defender of existing institutions, a maintainer of the cause of piety and tradition, a champion of "the old perfections of the earth." This apparent disproportion is a proper one. For, just as the things that do not exist are far more numerous than the things that do, so plans for the constitution of Utopias are far more frequent than reasoned vindications of things as they are. It is incomparably easier to expose the evils of the existing social order than it is to make evident to the insatiable mind of man the benefits that accrue to him under it. Moreover, not only have founders of imaginary commonwealths a simpler task than defenders of actually established states ; they are far less liable to destructive criticism. For they merely depict the visionary felicities that will be enjoyed *if* such and such conditions prevail in the future. They are as secure from attack as are the garrisons of castles in the air. The champions of things as they are, on the other hand, have the difficult task of appealing to ambiguous and disputable fact. They have to seek their weapons

7

in the sealed armouries of history, to gather heavy masses of protective statistics, to dig in the rock of reason rather than to fly on the wings of fancy.

Finally, revolutionary and utopian writings are, as a rule, far more interesting than writings of a conservative type. They have much of the fascination of fiction. It is natural and proper that the unknown and untried should have more charm for the spirit of man than the familiar and the explored. For dissatisfaction is the great incentive to progress, and from those (if such there be) who are wholly content with the present there can be no hope of future advance. Hence it is good, as well as natural, that revolutionaries should be more vocal and instrumental than conservatives. The conservative elements in the world are immense in their numbers and massive in their immobility. It is commonly sufficient for practical purposes if conservatives, without saying anything, just sit and think, or even if they merely sit. Certainly it is quite enough if, in a generation, they produce one supreme spokesman such as Burke.

F. J. C. HEARNSHAW

KING'S COLLEGE
UNIVERSITY OF LONDON
December 1930

CONTENTS

THE SOCIAL AND POLITICAL IDEAS OF SOME REPRESENTATIVE THINKERS OF THE REVOLUTIONARY ERA

I

THE THEORISTS OF THE AMERICAN REVOLUTION

IT was the habit of Elizabethan days, according to Sir Walter Raleigh, to begin even a nautical diary with "a few remarks on the origin of the world, the history of man, and the opinions of Plato." And the writer upon the theorists of the American Revolution should profit by this example; for there were few if any subjects of contention in the American Revolution which had not been debated, contested, and left unsettled in the days of the great Greek philosophers, if not long before their day. For instance, the Americans derived their independence in no small measure from the momentary freedom of the seas obtained by the first Armed Neutrality. But this was no new question. Had not Demosthenes charged Alexander the Great with violation of a treaty which guaranteed freedom of the seas? "One article," he said, "is thus expressed: 'The uniting parties shall all have the full liberty of the seas. None shall molest them or seize their vessels on pain of being regarded as the common enemy.'" [1]

Again, Americans sometimes think of the theory of natural right as borrowed by Thomas Jefferson from John Locke; and so, in a sense, it was. But it was a very ancient doctrine when Locke applied it to modern political problems. Indeed, Aristotle in his *Ethics* had advanced the theory with astonishing definiteness. "Political justice," he says, "is partly natural and partly conventional. The part which is natural is that which has the same authority everywhere, and is independent

---

[1] Demosthenes' *Orations*, Thomas Leland's translation (1829 edition), p. 109.

of opinion."[1] And in his *Rhetoric* he had advised advocates that if they have no case according to the law of the land they should appeal to the law of nature and argue that an unjust law is not a law,[2] advice which the American colonists followed with astonishing definiteness during the Revolutionary period.

Professor McLaughlin, in his excellent volume entitled *Steps in the Development of American Democracy*, declares of the philosophy of the Revolution : "The thing most nearly new . . . was that a law contrary to natural law . . . was not a law at all." The phrase "most nearly new" is well chosen, as the idea was not a novelty even from the point of view of British constitutional interpretation, since Coke had declared in the days of the first Stuart :

> The Common Law will controul acts of Parliament, and sometimes adjudge them to be utterly void : for when an act of Parliament is against common right and reason, or repugnant, or impossible to be performed, the Common Law will controul it and adjudge such act to be void.

Furthermore, the much discussed opening idea of the Virginia Bill of Rights, "That all men are by nature equally free," was stated centuries before by Ulpian in the words : "By the law of nature all men are born free";[3] while the famous phrase of the Massachusetts Constitution of 1780, " a government of laws, and not of men," was almost identical with that of Harrington, who in *Oceana* speaks of "the Empire of lawes and not of men."[4] Harrington owed the phrase to Aristotle and Livy; and its first freshness was therefore gone when John Marshall employed it in his powerful opinion Marbury *v.* Madison.

It is easy to fall into the error of thinking of American institutions as new because the American nation is new. But as a matter of fact the history of American political ideas, like that of English, is to be measured not in years, but in centuries.

---

[1] *The Nicomachean Ethics*, J. E. C. Welldon's translation, p. 159 (London, 1892).

[2] *The "Rhetoric" of Aristotle*, J. E. C. Welldon's translation, p. 101 (London, 1886).

[3] " Cum jure naturali omnes liberi nascerentur." *Cf.* Sir R. W. and A. J. Carlyle's *Mediæval Political Theory in the West*, i, 39.

[4] James Harrington, *The Common-wealth of Oceana*, p. 2 (London, D. Pakeman, 1658).

It is also true that whatever philosophical inheritance England had toward the middle of the eighteenth century belonged to the American colonists by the same right. It came to them from the fact that they too were Englishmen.

So much for the inevitable "few remarks on the origin of the world, the history of man, and the opinions of Plato." We are now ready to discuss our special topic, the theorists of the American Revolution.

It is said that a certain German scientist engaged to write a book on *Snakes in Ireland* opened his volume with the words, "Strictly speaking, there are no snakes in Ireland." And one may as properly begin a discussion of the theorists of the American Revolution with the words, "Strictly speaking, there were no theorists of the American Revolution." The philosophy employed by the leaders of the Revolutionary movement was not the product of the Revolutionary era. In so far as it was distinctly American it dates rather from early colonial days. Long before the beginning of the war of pens, which preceded the war of muskets, the American colonists, beginning with the Virginia Assembly of 1619, had developed and wrought into institutions their hereditary views upon such questions as the meaning of representation, the location of the taxing power, the relation of Church and State, the freedom of the Press, the freedom of the seas, and the relation of the executive to the legislative and judicial branches of government. Even the difficult question of the relation of local to central government had been faced by each colony separately, and it offered few new problems when presented by the Revolution to all of them at once. Thus Édouard Laboulaye was true to the facts when he wrote: "Before Locke had written the *Civil Government* and Rousseau the *Social Contract* the emigrants of Plymouth had founded a real republic under that rude climate, where Liberty alone was able to live." [1]

In seeking to trace the origin of America's Revolutionary philosophy, therefore, we must deal less with individuals than with forces, and of these forces nature, in the form of a new continent, was chief. Nature unadorned taught the pioneer to love personal liberty and to resent any sophisticated system

[1] *Histoire des États-Unis*, i, 35–36.

which social evolution had developed to fetter him. There are no orthodox methods of doing things on the frontier. If there is not a screw-driver at hand, the pioneer uses the blade of his hunting-knife. And the fact influences the thinking. The frontiersman sees no value in legal subtleties, which grow up so easily in urban communities. He is by nature a pragmatist, looking always at results. To him you look in vain for that consistency of method, that submission to logic, that adherence to precedent, which make up so large a part of the mental equipment of dwellers in settled communities. His attitude toward mere precedent is scornfully expressed by James Otis in the words: "Though all the Princes since Nimrod had been tyrants, that would not have established the right of tyranny."

Furthermore, from the first the English colonists in America had enjoyed an astonishing degree of freedom. This they adapted to their new surroundings; and they recast their inherited philosophy to suit their revised political institutions.

Moreover, the life of the settlements, especially in New England, tended to make political philosophers of the more intelligent. The colonists met frequently in village assembly or town meeting to deliberate upon public questions and to give instructions to their representatives. "It was in these assemblies of towns and districts," wrote John Adams in 1782, "that the sentiments of the people were formed."[1] The sentiments of the people inevitably became the philosophy of the Revolution, and John Adams was at least gazing in the direction of truth when he wrote, during his later controversy with Abbé Mably:

> The theory of government is as well understood in America as it is in Europe; and by great numbers of individuals is everything relating to a free constitution infinitely better comprehended than by the Abbé de Mably or M. Turgot.[2]

In the field of religion also the American colonists had allowed their new surroundings to modify their inheritance, and had developed ecclesiastical institutions quite distinctive in character and irresistibly democratic in political influence. Although it required generations for Roger Williams' liberal-

[1] Works of John Adams, 1863 edition, v, 495.   [2] Ibid., v, 491.

ism to blossom under the hands of Henry, Jefferson, Mason, and Madison into the separation of Church and State, the idea of sovereignty of the faithful early gave rise to the political conception of sovereignty of the people, and to the conception of an area of rights reserved to the individual and beyond the control of any Government. And this was in Revolutionary days, and still remains, the basic theory of all American constitutional law.

In this manner inheritance, nature, and the new theology combined to put behind all American colonial institutions a philosophy which could accept nothing less than political autonomy. Grotius says that under Rome the power which a nation exercised over its colony was *imperium*, or empire; while the Greeks described the same relationship as ἡγεμονία, hegemony, or leadership in judgment. The American colonies took the Greek view to describe the relationship of the American colonists to the Mother Country.

Thus it came about that the task of the American leaders of Revolutionary days was not the creation or elaboration of a set of theories, but rather the application of an existing American philosophy to the special emergencies called forth by the Writs of Assistance, the announcement of the Stamp Act, the Townshend Acts, and the Penal Laws. They felt called upon to furnish few new ideas, and their interpretations come much nearer to what we now call propaganda than to political theory. The need of the hour was not a new philosophy, but the bringing together of thirteen distinct, locally minded, mutually jealous communities, that each might secure not some new right, some reasoned liberty, but safety for rights long enjoyed and seldom disputed. In brief, they fought not to make but to defend a democracy already established and dearer even than their hereditary allegiance.

It is doubtful whether the word 'revolution' properly applies to so conservative a movement. Revolution involves the idea of basic alterations. The Revolution of 1688, for example, altered the whole theory of sovereignty in England. Before it sovereignty lodged with the Crown: but after it sovereignty lodged, in theory at least, in the House of Commons. It required a Locke to put the necessary philosophical theory behind so fundamental a change. Rousseau

15

and Karl Marx prepared their systems of philosophy with reference to basic changes as startling. But the American Revolution emerged and passed without the need of such a fundamental philosophy to explain or to defend it.

When the hour for abandonment or defence arrived every colony might have said to King George III what Massachusetts had said to King Charles II :

> For over a generation, with royal consent or by virtue of royal neglect, this colony has enjoyed the privileges of government as its undoubted right in the sight of God and man. . . . To be governed by rulers of our own choosing and lawes of our own, is the fundamental privilege of our patent.

Governor Hutchinson of Massachusetts described all colonies when he wrote shortly before the Revolution :

> It would not be easy to imagine a subordinate government less controlled by the supreme government than are the governments of the colonies. . . . Not only do penal laws, the method of administering justice, and the law of inheritance differ from the English Constitution, . . . but they have been allowed to establish a culture, a discipline, a Church, which one would scarcely tolerate in England.[1]

It was natural for such colonists, the freest in the world, to think of themselves with pride as Englishmen overseas, and to maintain a love for the English Constitution as they interpreted it. John Adams spoke for them as for himself when he declared it

> a settled opinion that the liberty, the unalienable, and indefeasible rights of men, the honor and dignity of human nature, the grandeur and glory of the public, and the universal happiness of individuals, were never so skilfully and successfully consulted as in that most excellent monument of human art, the Common Law of England.[2]

They were not conscious of the changes in England which had slowly taken the supremacy from both the common law and the British Parliament and placed them in the hands of an oligarchy which controlled Parliament by means of pocket-boroughs. But as the plans of King George III began to unfold the colonists found it increasingly necessary to rely less upon the English common law and their rights as

---

[1] É. Laboulaye, *Histoire des États-Unis*, ii, 14.
[2] Works of John Adams, 1863 edition, iii, 440.

Englishmen, since it was evident that neither the one nor the other would, under existing conditions, enable them to keep unimpaired their cherished institutions. And it is therefore not strange to find the colonists, when the crisis came, handling theory uncertainly and shifting their bases from time to time as the contest thickened.

Their first defensive position was taken in connection with the Writs of Assistance, in 1761. James Otis was the expounder of the American contention. He repudiated the statute of Charles II and that of William III which had given to Revenue officers in America the right to use general search-warrants. And, as Bancroft properly observes, that was equivalent to a declaration that "the Parliament of Great Britain was not the sovereign legislature." Otis summed up in striking language the accumulated philosophy upon which that contention was based; but there was little of novelty or original theory in his words. Three points stand out clearly:

(i) That there is a natural right, sacred beyond the power of any Government.

(ii) That what is vaguely called the British Constitution limits Parliament with respect to natural right.

(iii) That an act of Parliament contrary to the Constitution is null and void.

It is doubtless true, as John Adams wrote many years later, that at that hour independence was born. But it is also true, even in view of Otis's later pamphlet, *The Rights of the English Colonies*, a philosophical dissertation upon the principles of government, that Otis was not a political theorist. He was what he had been trained to be, a skilful and resourceful advocate seeking to make a case for a client whom he loved and trusted, not a philosopher consistently setting forth abstract truth.

The next spectacular interpreter of the American position was Patrick Henry, of Virginia, who denounced the Stamp Act in a set of resolutions which declare that the colonists had "brought with them, and transmitted to their posterity ... all the liberties, privileges, franchises, and immunities that have at any time been held, enjoyed and possessed, by the people of Great Britain," among which he listed self-taxation.

Every attempt, he declared, to vest the taxing power over Virginia in any body but the General Assembly of that colony "has a manifest tendency to destroy British as well as American freedom." It was easy to ridicule this claim, and to make specious arguments to show how absurdly much it proved. William Knox, in his famous pamphlet *The Controversy between Great Britain and her Colonies Reviewed*, pays mocking attention to this argument when he asks how the colonies could take to Virginia in 1607

> the Habeas Corpus Act which the people of England did not enjoy or possess till the reign of Charles II; or the Bill of Rights, which they did not enjoy till the reign of William and Mary.

Otis's argument from natural right is dismissed by Knox with the words:

> The native Indians in North America, the Hottentots at the Cape of Good Hope, the Tartars, Arabs, Kafirs and Groenlanders, will all have an equal title to the liberties and rights of Englishmen with the people of Pennsylvania, for all their constitutions of government are founded on the natural right of mankind.

As we read this deduction in connection with the eighteenth century it sounds fantastic; but as we see it in practice at Geneva to-day it seems practical politics.

While conceding to Patrick Henry high rank as an advocate and a propagandist, history does not claim for him, either, the distinction of being a political theorist. The philosophy which he advanced as to the nature of the British Constitution was not strong enough to overcome such official interpretation of its actual meaning as that of Lord Mansfield, who declared, during the Stamp Act controversy, that the Parliament of Great Britain represented the whole British Empire, and had full authority to bind every subject of the Crown, whether enfranchised or not. But in the face of even that authority upon the actual meaning of the British Constitution the colonists continued to adhere to their own views of its nature, and insisted that they were its real defenders. And in this view they had the openly expressed sympathy of great reform leaders like the elder Pitt, and of great non-reform leaders such as Burke.

THEORISTS OF THE AMERICAN REVOLUTION

In the American arguments, from first to last, there appears the same kind of inconsistency as that already pointed out. Sometimes the colonists argued that submission to external taxation was a duty, but that to accept internal taxation by Parliament would be to accept slavery. Sometimes they argued that the theory of virtual representation, which satisfied, or at least was accepted by, England's great unenfranchised cities, was but a mockery of representative theory; and William Pitt made his greatest speech upon that theme, but in closing it he showed himself true to the theory of absolute sovereignty in Parliament.

Thus, on varied lines, as the exigencies of the rising contest seemed to demand, did America's advocates on both sides of the ocean present, not a systematic philosophy, but a skilful defence of America's right to make her own laws. This position demanded the theory of a British Empire which would maintain its unity without subjection of outlying parts to the English Parliament. This was furnished in lavish detail; and when furnished it was but the philosophy of the present British commonwealth of nations. For example, Alexander Hamilton argues in *The Farmer Refuted*:

> We may deny [reject] his Majesty, in his political capacity, as a part of the legislature of Great Britain, and yet acknowledge him in a similar political capacity as a part of the legislature of New York. ... The Colony of New York therefore may be a branch of the British Empire, though not subordinate to the legislative authority of Britain. ... I deny that we are dependent on the legislature of Great Britain; and yet I maintain that we are a part of the British Empire—but in this sense only, as being the free-born subjects of his Britannic Majesty.[1]

And in another section of the same pamphlet he wrote: "When we say French Dominions, we mean countries subject to the King of France. In like manner, when we say British Dominions the most proper signification is, countries subject to the King of Great Britain." And in a note of explanation he adds this significant suggestion: "And, for the future, we may ... call the colonies his Majesty's American Dominions."

[1] Works of Alexander Hamilton, 1885 edition, i, 82.

Had the concessions then been made to the American colonies which were later so wisely made to Canada and the other Dominions, concessions of entire self-government, America might be to-day "his Majesty's American Dominion."

Secession has been defined as withdrawal from Church, federation, or similar body. When the thirteen American colonies seceded from the British Empire they had to make good their withdrawal by the harsh methods of the sword and foreign alliance. They forcibly seceded; but in as real a sense each of the present British Dominions seceded from the British Empire upon obtaining dominion status, although they required no force to make good their right to govern themselves. In withdrawing from the British Empire they became members of the British commonwealth of nations. Had it been possible in 1776 for England to say to any colony capable of self-government, "You are entitled to retire from the British Empire, and become a self-governing member of the British commonwealth of nations," there need not have been bitterness or bloodshed. But England, the first of modern States to perceive the wisdom of such a course, had not yet made the great discovery by which, as Laboulaye wrote in 1876, British colonies become "members of a confederation capable of expansion to infinity."

Perhaps the demands most nearly common to all types of American Revolutionary leaders are these:

(i) The right to government by their own chosen representatives.

(ii) The right to consider loyalty to the king the only bond between them and other parts of the Empire.

They did not secede in order to escape from an oppression too hard to be endured, for such did not exist. They did not secede on account of love of democracy, for there was little of such love apparent at that early day. They did not secede in order to found a nation, for the love of America as distinct from the love of the individual colony was long in arriving. They seceded because they were refused the right to be autonomous communities within the British Empire. "A handful of immigrants may accept the protection of the Empire," wrote Laboulaye in 1876.[1] But

> a group of three millions of men will not submit to a distant Government which exploits them, to an administration which disturbs their interests and their liberties! That is what England, taught by experience, understands to-day. She governs India, a nation enervated by her religion and her climate, and governs it by force. But Canada, the Cape, and Australia, though they be also a world, govern themselves; their union with the Mother Country is an advantage to both parties—and there is neither inferiority nor subjugation.

That was the considered judgment of an eminent French scholar intent upon teaching the next generation of Frenchmen how to succeed in colonial enterprise. And he added: " It is also the glory of England that she alone has realised that justice is a bond more powerful than force."

If you compare the Imperial Conference report of 1926 with the basic documents of the American Revolution, such as the resolutions of the Stamp Act Congress, you will see that what the British colonies of the eighteenth century contended for in battle has become the basic philosophy of the British commonwealth of nations. " The stone which the builders rejected, the same is become the head of the corner." The Imperial Conference report says:

> They [the Dominions] are autonomous communities within the British Empire, equal in status, in no way subordinate one to another in any aspect of their domestic and external affairs, though united by a common allegiance to the Crown.

In describing how an empire has in part changed into a commonwealth of free states the report says:

> The tendency toward equality of status was both right and inevitable. Geographical and other conditions made this impossible of attainment by way of federation. The only alternative was by way of autonomy, and along this road it has been steadily sought.
>
> Every self-governing member of the Empire is now master of its own destiny. In fact, if not always in form, it is subject to no compulsion whatever. . . . Every Dominion is now and must always remain the sole judge of the nature and extent of its co-operation.

Such a spirit if universally applied will solve most of the ills of colonial government. Colonies do not exist for the

---

[1] *Histoire des États-Unis*, ii, 2.

benefit of mother countries. They are the training-grounds for free nations; and in that conception every colony, however backward, may find hope and incentive to progress.

When Thomas Jefferson and his committee wrote the Declaration of Independence, designed to present the reasons for the American Revolution, they avoided the earlier and oft-repeated arguments from charters, and from British inheritance, concentrating upon reasons for repudiating the King. They leaped back to Aristotle and appealed to "the law of nature," arguing that "an unjust law is not a law." Jefferson himself tells us that for almost two years before the Declaration of Independence was drafted Congress debated the principles of the law of nature and of nations, and that the opening paragraph of the Declaration stated the conclusion which had been reached with virtual unanimity:

> We hold these three truths to be self-evident, that all men are created equal, that they are endowed by their Creator with certain unalienable rights . . . that to secure these rights, governments are instituted among men, deriving their just powers from the consent of the governed.

There was no more novelty in these doctrines than there had been 284 years before in Columbus's theory that the earth was a sphere. Aristotle had declared that as clearly as did Columbus, and Aristotle had proclaimed the theory of natural right as clearly as did Jefferson's Declaration of Independence. But Aristotle had not risen to the height of conceiving all men as "created equal"; that came into America's Revolutionary philosophy through Luther and Calvin, each of whom must therefore be placed among the so-called philosophers of the American Revolution, though each wrought out his philosophy generations before.

But the value of historical studies lies not in the knowledge of the past which it gives. It lies rather in the insight which it furnishes into the things of the future. Human thought has followed throughout the ages an ever-widening course. Things parochial have tended to become things national; and to-day things national are growing, or seem to be growing, into things international.

As there is a law in England, called the common law, which takes precedence of all other, as there is a law in America, called the natural law, which takes the same precedence, so there is in the world the fundamental law, which is above statute or constitution, which the religious mind calls the law of God, the philosophical mind calls the law of nature, and the judicial mind calls the law of human society. It is not a law; it is the law, supreme over all other law, and defending the individual against all human society. It defends, and for all mankind, the rights which every human being possesses, which follow him like his faithful shadow whithersoever he goeth. The nation which overrides them is the enemy not of one nation, but of all nations.

> Not of to-day nor yesterday
> Is this a law, but ever hath it life,
> And no man knoweth whence it came, or how.[1]

ROBERT McELROY

BOOK LIST

BECKER, CARL: *The Declaration of Independence: a Study in the History of Political Ideas.* New York, 1922.

CORWIN, EDWARD S.: *The "Higher Law" Background of American Constitutional Law.* Printed in *The Harvard Law Review*, vol. xlii, Nos. 2 and 3.

DUNNING, WILLIAM ARCHIBALD: *A History of Political Theories from Rousseau to Spencer* (especially chapter iii). New York, 1926.

FREEMAN, EDWARD AUGUSTUS: *History of Federal Government from the Foundation of the Achaian League to the Disruption of the United States,* vol. i. London, 1863.

FRIEDENWALD, HERBERT: *The Declaration of Independence: an Interpretation and an Analysis.* New York, 1904.

JAMESON, J. FRANKLIN (editor): *Essays in the Constitutional History of the United States.* New York, 1889.

LOCKE, JOHN: *Second Treatise on Civil Government.* Everyman's Library, 1924.

McILWAIN, CHARLES HOWARD: *The American Revolution: a Constitutional Interpretation.* New York, 1923.

McLAUGHLIN, ANDREW CUNNINGHAM: *Steps in the Development of American Democracy.* New York, 1920.

MERRIAM, CHARLES EDWARD: *A History of American Political Theories.* New York, 1928.

OSGOOD, HERBERT L.: *The Political Ideas of the Puritans* (*Political Science Quarterly*, vol. vi (1891)).

SCHLESINGER, ARTHUR MEIER: *New View-points in American History.* New York, 1922.

---

[1] *The "Rhetoric" of Aristotle*, J. E. C. Welldon's translation, p. 93 (London, 1886).

23

II

THE EARLY ENGLISH RADICALS

IN Maitland's playful use of a legal phrase this lecture is "a fraud on the title." For the Parliamentary reformers of the eighteenth century never, so far as is known, called themselves Radicals. To them and to their contemporaries 'radical' was an adjective. They applied it to the restoration of the body politic, much as the surgeon still speaks of the treatment of the human frame by a radical operation. The word graduated as a substantive mainly by way of insult or reproach. With the nineteenth century it crept slowly into currency, and was at first used, rather vaguely perhaps, of anybody whose politics the user chanced to dislike. As late as 1819 Sir Walter Scott is found explaining that it was "in very bad odour . . . being used to denote a set of blackguards." [1] Still vague, but more polite and a shade more precise, was the description given to the House of Commons in 1817 by J. W. Ward.[2] He defined the Radicals as being "not only those that are for annual Parliaments and universal suffrage, but that class that desire to alter the constitution upon some general, sweeping plan," in contradistinction to moderate reformers, "content with partial alterations applicable to . . . particular grievances." [3]

Ward still spoke of "Radical reformers," and shrank from the substantive radical. For the word only established itself firmly as a noun between Peterloo and the Great Reform Bill, possibly while the Radicals themselves were adopting the

---

[1] To T. Scott, October 16, 1819, Lockhart's *Scott* (Edinburgh ed., 1902), vi, 128. They become "Radical reformers" again in Scott's next sentence. See quotations given in the *New English Dictionary*.

[2] John William Ward (1781–1833), fourth Viscount Dudley and Ward (*s*. 1823) and first Earl of Dudley (*cr*. 1827); Foreign Secretary in Canning's Ministry of 1827. Best known for his *Letters* to Copleston and for his pleasant *Letters to Ivy*, ed. S. H. Romilly, 1905.

[3] Hansard, xxxvi, 761.

white hat of Orator Hunt as their ensign armorial. It is therefore frankly unhistorical to speak of Radicals in the eighteenth century. But the flaw in the title is one of terminology, not of substance. Radicals were active fifty years before the public learned how to name them, and in the eighteenth century the fathers of Radicalism taught the doctrines which were to furnish almost the whole political programme of later Radicals. Anticipation of their name is, therefore, harmless so long as it is understood. If it be misleading at all, it is so only in form, not in fact, for the licence has some warrant in custom and usage.[1] And even Ward's description of Radical doctrine will serve our turn. For some vagueness is essential, and even if the Radicals of the eighteenth century would not all have accepted his definition, it nevertheless represents the creed toward which many were moving and that some ultimately held.

No traffic commissioner fixes the routes of political ideas. And it is to William Pitt, Earl of Chatham, himself no Radical, and in the stuff of his political thinking perhaps even reactionary, that we must trace some of the creative force of early Radicalism. His most vitalising influence was, indeed, indirect. The dramatic force of his statesmanship and the glamour with which he so well knew how to envelop himself kindled political interest and imagination. It may be paradox to claim that eighteenth-century Radicalism sprang from the *annus mirabilis* of 1759, but no student of contemporary journalism would deny that the paradox contains more than a grain of truth. Pitt warmed the public mind to a temperature in which a movement for reform could begin.

More clearly the beginnings of Radicalism owed something to Pitt's assaults upon the Whig monopolists. In his fight against men solidly entrenched in the boroughs, where his own influence was scant, Pitt was forced to rely upon national

---

[1] It is a convenient, if inaccurate, custom to refer to the more advanced Parliamentary reformers of the period as Radicals. The late C. B. R. Kent entitled his book *The English Radicals*. In *The Age of Grey and Peel* (1929) the late Professor H. W. Carless Davis was more careful, though chapter iii, in which he deals with this topic, is entitled " Radicalism and Reform." The subject is slightly covered in the first chapter of *The French Revolution in English History*, by the late P. A. Brown (1918). See also Veitch, *Genesis of Parliamentary Reform* (1913), chapters ii–iv.

sentiment; to enlarge, as it were, the political public. "You have taught me," George II told him, in words that ring less like the monarch's than the Minister's, "to look for the sense of my people in other places than the House of Commons."

Pitt created opportunities, but he did not use them. His constructive powers fell far short of that immense executive ability which he revealed in his more glorious moments. Directly he contributed nothing new to the materials out of which Radicalism was moulded. He gave a fresh twist to old ideas, or put a new face on ancient devices. He toyed with notions of shorter Parliaments and of strengthened representation for counties or great towns : notions only taken up to be dropped at a hint of discouragement. But these were no more than clumsy weapons from the lumber-rooms of Tory country gentlemen, hastily burnished for war against the Court and policy of George III. Both, it is true, count for something in the theory of Radicalism. It may have been important that Chatham gave these ideas a new currency and a momentary respectability, free from the taint of earlier faction. But he placed them in no Radical setting. There could be no real affinity between later Radicals and a statesman who thought that representation was not " of person but of property " and that " in this light there is scarcely a blade of grass which is not represented." [1]

Chatham was to Radicalism a source of energy, therefore, rather than a fount of ideas. He created a public for it to work upon, but made no original contribution to its creed. Triennial Parliaments and county representation were already in the political museum, ready to be taken down and dusted by the first comer. Yet some of Chatham's followers were more vigorous than their master, the most persistent, as he was the most nearly Radical, being John Sawbridge, one of the personal links between Chatham and the City. According to a doubtful authority, Chatham and Sawbridge were old

---

[1] Reported March 13, 1766, in *Original Letters principally from Lord Charlemont . . . to Henry Flood*, ed. T. Rodd (1820), pp. 14–15. Chatham's views can be traced in *Chat. Corr.*, iii, 406–407 *nn.*, 457 *n.*, 464 *n.*, iv, 146, 148–149, 155 *n.*, 156–157, 174 *n.* ; *Grenville Papers*, iv, 534, 535 *n.* ; Junius, *Letters* (ed. 1902–3), i, 384 *n.*, 391–392, ii, 77–79 ; *Parl. Hist.*, xvi, 952–954, 966, 978–979, xvii, 219, 223 *n.* ; Thackeray, *Chatham*, ii, 162–163, 244 and *n.*; Fitzmaurice, *Shelburne*, ii, 224. Professor Basil Williams treats the subject briefly in *Pitt* (1913), ii, 266–268.

schoolfellows, and Chatham helped Sawbridge in 1768 to secure his election for Hythe. "Their mutual friendship," says the quaint *City Biography*, "reflected honour on each other." "The Peer aided by his influence one who wanted his patronage," and the commoner "repaid it by proper, but independent, exertions of gratitude and genius." [1]

Gratitude there may have been; genius must be taken in a biographical sense. But Sawbridge was a man of ability and resolution, and his family was not without note. His sister, once more famous than her brother, was Mrs Catherine Macaulay, the "republican historian," and 'quizz' of Dr Johnson. They came of a Kentish family, but had ties with the City through their maternal grandfather, George Wanley, the banker. These ties Sawbridge strengthened, as he enlarged his social and political connections and augmented his fortune, by lucky marriages; first with a daughter of Sir Orlando Bridgeman, who was therefore niece of the first Lord Bradford, and second with a daughter of Sir William Stephenson, Lord Mayor in 1764. The first is reputed to have brought to Sawbridge a fortune of £100,000, and we may perhaps suppose that the second was not portionless.

While still in the thirties Sawbridge had become a pillar of the City. Between 1769 and 1775 he was successively chosen Alderman, Sheriff, Master of the Framework Knitters, and Lord Mayor. Except for a few weeks in 1780, he represented the City in the House of Commons from 1774 to his death in 1795. Amid the storm and tumult of City politics he was ever a sturdy fighter, a Wilkite when Wilkes was in need, independent when the fortunes of Wilkes had risen, frequently in political hot water, and usually enjoying the heat. [2]

In 1771, just before Chatham raised the same subject in the Lords, Sawbridge moved in the Commons for leave to bring in a "Bill for shortening the Duration of Parliaments." Year after year, down to 1779, when shorter Parliaments

---

[1] *City Biography* (1800), p. 89.

[2] Dates of Sawbridge's career are best taken from A. B. Beaven, *Aldermen of the City*, vol. i, pp. 171, 308, 325–326, vol. ii, pp. xxvi, lviii, 134 and important note, 200, 281. The *Dictionary of National Biography*, following *City Biography*, pp. 88–89, has mistakes of chronology; Sawbridge's shrievalty being antedated by a year, the erroneous conclusion is reached that he was the sheriff who made the returns of Wilkes for Middlesex in 1768–69.

became merged in wider programmes of reform, he persisted in moving the same or similar resolutions.[1] Wraxall suggests that Sawbridge, with his "coarse Invectives," was one of the few speakers who could rouse Lord North. He was without doubt master of the cut-and-thrust of City platforms, could marshal an argument, and was not without logic when it served. But a eulogist only claims that he was "a useful speaker," and there is little evidence that his eloquence moved Lord North. More likely his speeches shared the fate of others, which always seemed to sink into Lord North, according to Wraxall, "like a Cannon Ball into a Wool Sack."[2] Sawbridge, in fact, made no impression upon Ministers. They conquered him by silence and by sleep, and year by year they left their followers to vote him down in the lobby.

Sawbridge has been described by a careful historian as "an advanced Radical of the Republican type."[3] I suspect that this is robbing Catherine to pay John. For the republicanism I have signally failed to detect, and even the Radicalism would scarce provoke a tremor in the most timid. But did it exhibit any new features? There is just this: Sawbridge may for a moment have coquetted with the heresy of delegation, though the evidence is a little tenuous.

In the "Protestant Tempest" of 1780 Sawbridge got into trouble. He shrank from the intolerance of Lord George Gordon, though he submitted, perhaps weakly, to the will of his constituents, who were strongly "Protestant." Conversely there were suggestions, true or false, that he was not too forward in the suppression of the Gordon Riots. It is likely enough that when that cauldron of strife boiled over with unexpected violence he was not averse from allowing those who had stirred the brew to realise the consequences of their intemperate zeal. However that may be, he contrived to satisfy neither party. At the general election of 1780 he had to suffer the penalty for blowing hot and cold. In a brisk defence he claimed that there was ample proof of his Protestant

---

[1] References in Veitch, *op. cit.*, p. 35; and see Sharpe, *London and the Kingdom*, iii, 128–132.

[2] *Historical Memoirs* (ed. 1904), p. 297 ; *City Biography*, p. 89, and the report of a speech by Sawbridge in the *Universal Magazine* for February 1772, pp. 102–103, attached to it in B.M. 10825, cc. 13.

[3] Beaven, *op. cit.*, i, 307.

zeal. "Whatever my private Opinions might be," he added, "I should always esteem it my Duty to submit them to your better Judgment." [1]

With this Sawbridge's opponents made great play. In a pretended *Last Dying Speech and Confession* he is represented as promising to have " neither a Will nor Religion of his own," but to " embrace any that his Masters should direct." [2] Another broadside makes him construct " a Wooden Machine, which will save the Expence and Trouble of Contested Elections, and by Means of Springs and Wires, answer every Purpose of a Representative, who is implicitly to obey his Constituents, and have no Will of his own." [3] All this may imply no more than that a candidate in trouble with his constituents sought rather desperately for a way of escape, and chose to extricate himself by means familiar enough to us, though not very usual in the eighteenth century. The evidence must not be pressed too hard. But from the controversy there emerges at least a hint of that theory of delegation which seduced some later Radicals, and there is in it the germ of the pledge-bound member, a germ capable of dangerous growth.

Alongside the gentle efforts of the Chathamites, and at moments converging with them, run the tempestuous agitations of John Wilkes, the second source of early Radicalism. But there were two kings in Brentford—Wilkes and Parson Horne—and the two kings did not always speak with one voice. Mr Gladstone said of Wilkes that he was "the unworthy representative of great causes," but the unworthiness of the representative here matters less than the significance of the causes. Like Chatham, Wilkes stirred the public mind. Once it was aroused, he helped to secure the material by which interest was sustained. His was probably the trick— for it was a trick—by which was gained the freedom to publish the reports of Parliamentary debates, an essential part of the

---

[1] *Haslewood Collection of Ballads and Broadsides*, No. 134 (September 12, 1780), in B.M. 1850, c. 10. See also Nos. 115, 117, 123–124, 127–131.

[2] *The Last Dying Speech and Confession . . . of Mr Alderman S——, together with a Copy of a very Penitent Letter that he sent to his late Masters this Morning* (September 15, 1780), *ibid.*, No. 135.

[3] *Guildhall Exhibition of 1780, ibid.*, No. 138 : a pretended catalogue of portraits, one for each candidate.

nutriment of later Radicalism. And he laid before Parliament the first comprehensive scheme of reform that can fairly be called Radical.

This plan was his most direct contribution to Radicalism, but two indirect influences are earlier in date. The repeated refusals of Wilkes as member for Middlesex, and even more the final determination of the House of Commons to give the seat to a candidate whom the electors had decisively rejected, disturbed many serious people who had little in common with the turbulent followers of Wilkes. Had Wilkes been chosen for a borough and deprived of his seat by the arbitrary action of the House the effect would probably have been negligible. When such things happened—as they did—no dog barked. But to meddle with a county was quite another affair. That the House had itself presumed to choose a county member, that it had tampered with the soundest part of the representation, with that part of it which was reckoned, in its superior purity, as a very bulwark of safety, was what made the decision appear sinister. It was this, rather than the transient ebullitions of the Wilkite mob, that turned thoughtful men to an examination of the principles upon which the representation ought to rest. For if the boasted independence of the counties were threatened, what confidence could the representation otherwise deserve? Here was the beginning of a discussion of general principles that was to go farther and deeper than the proposals of Chatham and Sawbridge.

Secondly, Radicalism called for organisation. The needs of Wilkes drove his friends to devise a political society on a model that could be imitated. The Society of the Supporters of the Bill of Rights might better have been called a society for paying the debts and election expenses of John Wilkes. It did, in fact, pay a great deal, but no society can fill the Serbonian Bog. It tired at last when Wilkes made plain his view that the support of liberty was a monopoly which covered no financial aid to any but himself. The society split, after a fruitless effort to dissolve it outright, and the dissidents withdrew to form a Constitutional Society of their own.

Possibly the Wilkite society was more important because it set the type of an organisation and of a method of propaganda, than because it led opinion or did much to win converts. But before it vanished into nothingness it laid down articles of faith. It is to be borne in mind that they were not adopted until after the schism. Horne and Sawbridge and other City politicians, who had already withdrawn, were not pledged by them. They represent only the slightly wavering opinions of the Wilkite remnant. Some of these articles—short Parliaments and war on corruption—are not new. But two points are notable. First, there is proposed a test for candidates which over a wide political field would have made them little more than delegates. Secondly, the short Parliaments of the Society's resolution are translated, in the words of the actual test, into *annual* Parliaments, and "a full and equal representation" is defined in terms which might mean no more than a household vote, but are equally compatible with universal suffrage.[1] Though it must be repeated that these are the opinions only of the Wilkite remnant of a not very numerous society—and Wilkes himself did not like the form of them—it is plain that they mark a stage in the advance of Radicalism toward a doctrine founded on principle.

So, also, did the one direct attempt made by Wilkes himself to secure Parliamentary reform. In 1776 he asked leave of the House of Commons to introduce a Bill for a "more just and equal representation." Leave was refused, and we have therefore no text of the Bill. But statement and argument are compatible with universal suffrage—perhaps, indeed, they even require it—though Wilkes might have been content to propose something less had he been driven to give practical details in a draft. "I wish, Sir," he said, "an English Parliament to speak the free, unbiassed sense of the body of the English people, and of every man among us. The meanest mechanic, the poorest peasant and day labourer, has important rights respecting his personal liberty, that of his wife and children, his property, however inconsiderable, his wage, his earnings, the very price and value of each day's labour."[2] This was getting near to the language of Cobbett. It is on the threshold of a doctrine of rights, if it does not cross it.

---

[1] Printed (as advertisements) in Woodfall's *Public Advertiser*, June 13 and July 25, 1771; reprinted in Junius, *Letters* (1903), ii, 71–74. Wilkes' opinion, *ibid.*, pp. 84–85. *Cf.* Stephens, *Horne Tooke*, ii, 164–166.

[2] *C. J.*, xxv, 673; *Parl. Hist.*, xviii, 1286–1298.

And it gives a glimpse of social feeling rare even in the writings of reformers before the advent of Mary Wollstonecraft.

Par'son John Horne, better known by his later name as Horne Tooke, the friend and foe of Wilkes, and as keen in enmity as he was warm in friendship, had more direct associations with the revolutionary age than Wilkes, who became Laodicean in prosperity. But he was always skilfully moderate. Gifted with an *aplomb* even more magnificent than Wilkes could command, he could get the results of an equal impudence without falling to an equal vulgarity. Like Wilkes, he was not a gentleman born, but a gentleman made. Both had to rise above the taint of 'trade,' and the hard shifts of the struggle may explain some of their Radicalism, but Horne, the son of a fishmonger and poulterer, had to rise from the retail trade, while Wilkes, the son of a distiller, had to rise only above the wholesale. Each father had been determined "to make Johnny a gentleman," but if Horne's father made some bad blunders, in the end he also made the better job of it. A pretty wit in the son counted for something. There is a legend that young Horne was hard pressed by his schoolfellows to name his father's occupation, when truth untruthful got him out of the difficulty. "A *Turkey* merchant" was his reply to his tormentors. The story may belong to the apocrypha of anecdote, but it is at least in character. In 1794, when he was on trial for his life, he wished to speak in his own defence. "If you do you'll be hanged" was the terse comment of Erskine, his counsel. "Then," came the reply, "I'll be hanged if I do." One wonders whether, in this instance, the temptation to joke may not have saved the neck of a wit.

To the elder Horne it had been plain enough that the way of escape from trade was through the gateway which led to a profession. But he was not so shrewd in judging the character of his son. He thrust him against his will into the Church, for which he was unsuited by both character and opinion, for his morals were lax and his theology was heterodox. Provided with a living at New Brentford,[1] young Horne had some success as a preacher, but any skill that he showed in the pulpit must have been purely intellectual. With the best intentions

---

[1] "Brentford, the bishoprick of Parson Horne," as Mason calls it in *An Heroic Epistle to Sir William Chambers* (1773), l. 112.

his father had barred the way to the exercise of the son's true genius. Young Horne loved the dust of controversy and delighted in the battle of argument. Had his character and interests been different this might have been no disability in the Church. As it was, he might still have flourished at the Bar and risen to prominence in the State, for his mind was political and legal. But in those days once a man had taken orders he was caged in a professional prison. He could neither go to the Bar nor enter the House of Commons. In a later generation the Rev. Leslie Stephen found himself barred in the same way from the family calling when his dissent from the family theology made him unhappy in the Church,[1] though in this case a bad rule made a good biographer and a sound critic. It may have been some slight fellowship of mind, though not of morals, that induced Sir Leslie Stephen to write the life of Horne Tooke in the *Dictionary of National Biography*. After he had passed middle life Horne endeavoured to contest the law which obstructed his ambition. But the only result was that he was more than once refused admission to the Bar, and that his election for Old Sarum in 1801 gave him a session in the House before clerical disqualification was confirmed by what is known as the Horne Tooke Act.[2]

To the thwarted lawyer and politician the Wilkes controversy came as a positive boon, while he was still at the height of his energies, though before his powers had ripened or his judgment had matured. In 1765, when he first entered the fray, he was still under thirty, and there can be no doubt that for some years he thoroughly enjoyed it. He probably planned the Society of the Supporters of the Bill of Rights, and some other ingenious and successful ideas of the Wilkites may have sprung first from his fertile brain. But in a different sense from that in which Wilkes told George III that Wilkes was never a Wilkite neither was Horne wholly a Wilkite. Quite genuinely he seems to have put principles before persons, though it is well-nigh impossible to separate opinions from the personal vendettas of the City Radicals, with which they were entangled. It was Horne, however, who led the Wilkite

[1] F. W. Maitland, *The Life . . . of Leslie Stephen* (1906), pp. 173–174. Means of renouncing orders, which removed this disability, were provided in 1870 by 33 and 34 Vict., c. 91.   [2] 43 Geo. III, c. 63.

schismatics in 1771, and formed the new Constitutional Society. Its history is dark, and it is difficult to establish a direct connexion between it and the later Society for Constitutional Information. But Horne was a member of the later as well as of the earlier society, and his share in the proceedings of the Society for Constitutional Information was the basis of the case against him when he was put on his trial in 1794 for constructive treason.

Horne Tooke has manifestly, then, a place in the history of Radicalism. But in what sense was he a Radical? In mind, as in manner, he belonged to the middle decades of the eighteenth century. If he were furniture he would certainly be classed as Louis-Quinze. Intellectually he had freed himself from speculative restraints, but his practical aim was to mend an old society, not to create any new and illusory Elysium. ". . . Your political principles," he makes Burdett say to him toward the end of his career, "are as much out of fashion as your clothes." "I know it," he replied. "I have good reason to know it. But the fashion must one day return or the nation be undone." [1] This is not the standpoint of a creative political philosopher. Horne Tooke's illusions are not about the future, but about the past, a past of imaginary perfections, which must be restored to cure the ills of the present. He will have nothing to do with equalitarian doctrines. He will not hear of any abstract 'right.' He is, indeed, almost at one with Bentham in the *Fragment on Government*. 'Rights' for him are founded upon the law and government of the country, and must be proved in accordance with them. He revered the "constitution and constitutional LAWS of England" because they were "in conformity with the LAWS of God and nature." "Upon these are founded the rational RIGHTS of Englishmen." [2] The wary critic may here suspect confusion

[1] In his *Diversions of Purley*, Part II (1805), p. 15. Part I appeared in 1798.

[2] *Ibid.*, Part II, p. 14. There survives an interesting scrap of a diary (May–October 1794), printed in *Notes and Queries*, 8th series, vol. xi (1897). Full references to Tooke would occupy much space. The best estimates are by Sir Leslie Stephen in the *Dictionary of National Biography* and in *The English Utilitarians*, i, 124–130, 137–142. *The Memoirs of John Horne Tooke*, by Alexander Stephens (1813), are of variable accuracy, but are based, in part, on personal knowledge. Something may be gleaned from *The Controversial Letters of John Wilkes . . . the Rev. John Horne, etc.* (1771), and from Horne's letters to Junius. Many anecdotes in *The Table-talk of Samuel Rogers*, pp. 83, 125–131.

of thought, for when a man has cast aside natural rights with one hand only to lead in God and nature by the other it frequently means that he is preparing to have it both ways without letting the right hand know what the left hand is doing. But a quotation from one of the discursive interludes in a philological treatise must not in any case be viewed too closely, and it seems clear enough that Horne Tooke recognised no rights that were not founded on law.

If a Radical Horne Tooke was certainly no extremist. He once declared, it is said, that in the cause of Wilkes he would "dye his black coat red." But this marks distaste for his uniform rather than any prescience of the future significance of red ties or red flags. At a dinner in 1790 to celebrate the anniversary of the fall of the Bastille Horne Tooke attempted to moderate the too enthusiastic language of an unguarded resolution proposed by Sheridan. He failed, but he persuaded the excited gathering to accept a second resolution, declaring that "thanks to the generous efforts of their ancestors the English have not a task so difficult to fulfil as that with which the French are at present occupied ; in a word, that they have only to maintain and perfect the Constitution which has been transmitted to them by their ancestors."[1] In July 1790 Pitt himself would have accepted this as a moderate utterance. Horne Tooke certainly kept company with Radicals, but there were Radicals and Radicals, and he explained by an illustration his co-operation with men who wanted reforms more drastic than to him seemed needful. "My companions in a stage [coach] may be going to Windsor," he said. "I will go with them to Hounslow. But there I will get out : no further will I go, by God ! "

So far English Radicalism was essentially native : untouched by the stimulus, uninfluenced by the pattern, of external events. So, in the substantial stuff of it, perhaps it always remained. But new events now gave it increasing force and a wider sweep. First of them was the American Revolution ;

---

[1] Stephens, *op. cit.*, ii, 113 ; diary, *loc. cit.*, p. 104. This affair excited some interest in France. There are accounts in *Archives nationales*, C. 42 (379), in the *Moniteur*, July 30, 1790, and in a dispatch of La Luzerne, *Archives des affaires étrangères, Corr. d'Angleterre*, 574, ff. 54–55.

but not because of the generalisations about natural rights which float like a flag of liberty above that edifice built up of grievances and stern determinations which is the Declaration of Independence. Natural rights, it is true, crop out unexpectedly here and there, as in the title of Granville Sharp's pamphlet of 1774 on the wrongs of Ireland and America, *A Declaration of the People's Natural Right to a Share in the Legislature, which is the Fundamental Principle of the British Constitution of State*, where the rider might be held to discount the declaration. Sharp is unquestionably to be counted a reformer, but his vague references in passing to the need for reform at home are of a moderate order. The main influence of America must be sought otherwhere than in its effect on the diffusion of any abstract idea of rights. It lies in the fact that discussions of American grievances centred on the problem of representation, and that sympathisers with the colonies turned quite naturally to consider also the true foundations of representation in general, and therefore to criticise the system, or want of system, at home.

One of the most prominent of the critics was Major John Cartwright.[1] His younger brother, who invented the power-loom, may to-day seem more important, but in the eyes of contemporaries John cut the greater figure. Down to his death in 1824 this old seaman and militia officer was for almost half a century in the van of political argument, and earned for himself the title of the "Father of Reform." He was full of oddities, and was frequently wrong-headed. His character, a strange compound of earnest persistence and an impishness almost Voltairean, is marked plainly enough on the curious statue erected to his memory near his home in Burton Crescent. And it is not without irony that municipal authorities, probably knowing little of Cartwright's history, should in the interests of respectability have changed the name of Burton Crescent in comparatively recent times to Cartwright Gardens. But Cartwright would certainly have been amused, and quite possibly gratified, had he known that one day, for

[1] *B.* September 17, 1740 (O.S.), *d.* September 23, 1824. *The Life and Correspondence of Major Cartwright*, 2 vols., 1826. was edited by his niece, Frances Dorothy Cartwright, minor poetess, who has herself a tiny niche in the *Dictionary of National Biography*. A brief *Memoir* was also published in 1831. See also the long characterisation by Francis Place in Add. MS. 27850, ff. 108–110.

the betterment of property, he would be accorded official canonisation.

On some subjects Cartwright was a cynic. He once told the astonished Wilberforce that he had been of thirty religions, and should, perhaps, be of thirty more.[1] Yet on questions of reform he was no cynic, but an unquenchable optimist. For him the millennium in politics was always just round the corner. To the end some new club or society was always going to accomplish the impossible, to be the agent of benign transformations, or the herald of some golden dawn. Disappointments made no difference. He fell only to rise; he hoped always to fight better. Victory might come in a night. "My opinion has long been," he wrote at the end of his life, "that reform, come when it will, will come suddenly."[2] And the event proved him right, though he did not live to see it. Doubtless his exaggerated optimism had a ridiculous side, and sometimes made him a troublesome colleague. But it helped to nourish patience, and it nerved him to persistence. Without it he could not have fought undaunted through the rebuffs of half a century, until he had linked the reformers of the eighteenth century to Radicals of a new generation. Even in the doldrums of 1797 he refused to believe that reform was dead and buried. "J. C.," he wrote on the margin of a pessimistic letter from Horne Tooke, "is a believer in the resurrection."[3]

Cartwright was a Radical who believed in history, which was good. But he also believed that he understood it, which was a mistake. No examiner could view his history with any economy of blue pencil. He treated it as a child does a bran-tub, from which drawings are without stint, casting aside the toys he did not want until he had drawn those which would best furnish his playbox. A blasting, but not uncommon, delusion that classical knowledge is a safe guide through the subtleties of English mediæval Latin may also have contributed to his errors, as it has been the undoing of better men. But his belief in history had this merit: though Cartwright

[1] *Life of Wilberforce*, i, 245. But his attitude varied. A strong belief in the providential order of the universe runs through *American Independence*, and even seems to be central to the argument.

[2] April 3, 1823. F. D. Cartwright, *op. cit.*, ii, 238.

[3] *Ibid.*, i, 240 and *n*. *Cf*. i, 300.

was Radical it preserved him from revolutionary methods in domestic politics. His strength was that he was an optimist; his weakness that he was doctrinaire. History did not quench the optimism, but it set bounds to the doctrine. Doctrine there is in plenty, particularly in his earlier writings about America,[1] but it is part of the furnishing of his vocabulary and a method of argument rather than a fundamental and consistent logic, which was, indeed, beyond his powers. It has to be squared with his strange conceptions of historical development. The history was often wrong, but despite his own exaggerations of language it saved him from some headlong plunges into abstract theory, by keeping him in touch with the past, upon which he had to build, however grotesquely he may have misinterpreted it.

This is ultimately plain even in his advocacy of American independence, where theory struggles for the mastery, and seems at first to be uppermost. He may flout the "appeal to ancient times,"[2] but he is ready enough to invoke "the warning voice of history."[3] He may be free in his resort to the "law of nature" and to "inherent, unalienable right,"[4] but he has to persuade himself that the law of nature is the "very soul of our constitution,"[5] and that he goes behind charter and precedent only to revive its principles in their original purity.[6] These principles, he argues, in terms that would be judged sophistical were he not so patently earnest and sincere, are not consistent with the maintenance of Parliamentary sovereignty over the colonies.[7] The Governments in America, he holds, " are no longer dependent

---

[1] *American Independence the Interest and Glory of Great Britain . . . in a Series of Letters to the Legislature*, 1774. (Full title-page is wordy and emphatic, as Cartwright's often are.)   It has not usually been observed that these ten letters had already appeared, signed " Constitutio," in Woodfall's *Public Advertiser*, March 30, April 4, 18, 22, 25, May 2, 9, 16, 23, June 6, 1774.   A second edition with two more letters from the *Public Advertiser*, January 19 and 23, 1775, a letter to Burke, and a postscript appeared in 1775.   *A Letter to Edmund Burke, Esq. . . .*, was also printed separately, 1775. This was commented on by Abingdon, to whom Cartwright replied in *A Letter to the Earl of Abingdon . . .*, 1778.   There is a list of his writings at the end of vol. ii of the *Life*.

[2] *American Independence*, p. 4.   [3] *Ibid.*, 2nd ed., App. 3.

[4] *Ibid.*, pp. 2–3, 7 (*cf.* pp. 15, 25) ; 2nd ed., App. 7.   *Letter to Burke*, p. 6.   *Letter to Abingdon*, p. 11.

[5] *American Independence*, p. 27.   [6] *Ibid.*, pp. 3–4, 7–8 (*cf.* p. 25).

[7] *Ibid.*, pp. i–ii, 30–31, 53 ; *Letter to Abingdon*, pp. 7, 17.

colonies; they are independent nations." [1] This is not because of their revolt, but is, it would seem, part of their natural order of development under our "inestimable constitution." People "cannot be free who are NOT governed by their own consent. Those who are . . . *choose their own governors*," he says, grafting something of the ideas of 1688 upon his own doctrine. ". . . It is an unalterable law of nature; that is, it is the law of God." [2] That the "law of God" is, at the moment, honoured very amply in the breach is part of his case. He would have it honoured in deed and in truth by a return to "this immutable, this divine standard" which has preserved our constitution. "This is a principle of renovation and recovery from all corruption and decays, this is a principle of immortality." [3]

His remarkable powers of self-persuasion thus enabled Cartwright to convince himself that a revolutionary solution of the American problem was a logical consequence of historic constitutional principles. And he would have no half-measures. For mingled with the confusion of twisted theories and historical delusions is a measure of practical, even of prophetic, sense. He is full of scorn for well-meant suggestions from Dean Tucker and others of an American representation in the Parliament of Great Britain. It is "the wildest of all chimeras." [4] "In the imagination of these visionaries," he says, "the vast Atlantic is no more . . . than a mere ferry." [5] The true solution must be a frank recognition of the colonies as self-governing states. Upon the basis of their independence could be erected a league of commerce and security under the leadership of Great Britain, to whom the Americans would grant "an equivalent in *exclusive trade*," [6] in return for the protection of her arms. Thus might American independence become "the interest and glory of Great Britain." [7]

It was through the gateway of America that Cartwright

---

[1] *American Independence*, p. 8 (*cf.* pp. 21, 32) ; *Letter to Abingdon*, pp. 4–6.
[2] *American Independence*, p. 9.   [3] *Ibid.*, p. 27.
[4] *Ibid.*, 2nd ed., App. 11.   [5] *Ibid.*, p. 19.
[6] *Ibid.*, p. 66.
[7] The king was to be head and sovereign of the confederacy. It was Parliamentary sovereignty alone that Cartwright denied. *Ibid.*, pp. 62–72 ; 2nd ed., pp. 9–14, *Postscript*, pp. 32–39, 49. *Letter to Burke*, p. 17 (cf. *Letter to Abingdon*, p. 31).

entered the arena of domestic reform. His plea for peace with the colonies engaged him in a constitutional warfare from which he had thereafter no discharge. Since it was "the right of a free subject not to be taxed without his consent," [1] the representation must clearly be made pure and equitable, or his theoretical right would in practice be defeated. Therefore the representation needed great amendment and much restoration. "It doth not appear to be very consistent with *the spirit of our constitution* . . . that a Dunwich or an Old Sarum, containing half a dozen cottagers, should have the chusing of as many . . . national representatives as a Norwich or a Bristol . . .," or that "indigent and corrupt men" should "make a trade of voting." [2] Political virtue may, perchance, be found in the existing House of Commons, where "it grows not very abundant" amid "the noxious weeds of prostitution and bribery." But "until there shall be opened clean doors into that House," by which men may enter "undefiled by the base arts practised in elections, . . . the real patriot . . . incapable of debauching or invading the rights of his fellow-citizens" is scarce to be looked for within its walls.[3] Let it be elected by "the unbribed, unbiassed suffrages of the freeholders," and the House would be once more "the terror, not the tool of bad ministers ; the bulwark, not the abusers of the people." [4]

Cartwright "dwelt long on the nature and excellence of the English Constitution" [5] because he believed it to be his mission to preserve, to restore, to amend it when in decay, but not to change it by rash innovations. For all his radicalism, his mind, like that of many another English reformer, was veined with conservatism, even with antiquarianism. He justified his hope for the future by his conception of the past. He told himself—perhaps he was constrained perforce to persuade himself—that he wanted to go back to "the antient practice of the constitution." [6] That these practices, as he imagined them, never existed, is beside the point. His

---

[1] *American Independence*, p. 4.   [2] *Ibid.*, p. 42.

[3] *Ibid.*, p. v.   [4] *Ibid.*, p. vi.

[5] *Take Your Choice* (1776), p. 18. The second edition (1777) is entitled *The Legislative Rights of the Commonalty Vindicated ; or, Take Your Choice.* In their main substance the many later writings of Cartwright, such as *The People's Barrier* (1780), are little more than amplifications or reiterations of these pamphlets.

[6] *Take Your Choice*, p. 15 ; *Legislative Rights*, p. 18.

imaginings kept him in the tradition, while enabling him to be a strong and thorough Radical. His proposals, set forth in October 1776 in the pamphlet called *Take Your Choice*, were never varied in substance in his later writings, though he occasionally supported milder measures for reasons of practical expediency. They are drastic and comprehensive—universal suffrage,[1] equal representation, annual Parliaments,[2] the ballot,[3] in certain circumstances the payment of members,[4] and something very like one man one vote.[5] Indeed, on all points save one it may be argued that he anticipated the Chartists. Rather curiously he favoured a property qualification for members of Parliament.[6] It is equally odd that this was abolished in 1858, before any part of Cartwright's own programme was fully established in law. Cartwright balanced this remnant of conservatism, however, by protesting against the view that wealth and property alone constituted a stake in the country, and maintaining that the true stake in the country was a wife and children.[7]

With Cartwright's pamphlet Radicalism had reached a point beyond which little further development was possible on the purely political or practical sides. It might yet be placed on a new basis of theory, or it might be reinforced by new energies. But it could not be—in fact, to this day has not been—very much amplified as a programme to be realised in constitutional Acts of Parliament. Yet from time to time Radicalism did augment its power from new circumstances or organisations, from new enthusiasms and new men. A part at least of its programme gained fresh support and respectability from its association with the great Economy Campaign, and it learned some lessons of organisation from the plan of

[1] *Legislative Rights*, pp. 28–29, 147 (though he is against women's suffrage, *ibid.*, pp. 45–47) ; *Take Your Choice*, p. 19.

[2] *Ibid.*, pp. xxv, 15, 77 ; *Legislative Rights*, pp. 18, 85, 105. Equal representation and annual Parliaments are generally commended in the same sentence, as if they were inseparables.

[3] *Ibid.*, p. 168 ; *Take Your Choice*, p. 70.

[4] *Ibid.*, p. 72 ; *Legislative Rights*, p. 171.

[5] *Ibid.*, pp. 32, 34–35, 173–174 ; *Take Your Choice*, p. 73.

[6] *Ibid.*, p. 69 ; *Legislative Rights*, p. 164. He proposed rather a high qualification, but modified his view later.

[7] *Ibid.*, p. 29 ; *Take Your Choice*, p. 19.

county associations which that campaign produced.[1]   Its leader, the Rev. Christopher Wyvill, non-resident incumbent of Black Notley, in Essex, and by marriage resident squire of Burton Constable, in the North Riding of Yorkshire, was himself a genuine reformer, in the State if not in the Church, and the six untidily arranged volumes of his published papers and correspondence are a valuable repertory of information on the reform movement at large.[2]   But the Economy Campaign was not, in itself, Radical.   It made use of Radical materials ; it enlisted the aid of some Radicals ; from it there sprang, in a transitory gleam, one sweeping proposal of Reform ; and it supplied much of the force that was behind the reform resolutions of the younger Pitt.   But it was a non-party movement provoked by the burdens of the American War ; its aim was to check extravagance and corruption, and thus to cut at the roots of illegitimate influence in Parliament and in the constituencies.   Its fruits are seen in Clerke's Act, in Crewe's Act, and in the two statutes which embody the economical reforms of Burke.[3]   But with those measures many of its supporters were satisfied, and once they were passed the Whigs in particular grew lukewarm.   Moderate reform was part of its public programme, and Pitt was certainly helped, if not pushed, by it.   But after Pitt's schemes had failed the movement tended to fade away.   Some of the individual leaders remained to the end reformers, but the county associations and other allied bodies vanished into the moorland mists from whence they had come.

One gleam of Radicalism did appear during the campaign. It came from a Westminster committee [4] in alliance with the county associations, and was a sweeping proposal for annual Parliaments, universal suffrage, and something like equal electoral districts.   But its sponsor in Parliament was the Duke of Richmond, who quarrelled in turn with political companions of every party, and in succession with most of his own political opinions.   He cannot, therefore, be counted a very steady recruit to the Radicals, though he did give an impetus to Radicalism.   His *Letter to Colonel Sharman,* first

---

[1] Veitch, *op. cit.*, chapter iii, and references.

[2] *Political Papers,* 6 vols., York and Richmond, 1794–1802.

[3] 22 Geo. III, cc. 41, 45, 81, 82.

[4] *Report of the Sub-Committee of Westminster,* p. 8 (B.M., E. 2101 (17)); *Parl. Hist* , xxi, 686–688 ; *L. J.*, xxxvi, 144 ; Walpole, *Letters*, ed. Toynbee, xi, 233.

published in 1783, became a classic with Radicals and reformers, and in 1859 it was even reprinted in support of the
movement for the 'household franchise,' though few then
wanted universal suffrage and the time was fast approaching
when annual Parliaments would be a boon that no party could
ask, or, indeed, endure.

In 1780, possibly under the stimulus of the Economy
Campaign, a number of reformers set up the Society for
Promoting Constitutional Information. Some of its members,
like Cartwright and Horne Tooke, were already well known,
and for the rest the society was almost painfully moderate and
respectable. But it was the means of recruiting or bringing
into prominence some new prophets of reform. Among its
more able and energetic promoters was Dr John Jebb, a remarkable man, who at forty years of age had abandoned on
grounds of conscience his calling as a don and a cleric, had
taken to the study of medicine, and had rapidly won a measure
of success in his second profession. It is possible that Wyvill
owed the idea of county committees acting in correspondence
and consultation, a device from which the Economy Campaign
drew much of its strength and collective influence, to a suggestion from Dr Jebb.[1] He had proposed such a plan to
Sir George Savile in 1776, and he had recommended it again
to a meeting of the freeholders of Middlesex in December
1779.[2] That he helped in the Economy Campaign is certain,
but he wanted Parliamentary as well as economical reform.
"Moving the People of England to carry so small a Reform"
as Burke's Bill of 1780 would, it seemed to him, "be tempesting
the ocean to drown a fly."[3] His major object was "to maintain and support the freedom of election" by shortening
Parliaments and extending the suffrage. Wyvill he thought
"a good man, spirited, manly, and persevering," but he was
in deeper sympathy with Cartwright, and there was close
friendship between them. Like Cartwright and Wyvill, he
was present at the famous meeting held on May 18, 1782,
to encourage Pitt in new projects of reform after his first
rebuff in the Commons. Like Cartwright and Wyvill, he put

[1] But cf. Veitch, op. cit., p. 63.
[2] An Address to the Freeholders of Middlesex . . . [on] . . . 20th December, 1779 . . .,
especially pp. 11–12, 21. Cf. Wyvill Papers, iv, 505.
[3] To Wyvill, December 19, 1780 (ibid., iv, 500).

his trust in Pitt instead of in Fox. But earlier than either of them, it would seem, he harboured a suspicion of Pitt's sincerity, and came to place little reliance on his perseverance. Yet on some points Jebb was a moderate. For all his Radicalism he would have no truck with the theory of delegation, and was at pains to demolish it. But he was impatient of men who made parade of their moderation. "Don't tell me of a moderate man," he used to say to Cartwright; "he is always a rascal."

Another among the founders of the Society for Constitutional Information was Capell Lofft, of Troston Hall, near Bury St Edmunds, whom Boswell called the "little David of popular spirit." "Though a zealous Whig," says Boswell, he had "a mind full of learning and knowledge."[1] Lofft was a county gentleman, an active Justice, a student of law and of literature, a translator of Virgil and of Petrarch, a writer on political, legal, and constitutional subjects, and in his own view a poet. His poetry cannot now be read without a struggle, though the struggle is sometimes for gravity. He is capable of such lines as

> Cities arose : society began,

which is chronologically doubtful ; and worse, if more amusing :

> Whether my head be bald or no
> Or grey, or black hairs on it grow,
> This know I not, nor care to know.[2]

Indeed, the good gentleman had no sense of humour, and probably not much real understanding of his fellow-men. He was, in fact, a doctrinaire, like many of the chosen pamphleteers of the Society for Constitutional Information. On occasion he could sway an audience, as Crabb Robinson testifies,[3] though his voice, if sweet, was feeble. In politics

---

[1] Boswell's *Johnson*, ed. Birkbeck Hill, ii, 278.

[2] *The Praises of Poetry* (1775), which never rises above the level of "The venerable pile our Chaucer wrought," possibly the best line in it. *Eudosia ; or, A Poem on the Universe* (1781), contains the line, "What should I speak of *vegetable* juice ?"

[3] *Diary*, i, 33. For an odd catalogue of Lofft's literary heroes see iii, 283. Robinson never quite lost an early respect for Lofft, who at times offered him advice. In 1811 he urged Robinson never to marry "a woman of what is called a strong mind," advice which Robinson followed by refraining altogether from matrimony (i, 365). Does this exhortation throw light on the character of Sarah Watson Finch, herself an authoress, whom Lofft had married as his second wife in 1802 ?

his veneration for Cartwright was only a little less than for Fox and Dr John Jebb.[1] In 1780 he even wrote an abstract of one of Cartwright's verbose pamphlets, *The People's Barrier*, and it was published and distributed gratis by the society. In this leaflet he accepts, of course, the full gospel according to Cartwright.[2] From his own independent writings one gets the impression of greater moderation, but his political opinions were strongly held, for he could not keep them out of his legal works, nor even out of his poetry. Lofft had less importance as an individual, however, than as one of a group. By himself he could have made little impact on the public mind. His significance, like that of some other writers for the Society for Constitutional Information, is that he helped to bridge the years between the Economy Campaign and the French Revolution. Together they kept reform, if not Radicalism, in the foreground of popular interest.

Lofft had on one occasion to defend the Society for Constitutional Information against the suggestion that it was a mere organisation of Dissenters, a charge quite certainly untrue.[3] A similar charge was made against the Revolution Societies, the dining societies which met year by year to celebrate the Revolution of 1688. It is true that in some places Churchmen and Dissenters met separately, though this was not everywhere the case, and it is true that Dissenting preachers were specially prominent as the chosen orators of such societies. Most prominent of them was Dr Richard Price. One is apt to think of Price as a grim figure, brooding over those necrological data on which are founded the actuary's tables of the expectation of life, or at best juggling with compound interest and inventing the Sinking Fund. A great lady who had asked for an opportunity of meeting him said, "I expected to meet a Colossus with an eye like Mars, to threaten or command." She was surprised to find him a small, unassuming man, even

[1] *On the Revival of the Cause of Reform* (1809), p. 6. He had, however, disliked Fox's coalition with North, as did many reformers.

[2] *A Summary of a Treatise by Major Cartwright, entitled "The People's Barrier against Undue Influence,"* in which he insists upon Cartwright's doctrine of personal representation. Lofft's considered opinions did not always go the full length of Cartwright's. He was, perhaps, too pedantic for the round generalisations demanded in the rough-and-tumble of political controversy.

[3] *An History of the Corporation and Test Acts*, Bury, 1790, p. 28.

a little ridiculous when his wig was awry, as it frequently was. But his kindly nature drew out the geniality of others, and as he rode the streets of London on his old, half-blind white horse even the orange-women used to cry "Make way for Dr Price!"[1] He loved children, and was not above romping with them, running a hopping race across a field, or leaping bushes in the garden with all the zest of a boy. His political writings are not all negligible. His *Observations on Civil Liberty*,[2] in which he contested the justice and wisdom of the American war, is not without merit as a piece of controversial writing, and had a circulation, it is said, of 60,000 copies. A full discussion of his political principles might, however, trench upon the exposition of Burke, who not only criticised the *Observations*, but also made Price's famous sermon in *Love of our Country*[3] a ground of attack in his *Reflections on the French Revolution*. The point to be noticed here is that Price and other Dissenting orators contributed to the theoretical armoury of the reformers, and, either individually or as members of the Revolution Societies, form links between the eighteenth-century Radicals and the new model of Radicalism which emerged during the French Revolution. Their importance is perhaps the greater as the Revolution Societies experienced a revival on the very eve of the French Revolution, through the special zeal which they showed and the fresh support which they won at the celebrations in 1788 of the centenary of the English Revolution.

Price and the Revolution Societies have brought us to the French Revolution, and with it once again to unquestioned Radicals, for when Thomas Hardy, the Scottish shoemaker of Piccadilly, founded his London Corresponding Society in January 1792, with its penny a week subscription and its constituency of working men, not only was Radicalism set again upon the full tide of universal suffrage and annual Parliaments, but it had begun to appeal not merely to agitators and doctrinaires of the middle and educated classes, but to men fashioned of the stuff out of which genuine Radicals were made.

G. S. VEITCH

[1] In P. W. Clayden's *The Early Life of Samuel Rogers* (1887) there are many pleasant glimpses of Price.
[2] *Observations on the Nature of Civil Liberty and the Justice and Policy of the War with America* (1776).
[3] *A Discourse on the Love of our Country* (1789).

THE EARLY ENGLISH RADICALS

BOOK LIST

GENERAL

W. E. H. Lecky, *History of England*, vols. iii–v, chapters x, xi, xv, xviii (vols. iii and v, chapters x, xv, xvi, in the Cabinet edition), is interesting and still valuable, though modified by accessions to knowledge. Sir G. O. Trevelyan, *Early History of Charles James Fox* (1st ed. 1880, "Silver Library" ed. 1901). Professor J. Holland Rose, *William Pitt and National Revival* (1911), and Dr Rose's brief *Short Life of William Pitt* (1925), which contains some revisions. Sir Leslie Stephen, *History of English Thought in the Eighteenth Century* (1881), vol. ii, chapter x, and *The English Utilitarians* (1900), vol. i, chapters i–iii, a compact but illuminating survey of the relevant conditions in the later eighteenth century.

ON THE REFORM MOVEMENT IN THE EIGHTEENTH CENTURY

H. W. Carless Davis, *The Age of Grey and Peel* (1929), especially chapter iii. P. A. Brown, *The French Revolution in English History* (1918), especially chapter i. G. S. Veitch, *The Genesis of Parliamentary Reform*, especially chapters i–v. C. B. R. Kent, *The English Radicals* (1899). Henry Jephson, *The Platform : its Rise and Progress* (1892), especially chapters ii–iv. Graham Wallas, *The Life of Francis Place* (1908; 2nd ed. 1918), especially chapter i.

ON WILKES

W. Fraser Rae, *Wilkes, Sheridan, and Fox* (1874), Introduction and chapters i–iii, vigorously written, and despite its age still worth reading. Horace Bleackley, *Life of John Wilkes* (1917), adds much from the Wilkes manuscripts in the British Museum and from other sources. Biographies by O. A. Sherrard (1930) and Raymond Postgate (1930) appeared after the completion of the text. For an odd story about Wilkes, related on the authority of Lord Sheffield, see Wilfred Partington, *The Private Letter Books of Sir Walter Scott* (1930), p. 276.

ON HORNE TOOKE

Alexander Stephens, *The Memoirs of John Horne Tooke*, 2 vols. (1813). J. Horne Tooke, *The Diversions of Purley*, vol. i (1798), vol. ii (1805). Sir Leslie Stephen, *The English Utilitarians*, chapter iv. See also the references in the notes.

ON MAJOR CARTWRIGHT

F. D. Cartwright, *The Life and Correspondence of Major Cartwright*, 2 vols. (1826). Graham Wallas, *op. cit.* Further references in the notes to the text.

ON DR PRICE

See the long list of works cited in the *Dictionary of National Biography*, and add P. W. Clayden, *Early Life of Samuel Rogers* (1887). References to Price's writings are given in the footnotes to the text of the article.

III

THE REVOLUTIONARY ERA IN FRANCE

IN the course of history there occur at long intervals great crises which set at defiance the comfortable teaching as to the normal development of the human race. At such times vital forces which should make for progress may be brought into collision, and then they engender strifes which in their turn cause politics to gyrate as in a cyclone. In this state of things great and imposing institutions may be whirled aside, and new ones may arise, only to meet the same fate if they chance to obstruct the whim of the hour. Finally only those will survive which meet the fundamental and permanent needs of mankind.

Such, in brief, are the main outlines of the story of the French Revolution of 1789–99. That great movement draws into itself, as it were, the new forces of eighteenth-century thought. The resulting current, gathering strength, finds itself obstructed by obstacles which it finally sweeps away, only to meet with others further afield and more formidable, which deflect its course and drive it back on itself. Hence, as a result, something approaching to political stagnation.

It is on the early stages of this movement that I propose to speak here; for their interest can never be exhausted. In them we witness the wreck of the absolute monarchy of France and the beginning of a series of political and social experiments most of which had been outlined by earlier thinkers. At first sight the collapse of the old *régime* and the successes of the new are almost inexplicable. But on inquiry the downfall of the old institutions will be found not to antedate the loss of their usefulness and therefore of their vitality; while the temporary success of several of the new experiments will also be found to be due largely to the fruitful studies of earlier thinkers and administrators.

Let us try, first, to understand the inner weakness of the old *régime*, which disappeared in the uprising of 1789; next, to appreciate the high hopes which prompted the establishment of a new order of things ; and, finally, to examine briefly the obstacles which were destined to drive France back along the path leading to autocracy.

We shall understand the weakness of the old *régime* in France if we take note of the material and intellectual causes tending to undermine it. For the material influences affected the masses of the people and prepared them for some kind of movement; while the pressure of the hard facts of everyday life also set the thinkers on their intellectual quest and led them to point out the lines which reform might take.

Let us therefore glance briefly at the conditions of life of the non-privileged Frenchman before the year 1789, for it was these conditions which produced the alliance between the thinkers and the masses; and when the thinkers and the masses move in unison their momentum is irresistible. When political reformers have no message that attracts the multitude their theme is bounded by the study; but when their message reaches a multitude that is longing for movement then events march rapidly and with conquering stride.

It is well to remember that such union between the thinkers and the masses is rare. The saying " When the hour strikes then comes the man " is a pleasing fiction. As if, indeed, the progress of mankind resembled one of those mechanical clocks that always put forth the hero or saviour at the appropriate hour ! No ! Human history has often taken a course that is tragically different. The hour of man's deepest longing has often summoned forth no fit champion. Or else, only too often, the champion came forth long before the human need became clamant; and the would-be saviour was forthwith jostled aside by a tiresome procession of punctual puppets.

Things went differently in the French Revolution. Then the course of events was rapid and decisive, because, long before 1789, man's need had begun to arouse thinkers, men of action, and at last the usually inert masses. In order to understand how this rare union of aim came about we must glance at the predetermining facts. Briefly they were as follows:

In France the reforming process was a century and a half overdue. The similar movement which in England began with the early Stuarts and continued with few breaks was dammed up in France. In England feudalism was gradually whittled down during the Commonwealth and the following reigns, but no similar change took place in France; and it may be said that there the land laws, the game laws, and class distinctions in general were as rigorous as they were in England during Tudor times. In regard to the power of the monarch, the contrast between the two countries was still more marked. No English king after Henry VIII wielded the authority which Louis XV wielded down to the end of his reign (1774). Indeed, right down to the Revolution Louis XVI was in theory absolute, ruling without participation of the States-General and with only spasmodic interference from the Paris *Parlement*. Thus, in France reform was delayed far too long; and, naturally, when it came it came with a rush.

It is indeed strange that in the midst of the most logical and critical people in the world two systems of government still co-existed; and these two systems were irreconcilable. I refer to the absolute monarchy and to feudalism. When Louis XIV became absolute he should have abolished feudalism root and branch, but he did not do so; nor did Louis XV or Louis XVI do so. Thus it came about that the weakened monarchy of Louis XVI struggled along, tied by the knee, so to speak, with the limping spectre of moribund feudalism. And this unequal tie not only hampered progress; it threatened an ignominious fall. For both runners were heavily burdened. Feudal France bore all the feudal dues and customs belonging to a vanished past; while monarchical France, still pulsating with life, had to bear the heavy load of war-taxes, palace-building, and other expenses of the most sumptuous Court in Europe. The wonder is that this strange three-legged race had not long ago ended in an ignominious fall. But, in spite of various efforts at reform, especially under the well-meaning Louis XVI, this glaring injustice persisted right down to the year 1789.

The result of this absurd anomaly was a State bankruptcy; and there is a depth of meaning in Carlyle's apostrophe:

> Honour to Bankruptcy; ever righteous on the great scale, though in detail it is so cruel. Under all Falsehoods it works, unweariedly mining. No Falsehood, did it rise heaven-high and cover the world, but Bankruptcy, one day, will sweep it down and make us free of it.

This consideration brings us to our second material cause—viz., the failure of the French monarchy to redress this singular wrong. What are we to say of an absolute monarch—for Louis XVI was absolute—allowing the mining process to go on under his throne and taking no energetic and efficient steps to stop it? True, he did try, but he failed ignominiously. Therefore in the financial sphere the Revolution was due to the resolve of the whole nation to do what the King had failed to do—viz., sweep away the inequalities of taxation dating back to feudal times. In those far-off days it was both true and not unfair to say, "The nobles fight, the clergy pray, and the people pay." But by the beginning of the reign of Louis XIV the French nobles ceased to fight at the head of vassals whom they had equipped at their own charges, and they now figured as well-paid officers in the royal army. As to the clergy, the titled clerics both then and far later remained free from taxes owing to an age-long immunity ; but rumour said that they were not over-earnest at prayers, and that most of the praying was done by the untitled clergy, who, as plebeians, were taxed. Finally, it was unanswerably true that the people paid—paid heavily—for the support of an extravagant Court and an expensive administration.

This lop-sided system received little real support from the Church ; for the Roman Catholic Church in France was still in the grip of feudalism. There were glaring differences between the titled and the untitled clergy. Down to the year 1789 the titled clergy absorbed nearly all the high places in the Church, while the rank and file, on whom fell the burden of work, were often miserably underpaid. It was only natural, then, that both thinkers and workers should clamour for sweeping changes in the Church. They also objected to its exaction of tithes, which to cultivators were often burdensome and always annoying. Hence the reformers in France tended to become anti-clerical—a tendency which has had far-reaching results in French life.

We can now see why both the thinkers and the masses desired drastic reforms of these galling inequalities both in Church and State. Inquirers into social questions, economists who pointed out the right and the wrong way of land tenure and tax-paying, along with the traders and peasants who knew where the yoke galled the shoulders, all united in the demand for an entire change. If the monarchy could enact the needed reforms, well and good ; but, if not, let the nation do what Louis XVI and his Ministers had failed to do. Above all, let the *noblesse* surrender their hated privileges ; and, so far as class privileges prevailed in the Church, let her give them up as contrary both to Christian teaching and to the dictates of humanity.

In all these demands, I repeat, the thinkers and the workers were at one ; for the old system was both irrational and very burdensome. Of its unreasonableness Voltaire, Montesquieu, and scores of lesser men had given scathing proofs. Of its burdensomeness Jacques Bonhomme had no need of any proof. On this subject I will quote M. Taine ; for that distinguished writer will not be accused of pro-Jacobin bias. Indeed, no French historian has more mercilessly exposed the inconsistencies, the brutalities, and the ghastly failures of the extreme Revolutionaries ; but he is equally severe on the stupidities of the old *régime*. To his book on that subject he adds an appendix as to the incidence of taxation on the average plebeian. He sums it up thus : that the total of all the royal taxes, of the tithes payable to the Church, and of feudal dues payable to the feudal lord amounted on the average to about $81\frac{3}{4}$ per cent. of the income, the taxpayer retaining only $18\frac{1}{4}$ per cent. of his earnings. This appalling system prevailed in full severity in old France. It pressed less severely on the outlying provinces, such as Brittany, Provence, Dauphiné, Alsace, and the North-east and North. But the contrast between the most burdened and the less burdened provinces was so glaring as to intensify the demand for assimilation in what would then be a national system.

Hence in France the democratic movement became also a movement for national unity. Thanks to her absolute monarchy, Frenchmen had long been conscious of an inner unity. Their victories and their defeats, their glory and their peril, as well as their achievements in literature and the arts, had endowed them with the same pride or fear, the same longings or enthusiasms ; so that all educated Frenchmen shared like feelings and aspirations ;[1] only the uneducated masses re-

---

[1] " A travers les diversités qui existent encore, l'unité de la nation est déjà transparente " (De Tocqueville, *Ancien Régime*, Book II, chapter viii).

mained provincial or parochial in outlook. But in 1789 both the educated and uneducated began to long for a close political union, which, by freeing them from the old provincial restraints, would give them freedom of movement as well as freedom from old feudal customs. Thus, owing to the glaring inequalities of the old order of things, both the thinkers and the peasants demanded its abolition; and as those inequalities were bound up with the old provinces, there arose an overwhelming cry (first voiced by the *économistes*) for the sweeping away of the provincial system and the merging of the old provinces in a national system. Only when France became politically what she had long been ideally—a nation—could there be one law for all. Accordingly there grew in volume a demand that where feudalism and provincialism had made for injustice and chaos the nation should step in and proclaim the sovereignty of one national law. Let there be an end to feudal confusions; and let the nation bring order out of chaos, light out of darkness.

Here the farmer and the thinker, the merchant and the theorist, were at one. Hence the impulse toward simplifying the old provincial tangles and merging all in a larger unity was overwhelming. This impulse or instinct we term nationality. It aims at the formation of one united nation. This national aim is not always allied to the democratic aim. Often it becomes opposed to it, and has even overcome it. But in France during the better and happier phase of the Revolution nationality was closely allied to democracy; and the two, acting together, account for the irresistible power of the combined movement, which swept away the weak barriers of an effete feudalism and an impotent absolutism. The whole world was astounded at the speedy collapse of the old *régime* in France. But, in reality, there was nothing surprising in it. All that was living in France called out for the change. How absurd to suppose that Louis XVI, after sending an army to America to help found the United States, could remain an absolute monarch in France! For that army came back imbued with ideas of liberty and equality; and the returning troops were perhaps as effective missionaries of the new ideas as all the philosophers had been. Thus the absolute monarchy was doomed to disappear.

THINKERS OF THE REVOLUTIONARY ERA

So too was the old order of things in the Church of France. For even in that body a large majority of the *curés* and a few of the bishops, led by Talleyrand, demanded drastic changes; and it was the secession of these malcontents from the order of the Clergy in mid-June 1789 which decided the day in favour of the union of the orders. Thus, in that summer the days of class privilege were over both in Church and State. The funeral pyre of the old *régime* was lit by peasants in the first great Jacquerie of the Revolution, while the deputies of France gave a show of legality to the holocaust by a series of self-sacrificing decrees known as the St Bartholomew of Privileges (August 4).

Meanwhile the old royal army was rapidly falling to pieces. The leaven introduced from America, added to the ferment of decaying feudalism, worked strongly in the rank and file, with the result seen in the capture of the Bastille (July 14), which crushed the feeble attempt at a royalist *coup d'état*. The consequence was the emigration of most of the officers, accompanied by the princes of the blood and the reactionary nobles.

Thus at the crisis the old monarchy found effective support neither from the army, which had become democratic at heart, nor the Church, whose customs were too feudal to render it popular, nor the *noblesse*, pampered as it had been by a century of courtly subservience. Very truly did De Tocqueville sum up the situation:

> Nothing was any longer organised to check the Government; nothing, any more, to help it. Therefore the whole grandiose edifice built by these princes could all together and in a moment crash to the ground so soon as the society which served as base quaked. [1]

No less remarkable than the collapse of the old order was the constructional power displayed by the new. The reformers, being at first both united and inspired by the feeling that they spoke for the masses, speedily asserted their authority as supreme. Gone were the days when the Tiers État knelt submissively at the entrance of the King. The commons of France had so knelt in all the former seventeen States-General; [2]

[1] De Tocqueville, *Ancien Régime*, Book II, chapter xii.
[2] Mme de Staël, *Considérations sur la Révolution française*, Part I, chapter xi.

but in this eighteenth States-General, of May 1789, the thrills sent through the body politic by the new thoughts of the age, as also by the sense of innate strength, forbade any such sign of submission. Further, when the two other orders refused to join them the Tiers État boldly declared itself to be the National Assembly—a term hitherto applied only to the States-General as a whole. It is significant that this bold claim was proposed by an almost unknown member, Legrand of Berri; but on June 17 the proposal carried all before it, and was adopted by 491 votes to 90. The statement in which the theorist Abbé Sieyès set forth this claim asserted that the Tiers État represented ninety-six-hundredths of the nation, and must therefore act, whatever the other four-hundredths might do or not do. It then formulated the following remarkable declaration: "The National Assembly being *one* and indivisible, no deputy, in whatever order he may be chosen, has the right to exercise his functions separately from the present Assembly."

It is worth while to compare this Declaration of Rights with the passages in the *Contrat social* of Rousseau, by which it was evidently inspired. In that work the Genevese thinker had said, "Sovereignty, being nothing but the exercise of the general will, can never be alienated"; and again he declared, "For the same reason that sovereignty is inalienable it is indivisible."[1] These two very doubtful axioms (which Rousseau never deigned to prove) evidently inspired Sieyès to make his celebrated Declaration, which flung down the challenge both to the King and to the two other orders; for the Tiers État now calmly took the place of Louis XVI, and also swallowed up the two orders. Well did that acute observer Mme de Staël say that this action of the Tiers État constituted the Revolution. She was right; for that body now virtually abrogated the authority of all other bodies in the State, and accordingly seized on power. Clearly, if the commons of France could make good this claim they would *ipso facto* inaugurate democracy of a type more thorough than that of the United States, where Congress consisted of two

---

[1] Rousseau, *Contrat social*, Book II, chapters i and ii. Note, too, this rigid definition, "The sovereign, being formed only of the individuals that compose it, neither has, nor can have, any interest contrary to theirs" (Book I, chapter vii).

Chambers and was to some extent balanced by the powers of the President. In France, on the contrary, events moved strongly toward a unitary republic.

The French claim was bold in the extreme; but its very boldness ensured success; for the French, perhaps more than any people, are attracted by a swift and decisive exercise of authority.[1] With Gallic enthusiasm they rally to a rousing lead. This characteristic of theirs—the pack instinct shall we call it?—renders them listless in the absence of a spirited lead, but swiftly and terribly militant when it is given. Then they can accomplish in weeks what it takes the slower British or Germans painfully to attain in the course of as many decades or centuries.

There are, however, occasions when the success of a revolutionary movement is so overwhelming as to be a misfortune; and it was so in the summer of 1789 among that excitable people, totally unaccustomed as it was to political activity. That form of activity more than all others calls for prudence and moderation in the hour of triumph. But these qualities were lacking in the Frenchmen of that time—a consequence of their inexperience even more than of their temperament. Accordingly we find that nearly all their actions in this revolution were marred by excess. Now, there is a half-truth in the paradox (coined, I believe, by Mr G. K. Chesterton) that nothing succeeds like *excess*. But that *mot* is a perilous half-truth, especially for ill-balanced, sentimental people. And in the case which we are considering it would be wholly true to say that the French Revolution erred everywhere by excess— excess in the manner in which the politicians applied the dicta of the foregoing thinkers; excess in the way in which they sought to coerce the recusant minority; excess on the part of the mob at every political crisis; and excess on the part of the *émigrés*, who sought to crush the Revolution by the help of foreign armies.

This tendency toward exaggeration is the more singular because Montesquieu had ably emphasised the need of political moderation, and had pointed out the evil results of excess.[2]

---

[1] Mme de Staël, Part I, chapter xviii.

[2] Montesquieu, *Esprit des lois*, Book III, chapter iv; Book V, chapter viii. He applies it especially to an aristocracy; but it is implicit in his comments on monarchy

Indeed, he had extolled the English Constitution because it established a balance of powers between monarch, nobles, and commons, which provided security against tyranny, oligarchy, and mob rule. These forms of rule, he declared, were perversions of monarchy, aristocracy, and popular government. All pains must therefore be taken to guard against them; and of those three perversions he judged mob rule to be the worst. Even Rousseau, though strongly inclined toward democracy, declared pure democracy to be impossible in a great nation; and all his arguments for popular rule were based on the assumption that he was legislating for a small community like that of a Swiss canton, or a primitive society like that of Corsica.

Thus, several of the pre-Revolutionary thinkers deemed pure democracy dangerous, especially in a great State. Yet the French Revolution, even in its earliest stages, showed signs of sweeping on far beyond the limits which its intellectual precursors had prescribed for it, and all attempts at imposing such limits as an English constitution would have imposed were very speedily thrust aside. I repeat that this phenomenon deserves careful attention; for it shows how partial is the influence which political thought may exert at a crisis. We should therefore beware of studying such speculations as if they furnished the chief key to the explanation of political crises. The events of the French Revolution should, I think, guard us against over-estimating the influence of abstract political thought, and should induce us to correlate our studies of political science with a close observation of the men of action of the period and with the impulses of the unthinking masses.

In times of popular excitement politicians who have read about political speculations are apt to set forth, with much parade of learning, just as much of certain doctrines as suits their purpose, and leave unmentioned the warnings and limitations with which the political thinker in question sought to safeguard them. How often must that thinker have turned in his grave to see the reckless or tricky use made of his teaching! Unhappy Rousseau! He wrote a series of rather

and democracy. So too in the *Lettres persanes* : " Nature always acts slowly, and, so to speak, sparingly. Her operations are never violent, and she is moderate even in production."

loose and illogical speculations for possible use by a Swiss canton or by Corsica, and in less than forty years they were being rigidly applied to the largest and most complex community in the world. Could purblind literalness or tricky eclecticism lead a people more wildly astray?

Yet the progress of 'enlightenment' in the eighteenth century, added to the practical experiences gained by some of its votaries, like Turgot, enabled the new legislators of France to proceed both swiftly and surely toward certain reforms destined to have a widespread acceptance. In no sphere was their success more marked than in that of local self-government—a subject whose width and complexity must exclude it from this survey.

Less obvious but equally important in its far-reaching influence was the swift rise of a new institution—the national army. It arose thus. In order to combat both reaction and the anarchy which threatened France on the break up of the old royal army, La Fayette, the "hero of both worlds," began to organise the bands of deserters from the King's regiments, along with crowds of volunteers, into a force which soon became the National Guard. Few events of the French Revolution had more momentous consequences than this voluntary arming of the newly enfranchised nation. La Fayette himself prophesied that the arming of a free people would involve the downfall of all despots. For, said he, the new force, the armed nation, must "prevail over the old tactics of Europe ; and will reduce arbitrary Governments to the alternative of being beaten if they do not initiate it, or overthrown if they dare to imitate it." [1]

Of all the prophecies uttered during the French Revolution none was more correct. The portentous outcome of that movement—viz., the citizen army—did overthrow the thin parade-ground array of the kings, and did compel them in the last resort to adopt conscription. What La Fayette did not foresee (though Burke did) was the growth in France of a military despotism founded on the new force.

We must now refer to the chief influences detrimental to the success of the Revolutionary movement. Time fails me to notice more than three. These are—the lack of suitable

[1] La Fayette, *Mémoires*, ii, 267.

leaders, the prevalence of an almost blinding fanaticism, and the triumph of the crusading spirit, which largely determined the collision with the neighbouring States.

The human factor in that difficult problem was singularly embarrassing. To state the case briefly, there was no leader who combined the faculty of clear and well-balanced thought with firm but tactful action. Now, to translate thought into action is the central and underlying fact in politics, as it is in life in general. But politics, being the most difficult of all the tasks that man can undertake, needs a union of clear thought with wise action; and such a union is rare indeed. Now, what of the leaders in the France of 1789? We have seen how, at the outset, the theorist Abbé Sieyès gave a sharp twist to events. But what of the King? Louis XVI, it is generally admitted, was a kindly man, with just enough of brain capacity to know that he was unfit to be king at that crisis. Yet, unlike the case of Richard Cromwell in 1658, his retirement was unthinkable, in view of the exacting demands of French kingship and the eager promptings of his ambitious consort. During fifteen years he had wavered between his own desire of effecting economical and other highly needful reforms and the determination of Marie Antoinette to maintain the monarchy in its pristine splendour. Accordingly he zig-zagged along, more than once sacrificing to her caprice or prejudice a sage counsellor who could perchance have saved both them and the monarchy. The last scapegoat was Necker, a possible saviour even at the eleventh hour, in mid-June 1789, but soon to be exiled. As for a saviour after the King and Queen and Court were brought prisoners to Paris in those dread days of October 1789, there was only one. Mirabeau was the nearest approach to a strong man produced by the France of the old *régime*; and he was too honeycombed by its vices ever to be trusted either by King or people. How a man who was generally distrusted for his ill-concealed venality could save a tottering monarchy has never been explained by Carlyle, Morse Stephens, and the other admirers of Mirabeau. I, for one, venture to state my conviction that Mirabeau at the time of his death, in April 1791, was both politically and morally bankrupt, and therefore could not have saved the monarchy. As for the other possible leaders,

La Fayette was the most promising. He was a good soldier and a straightforward man, who for a short time enjoyed considerable popularity. Unfortunately he lacked the faculties which either attract men or dominate them. Therefore in every sphere of life he achieved only a half-success, and was soon left behind. Nevertheless, it is possible that if La Fayette, Mirabeau, and Necker could early have acted together (which their vanity or distrust prevented) such a triumvirate might have stemmed the torrent. As it was, they sank, or were swept aside.

There is, indeed, much truth in Mme Roland's bitter complaint that in 1789 France was exhausted in men; that the men of that decade were scarcely more than pygmies, having plenty of philosophy, knowledge, intelligence, and charm, but endowed with none of that force of soul, sustained by breadth of vision and faculty for right judgment, which marks out the truly great man, the hero.[1] Him she looked for eagerly among the would-be champions of freedom, and found not. Alas! the nearest approach to him was that little Corsican lieutenant of artillery, then growing up and biding his time, until the pitiful dearth of great men gave full play to his mature powers and his Cæsarian instincts. Truly, the history of the French Revolution and its sequel resides more in the annals of its men of action than in the philosophisings of its prophets.

Here, however, I must point out that some of the preceding French thinkers had kindled a perfervid faith in the perfectibility of mankind, and that this faith, raised to the nth degree during the French Revolution, became the parent of its besetting vice—fanaticism. To trace the intellectual sources of this fatal defect would require a volume; for they lie deep in the character of that nation, cradled in absolutism and nurtured in the creed of an easily attainable millennium. Even the *économistes* had inspired exaggerated hopes of what might be accomplished by agrarian and fiscal reforms, so that the demand for *l'impôt unique* found expression in some of the rural *cahiers* of 1789; but hopes in that direction paled before those aroused by the social architects Mably and Morelly,

[1] *Mémoires de Mme Roland* (ed. Barrière), p. 264. See, too, Dumont, *Souvenirs sur Mirabeau*, chapter 17.

who beckoned mankind on to a veritable Eden; while Rousseau by dextrous logic proved that the sovereignty of the general will must lead to an improved Swiss Arcadia.

The ease of these politico-social architectonics constituted the chief danger for the untrained and therefore fascinated observers. "It is difficult not to become impassioned in a Revolution," wrote Mme Roland.[1] And how much the more so when its methods were syllogistic and its conclusion celestial! The creed became fixed (for the first time) in the month of September 1789, which witnessed the Declaration of the Rights of Man, including the absolute sovereignty of the nation. It would be of interest to trace the source of this potent idea back to Rousseau and earlier thinkers, and then to examine its development from 1789 to 1793. In the first Declaration of the Rights of Man the dogma runs thus: "The principle of all sovereignty resides essentially in the nation. No corporation (*corps*), no individual, can exercise authority which does not emanate expressly from it." The full-fledged doctrine appears in Robespierre's version of the Rights of Man accepted by the French Convention and the Jacobins Club in April 1793: "The people is the sovereign: the government is its work and its property: the public functionaries are its clerks (*commis*)." [2] As Buzot pointed out in notes written shortly before his execution, sovereignty during the resulting orgies of 1793 "was buried in the Assemblies of the sections of Paris composed of madmen or scoundrels who had daringly seized the will of all Parisians." [3] Such was the *finale* of this theory.

Even in 1789 it served as full warrant for the capture of the King, the attacks on all important corporations, especially the Church of France, and the erection of the constitutional fabric based on the first Rights of Man.

Much of this work, notably the anti-clerical decrees, was marked by hatred of the old order of things and frenzy for the new logical system derived from Rousseau. Nevertheless, the new order, founded by the autumn of 1791, was conceivably workable provided that its designers, who now had gained some experience, remained to work it. But by an act

---

[1] *Mémoires de Mme Roland* (ed. Barrière), p. 256.
[2] *Histoire parlementaire*, xxvi, 95.   [3] *Mémoires de Buzot* (ed. 1866), p. 30.

of incredible folly the "Constituents" declared themselves ineligible for the next, or Legislative, Assembly.

To it there now come inexperienced deputies, whose chief recommendation at the polls has been their eloquent promises to push on a Revolution which they regard as only just begun. Moreover, nominees of the Jacobins Club, which now has a network of branches throughout France, often prevail over moderates who regard the programme of 1789 as completed, and are therefore hissed and hustled aside. Accordingly another cyclone of fanaticism sets in. The Legislative Assembly soon relegates the " Constituents " to oblivion. The new members are remarkable for their inexperience, their gusty enthusiasms, and other engaging qualities of youth. Many are provincial lawyers or barristers ; and a still larger number, I regret to say, are literary men, or at least journalists. Eloquence of a windy type having won them their seats in the Legislative Assembly, blasts of eloquence fly forth daily from its tribune, while near by in the Jacobins Club the more radical of the old "Constituents" work hard and successfully to make that club a rival to the Assembly. The competition between the two bodies, first to gain, and then to keep, the lead as champion of liberty, ever accelerates the pace.

Thus, politics, which should have been an upbuilding process, resembled rather a party or a personal auction, in which the prize went to the most daring or persuasive bidder. Hence the floods of talk, the blatant appeals to the packed and expectant galleries—the result being seen in some 2000 decrees passed in less than eleven months. Hence, too, the collision with the Germanic Powers.

We cannot here review the lengthy negotiations with Austria concerning the bodies of armed French *émigrés* which were assembling in her Rhenish and Flemish domains for the purpose of invading France. For some time those bands had caused concern, even indignation. But there is little proof that Francis II of Austria wanted war with France. His dominions were in too much confusion to make an aggressive policy anything but a highly risky adventure ; and the disturbed state of his Belgic provinces seemed to offer them as an easy prize to the French arms. But the debates in the Legislative Assembly touched his pride. Finally they became so warlike in tone as to convince him that the extremists in France wanted war.[1]

The outbreak of hostilities with Austria, which soon widened into a general war, exerted so important an influence on the Revolution that a calm and detailed estimate of that influence is much needed. For such a study has, I believe, never been thoroughly made. Even Sorel, with all his power of illuminating survey, has attempted no complete estimate of the deadly blow dealt to the liberties of France when she plunged lightheartedly into a crusade for the liberties of mankind. Yet what a theme is this for the philosopher, the student, the lover of peace ! To follow the mingling of generous impulses and mean intrigues which lead to the declaration of war against Austria ; to trace the speedy sluicing of the democratic movement into militarist channels ; to note how the victories or defeats at the frontiers lead in Paris to spasms of intoxicating joy or fell butcheries in the prisons ; to show how the armies of France, while beating back the would-be invaders, yet also begin to threaten her newly won freedom, until the reasoning of the legislator is more and more silenced by the commands of the soldier—all this would tax the analysing power of a Taine, the philosophic faculty of a Sorel, the dramatising power of a Macaulay.

Let me try, first, to picture to you the scenes in the Legislative Assembly which on April 20, 1792, led up to the declaration of war on Austria. Imagine the 700 or more members seated in a great semicircle. Fronting them is the President's seat and the tribune, where the speakers deliver their orations. But above them are spacious galleries, which are crowded with eager spectators, who frequently cheer or hiss the orators. Remember that on April 19 the Assembly and also Paris has been excited by the reading out of the last dispatches between Paris and Vienna. They were read out by that questionable schemer General Dumouriez, now Minister of Foreign Affairs, who announced that on the morrow the King would visit the Assembly.

On that day, then, enter Louis XVI and his Ministers. A thin little figure, that of Condorcet the philosopher, is reading out a report on national education, when the spirit of

[1] For details see J. H. Clapham, *The Causes of the War of 1792.*

war enters and education is snuffed out. Dumouriez reads out a report on foreign affairs which tends strongly toward a rupture with Austria. At the end of it Louis rises ; and in a calm manner, which, thought Mme de Staël, betokened either resignation, dignity, or mediocrity, he proposes the declaration of war against Austria. He retires, and for the last time some cries of "*Vive le Roi !* " are raised.[1] It is the last time that he will hear them.

Did the King secretly share the hope, certainly cherished by Marie Antoinette, that the Austrians would speedily march in, crush all resistance, put down the Revolution, and restore the monarchy to its pristine splendour ? We do not know. But wild hopes of revenge certainly prompted her and several extreme royalists, who saw their chance in the war fever now rising throughout France. It appears, too, that some of the constitutionalists favoured a resort to arms as a means of strengthening authority and establishing the now tottering constitution. But the chief impulse making for war was that of their opponents. These, whether Girondins or Jacobins, sought by an attack on Austria to upset that same constitution and overthrow the French monarchy. Enthusiasts like Mme Roland, Vergniaud, and Gensonné might preach a crusade for the liberation of all peoples ; but sinister motives urged on the intriguers of the Girondin party, headed by the wire-puller Brissot. His blow, aimed ostensibly at Austria, was designed to ricochet and strike down *l'Autrichienne* and her feebler consort.[2]

Never, surely, has a war been brought about by motives so diverse. Yet though moved by very diverse reasons, the Legislative Assembly was eager for war. In the evening sitting of April 20 only one or two voices were raised for peace. Chief was that of an almost unknown member, Becquet ; and he seems to have gained the ear of the Assembly by suggesting that a motion for war, coming from the King, ought to be very carefully examined. This skilful hint even produced dead silence—a rare event. But when Becquet proceeded to argue that the work of the Revolution would be retarded, or even jeopardised, by a war murmurs arose. They redoubled when he declared that French finances needed years of peace

[1] *Histoire parlementaire*, xiv, 27–37.   [2] Sorel, Part II, pp. 398–401.

to regain stability: and Cambon, the Finance Minister, interrupted him with the singular remark, "You know nothing about the finances; we have money, more than we need." Undismayed by this ministerial bluff, Becquet declared that if the war became general their armies and fleets might inspire disquiet—*i.e.*, as to the liberties of France. (Again a storm of protests.) But he continued with an argument which won a little attention—that if they conquered Austria's Belgic provinces such a conquest would arouse the fears of Englishmen for a French conquest of Holland; and so France might find England and finally the whole of Europe against her. He also pointed out that Austria was not supporting the armed bands of French *émigrés*, and in other respects seemed still inclined to negotiate on reasonable terms, as well she might; for war would be ruinous to her. Let us, he said in substance, limit ourselves to defence if any Power attacks us; and probably we shall not have war; otherwise we shall be called the aggressors, a restless people, disturbers of the peace of Europe. Let, then, the King be invited to renew the negotiations and prevent a rupture of the peace.

Such was this able plea for moderation and delay, which might have saved France and Europe nearly a quarter of a century of war and eventual reaction. The Assembly would have none of it. The passions of the moment, again fanned by Guadet, Mailhe, and Merlin de Thionville, drown the voice of reason; and the war vote is carried with only seven dissentients—Théodore de Lameth, Jaucourt, Dumas, Gentil, Baert, Hua, and Becquet. Thereupon Condorcet, champion of national education, reads out a philosophic treatise which he has drawn up in favour of a crusade for the liberation of the enslaved peoples of the world. At the end he declares that every man is a soldier when he fights against tyranny, and that France will conquer or else will perish utterly along with her liberty and her laws.[1]

As in these articles we are seeking to assess the influence of the thinkers, we should remember that the most intellectual group among the French Republicans, that of the Girondins, was chiefly responsible for the outbreak of war. And in this

[1] *Histoire parlementaire*, xiv, 37–53. See, too, the sage comments of Sorel, Part II, pp. 430–438.

action they were guided not by any of the preceding political thinkers, but by party and personal motives. "La Gironde voulait la guerre et, par la guerre, le pouvoir."[1] In those damning words Sorel sums up the governing motives of the men who launched the Revolution into war. It is mere playing with adjectives to say that the war with Austria was 'inevitable.' No war is inevitable until it is actually declared. Yet these Girondins were well-read men. Their speeches are full of appeals to Aristides and Brutus. But they forgot that the war spirit is almost always destructive, rarely constructive; that, though their crusade might dethrone Louis XVI and other kings, it would not found the French Republic on a sure basis. They forgot also the wise warning of Burke, that the worse the turmoil in France, the stronger would be the trend toward a military dictatorship.[2] Alone among the French Republicans, Robespierre discerned this danger; but, with his almost feline capacity for survival, he uttered scarcely a single protest against the Gironde's very popular war policy, probably because he foresaw the ruin of that party in the storm which it had raised, but could not control.

Certainly the contact of those wordy rhetoricians with hard facts was staggering. It produced a state first of dismay, then of fury. When Paris seemed in danger from the Austrians and their Prussian allies the parties in the Assembly which had light-heartedly voted for war began to accuse each other of treachery. As Mme Roland noted in her *Mémoires*, "this was the time of the great division between the patriots."[3] Such a schism was but natural. When hopes of a liberation of the human race beat high it is exasperating to hear of the soldiers of liberty running away before the slaves of tyrants. Such an event must be due to treachery. Forthwith there begins an eager treason-hunt. All who are in office speedily become unpopular.[4] After Louis and Marie Antoinette are dethroned and immured in the Temple the new Girondin Ministers become suspect. Hoping to avert suspicion, they declare the Republic; but still, even after the victory of

---

[1] Sorel, Part II, p. 395.

[2] Burke, *Reflections on the French Revolution*, ed. E. J. Payne (Oxford 1886), p. 260.

[3] *Mémoires de Mme Roland* (ed. Barrière), p. 451.

[4] "La Gironde avoit touché le pouvoir. . . . Cela suffisait à la rendre suspecte aux yeux des démagogues" (Sorel, Part II, p. 511).

Valmy, suspicion clings about them. To recover popularity they again fan the war spirit. Now, thanks to French bravery and Allied lethargy, they succeed, and when the victory of Jemappes lays Belgium at their feet Brissot and his colleagues widen the bounds of the crusade. All the kings are now threatened; and, as Danton says, Frenchmen hurl down the head of their king as gage of battle. Meanwhile the Girondins, who have been hustled into regicide, adopt, from party necessities, a policy of aggression against the Dutch Netherlands, which brings Great Britain into the war.

At this second and even greater crisis the war spirit prevails over all the counsels of prudence. Brissot, in a lengthy report of the " Comité Diplomatique," accuses the British Government of conspiring against the liberties of France, and therefore proposes a declaration of war. With little or no discussion of this vague charge the Assembly approves it unanimously (February 1, 1793). The declaration of war includes Holland, because " her stadtholder is more the subject than the ally of the Cabinet of St James's." On this occasion not a single deputy questions the wisdom of a war policy; and at the Jacobins Club the same unanimity prevails.[1] After war is declared Cambon, Minister of Finance, admits that the financial outlook is not altogether satisfactory; but he states that it was the Dutch who had lent money to the Continental Powers for the war, and they also sustained the public credit of England. Therefore the French must seize Amsterdam.[2] Probably the desire of overrunning the Dutch Netherlands and of seizing their banks and their fleet explains that singular war vote of February 1, 1793. But the crusade for liberty quickly degenerates into a war of conquest; and this degeneration proceeds apace in the years 1794, 1795, when the French hosts—a nation in arms—push back the thin array of the Allies and break up that always unsteady Coalition. La Fayette's prophecy came true. The armed nation was more than a match for the kings.

But the victory cost France dear. The quick alternations between hope and fear shook the mental stability of a people not very remarkable for that virtue. Still, it is fair to say that no nation has ever experienced such violent oscillations of the

[1] *Histoire parlementaire*, xxiv, 204–207.   [2] *Ibid.*, p. 222.

political thermometer. Raised to fever heat in April 1792; then chilled by defeats; then exalted by the news of Valmy, Jemappes, and the conquest of Belgium; then in the spring of 1793 depressed to zero by the advance of the armies of the Coalition; then again masters of Belgium; and finally, in 1795, masters of the natural frontiers—the Rhine, Pyrenees, and ocean. Have the spirits of any nation ever sunk so low or soared so high? [1] What wonder, after all, that King and Queen, all the nobles and refractory priests that could be seized, Minister after Minister, general after general, official after official, were hurried off to the guillotine? The Terror was possible only because a large part of France was half mad with terror or fanaticism. A deputy of the Convention revealed the purpose of the extremists when he asserted, "We must continue the war that the convulsions of liberty may be the stronger." [2]

How much wiser were the Russian revolutionaries in 1917! After seizing on power they made peace—an ignominious and shameful peace, it is true—but by that act they gained a better chance to carry through their revolution. We may go farther, and say that few if any great revolutions have been successful if they have been complicated by a great and at times dangerous foreign war. The lot of England has in this respect been fortunate indeed; for the critical parts of our two revolutions were not warped by foreign war, and these movements therefore ran a normal course. It was the foreign war, I maintain, which made the French Revolution abnormal. But for the danger on the frontiers there would have been no sufficient excuse for the Reign of Terror; and possibly France would have been spared that ghastly episode.

In fine, it was the fears, the hopes, the passions aroused by war which intensified the Revolutionary cyclones. Always terrifying, that movement now gyrated bewilderingly. For a time all attempt at guidance seemed alike futile and fatal; for official responsibility became a sure passport to the scaffold.

In such a state of things the struggle was mainly one between the 'ins' and the 'outs'; and the nuances of a political creed became a secondary question. After all, there was at

---

[1] See Sorel, Part II, p. 530; De Tocqueville, *Ancien Régime*, Book I, chapter iii.
[2] Mme de Staël, *Considérations*, Part III, chapter xvi.

first no very decided difference between Girondins and Jacobins; and M. Aulard has shown that few differences of principle separated them over the new constitution of June 1793.[1] The much bruited charge that the Girondins were bent on splitting up France into a set of federal republics was also palpably false, as was shown by some of their leaders, no less than by Mme Roland in her *Mémoires*.[2] But in the urgent war crisis of the summer and autumn of 1793, which that party failed to stem, the charge was good enough to get rid of them; and they perished at the hands of men who shouted more loudly for "la République une et indivisible."

Next the victorious faction of the Jacobins split in twain. It is often said that the schism was due to questions of religion and morality. In reality (so it seems to me) it was the ill-fortune of the so-called atheistical group to come to the top in the spring of 1794, when the fortunes of France were still doubtful, and when the blockade by the British fleet began to tell heavily on prices. The orgy of suspicion being accentuated by want, the governing group became unpopular and could be disposed of by any specious charge well driven home by that skilful tactician Robespierre. A victory of theism over atheism, of Rousseau over Holbach? Be it so, if you will. For my part, I suspect that it was again a question of the 'outs' getting rid of the 'ins,' who were held responsible for the depressing outlook. And note that when theistic respectability in the person of "the sea-green incorruptible" tries to play the dictator his life is worth four months' purchase over that of the Hébertists and Dantonists.

By the time of the overthrow of Robespierre, on July 28, 1794, France had run through the whole gamut of political thought and found it all more or less vain. She therefore began painfully and wearily to pick her way back to more ordinary methods of government. But while her civilians were utterly tired of constitutional experiments, her soldiers triumphed on the frontiers. The tricolour was waving along the Rhine and beyond the Alps and Pyrenees. In this glaring contrast between the seeming bankruptcy of political ideals and the brilliant successes of her armies lay the unique

[1] Aulard, *The French Revolution* (English translation), ii, 174–202.
[2] *Mémoires de Mme Roland*, pp. 281–282.

opportunity which presented itself to the greatest soldier and the greatest organiser of the modern world.

In this article I have attempted a brief survey of the Revolutionary era from the point of view of the working out of the contributory political thought. That thought has often been praised or blamed as the chief factor determining the events of 1789 and later. While not denying its importance, I maintain that we must also assign even greater importance to the condition and therefore the conduct of the masses, which knew little or nothing about political ideas. I have shown how from the start the masses and the demagogues pushed on events at a rate certain to produce political dizziness in a people who had long been unaccustomed to any political action at all. The suddenness of their triumph in 1789 was a misfortune; for no movement can succeed unless it meets with intelligent criticism and opposition; and such opposition as the French Revolutionists encountered from the privileged classes was no less weak than foolish. Finally, when crusading enthusiasm led to the rupture with neighbouring Powers the events of the war not only whetted that enthusiasm, but insensibly brought France back to the autocracy from which she seemed for ever to have escaped.

On the other hand, no one who studies that great movement can fail to admire the lofty ideals of 1789, the generous impulses on behalf of the poor and oppressed in all lands, and the mighty sweep of its aims; for no people has attempted, and in part achieved, so much in a short time. Also there hovers over its earlier actions a romance which is truly French. How affecting are those fraternal federations of townsfolk and villagers before "l'autel de la patrie," on which they swear to obey and to defend the new order of things! But, like Wordsworth, who danced with the *fédérés* in the Rhone valley, we deplore the civil strifes that followed and the acrid suspicions that speedily corroded the universal joy; and I maintain that the chief cause of this change was the war with the Germanic Powers, and thereafter with Great Britain and Holland. Before those events there was a chance that the best of the teachings of the foregoing thinkers might take root. But the seed-bed is as important as the seed cast on it; and

THE REVOLUTIONARY ERA IN FRANCE

war never yet provided a suitable seed-bed for reforming ideas. It provides either arid rock or an unnatural forcing-bed, in which the best seed takes on a rank and noxious growth. Wrongly, then, did Napoleon, as he stood before the tomb of Rousseau, blame him as the chief cause of the misfortunes of Europe. Rather should those misfortunes be attributed to the war spirit, which became incarnate in the warrior-emperor himself.

J. Holland Rose

BOOK LIST

Acton, Lord : *Lectures on the French Revolution.*
Aulard, A.: *The French Revolution* (English translation, 4 vols.).
Carlyle, T. : *The French Revolution,* edited with notes by J. Holland Rose.
Dickinson, G. L.: *Revolution and Reaction in Modern France.*
Faguet, M. E.: *L'Œuvre sociale de la Révolution française.*
Fling, F. M. : *Source Problems on the French Revolution.*
Lefebvre, C., Guyot, R., and Sagnac, P. : *La Révolution française.*
Mignet, F. A.: *The French Revolution.*
Rocquain, F. : *The Revolutionary Spirit preceding the French Revolution.*
Rose, J. Holland : *The Revolutionary and Napoleonic Era.*
Rousseau, J. J.: *The Social Contract* (either the French text, edited by C. E. Vaughan, or the English translation by H. J. Tozer).
Sorel, A.: *L'Europe et la Révolution française,* Parts I, II.

EDMUND BURKE

EDMUND BURKE has been described as "one of the greatest men, and—Bacon alone excepted—the greatest thinker who ever devoted himself to the practice of English politics." This high eulogy does not appear to be excessive, even if one, in repeating it, bears in mind that Burke has to stand comparison with men so eminent intellectually as Clarendon and Bolingbroke; Canning and Peel; Gladstone and Disraeli; Salisbury, Asquith, and Balfour. One cannot, indeed, rise from a perusal of Burke's voluminous writings without a profound conviction that their author was a man of pre-eminent character, lofty patriotism, superb intellect, fiery zeal, and that "infinite capacity for taking pains" which has been curiously termed genius.

The feature, however, that specially distinguishes Burke from the other writers dealt with in this series of studies is not his character, his ability, or his diligence; it is the fact that he was not only a thinker of the first rank, but also a practical politician who for the thirty most active years of his life played a prominent part on the stage of great affairs. Of our other thinkers, Paine never reached in England a more exalted eminence than that of an excise officer; Godwin at the end of a long and unsuccessful career was nothing more lofty than a yeoman-usher of the Exchequer, living in New Palace Yard, and drawing £200 a year as a sinecurist; Bentham, a man of independent means, lived to the age of eighty-four without holding any sort of public office—a semi-recluse, spending his days in a house appropriately called the Hermitage, occupied like a lonely spider in spinning utilitarian webs.

Some there were who regretted that Burke allowed himself to be lured from the calm heights of philosophical speculation down to the plains whereon party politicians contended noisily, "not without dust and heat." Goldsmith, for instance, in well-known lines lamented that he who was

> born for the universe, narrow'd his mind,
> And to party gave up what was meant for mankind.

In a similar strain, one of Burke's early biographers, Dr Robert Bisset, a deep-dyed Tory, confessed, not unnaturally, that he did not "rejoice at the commencement of his connection with the Marquis of Rockingham" (1765), adding that "from that time he may be considered as a party man." "Burke," he continued, "ought not to have stooped to be the object of patronage. Like his friend Johnson, he should have depended entirely on his own extraordinary powers."[1] It is impossible not to sympathise with the spirit of these remarks. For on the one hand Burke had a philosophic mind of such strength and clarity that, if he had dedicated it to the unprejudiced pursuit of political principle, he could probably have produced works worthy to rank with the masterpieces of Plato and Aristotle, and far above the amateur lucubrations of Hobbes, Locke, and Rousseau. His essay on *The Origin of our Ideas of the Sublime and the Beautiful,* begun when he was an undergraduate in his teens and published when he was but twenty-seven, shows powers of independent thought of a high order. His ironical *Vindication of Natural Society,* issued anonymously in 1756, displays so complete and so contemptuous an acquaintance with both the reactionary principles of Bolingbroke and the revolutionary speculations of Rousseau as to indicate that even at that early date Burke stood fully equipped as a champion to defend civilised society against either those who would stop its steady advance, or those who would stampede it into a reckless abandonment of its base. The story that at one time, the exact date of which is a matter of much controversy, he was a candidate for a philosophical chair at Glasgow University—whatever element of truth it may contain—suggests that in the fifties he was a figure of some prominence in the world of metaphysicians. On the other hand, there can, unfortunately, be no doubt that his immersion in party controversy, from 1765 to his death, thirty-two years later, adversely affected the quality of his work. He became

[1] R. Bisset, *Life of Edmund Burke* (1798), p. 69.

an Old Whig apologist, and his zeal to maintain the Old Whig cause against all comers led him not infrequently to make assertions and develop arguments that in philosophical quietude he would emphatically have repudiated. From 1765 to 1783, probably, his official Whiggism put no strain upon his scientific conscience; the Whigs, as opposed to George III and the King's Friends, were the "men of light and leading." In 1783, under the reckless and unprincipled command of Charles James Fox, the Whigs made the fatal mistake of combining with the Tories of Lord North's reactionary rout for the purpose of driving Lord Shelburne from office and imposing their will upon the King. Burke, unhappily, although his alienation from Fox and the New Whigs had already begun, lent his support to the deadly Fox-North coalition, and for eight years his conduct in Parliament displayed a factiousness and unreason that no excuses can palliate. He attacked the younger Pitt with sustained and unpardonable animosity; he opposed his wisest measures—*e.g.*, the Eden treaty with France—and his various proposals for cautious Parliamentary reforms; he supported with sophistical arguments—*e.g.*, in the matter of the Regency Bill of 1788— principles plainly subversive of the Constitution; in general, he showed a passion and a prejudice that made even his friends ashamed of his aid. In 1790, however, the development of the French Revolution, by severing his uneasy and improper association with Fox and the New Whigs, restored him to sanity and sobriety and enabled him to do an imperishable service to humanity in exposing the true nature of the Jacobinism that was devastating the Continent.

If, then, Burke's political utterances—speeches, letters, dissertations, memorials—suffer from lack of detachment and philosophical impartiality, they gain from the fact that they are intimately associated with the actual course of current events. They are models of applied philosophy. They deal with the controversies of the passing moment *sub specie æternitatis*. They reveal the workings of a powerful mind that was never content until it had traced an argument back step by step to its ultimate source in "the eternal laws of truth and right."

This intimate association, however, in Burke's writings of the abstract and the concrete, the theoretical and the practical, the eternal and the temporal, has two consequences of an embarrassing nature. First, it compels every reader who wishes to understand Burke's works to make an exhaustive study of both his life and his times. Secondly, it imposes upon him the task of attempting to extract Burke's social and political ideas from masses of irrelevant and obstructive detail that have long since ceased to be either interesting or important. Thus Burke, in spite of his eloquence and lucidity, tends to be a weariness to the flesh. And the weariness is unnecessarily increased by the fact that there is no satisfactory life of Burke extant, and no properly edited collection of his works. In spite of the labours of Mr Bertrand Newman, Lord Morley, and Mr Thomas Macknight, the best biography still is that of Sir James Prior, first published in 1824. As to the various editions of the works of Burke, their name is legion and chaos. The first edition, sponsored by Lawrence and King (1792–1827), was never properly completed. Of the numerous later editions no two that I have examined are alike.[1] The four-volume edition of Burke's speeches, issued anonymously in 1816, is beneath contempt. The four-volume edition of Burke's correspondence, laboriously collected by Earl Fitzwilliam and Sir Richard Bourke, and published in 1844, although incomparably better than the edition of the speeches, is painfully incomplete (especially for the period 1745–65) and lacking in adequate elucidation. Few greater services could be rendered by a scholar, or group of scholars, commanding leisure and money than that of preparing for the world a definitive edition of Burke's speeches and writings, accompanied by a critical survey of his life and times. For the rapid process of the world along the course which Burke with prophetical prescience foresaw, and the successive fulfilment of his predictions, makes it every day increasingly evident that he has still a message to deliver of primary significance to modern man.

II

The fact that Burke wrote no formal treatise expounding his political and social ideas, but left his principles to be dis-

[1] My references in this essay are all made to Bohn's eight-volume edition of 1854–57.

covered inductively from a study of his occasional words and his expedient deeds, renders it necessary for us—as in the case of Rousseau—to make a cursory survey of his career and of the circumstances in the midst of which it ran its course. For purposes of examination it may be divided into three periods, as follows : first, A.D. 1729–65, the period of preparation ; second, A.D. 1765–89, the period of advocacy of reform ; third, A.D. 1789–97, the period of opposition to revolution.

The date and place of Burke's birth have given rise to much controversy : seven places dispute the honour of having presented him to the world, while six different dates (ranging from January 1, 1728, to January 12, 1730) have been assigned for his nativity. It would be irrelevant to discuss the question here ; enough to say that the best opinion tends to support the claims of January 12, 1729, and of 33 Arran Quay, Dublin.[1] His father, Richard Burke, was a Protestant attorney of good ability and high integrity, but of a passionate and overbearing disposition ; he was a loyal member of the Episcopal Church of Ireland. His mother was, and remained, a devout Roman Catholic. Her maiden name was Mary Nagle ; her parental home was Ballyduff, near Castletown Roche, in County Cork. Her kindred had been among the most faithful and persistent supporters of James II in the conflicts of 1689–92, one member of her family, Sir Richard Nagle, having been James's Attorney-General. Of the fourteen or fifteen children of Richard and Mary, only four—three sons and one daughter—survived infancy. The sons were brought up in their father's faith, the daughter in her mother's. But Edmund, the second of the three sons, although reared as a Protestant, spent (for reasons of health) five of his early years among his mother's relatives in Ballyduff, and he there learned that respect for Catholicism that made him so strenuous an advocate for the abolition of the penal laws in later life. His wide religious sympathy and his broad tolerance were further enlarged when he was sent, at the age of twelve, to an excellent school established some years before at Ballitore, in County Kildare, by a pious and scholarly Quaker, Abraham Shackleton by name.

---

[1] Those interested in this question will find the best treatment of it in A. P. I. Samuels' *Early Life of Edmund Burke* (1923), pp. 1–7.

EDMUND BURKE

In April 1744[1] Burke entered Trinity College, Dublin, and there he remained for some five years. During this period his genius unmistakably displayed itself. Not only did he win a scholarship (June 1746), carry off various college prizes, and secure a good degree; but outside the routine of the schools he read widely, wrote voluminously, and showed a keen interest in current affairs. In particular, he was one of four enthusiasts for controversy who, in April 1747, founded "The Club," the first students' debating society that history records, the minute-book of which (now treasured in Trinity College) is mainly in his writing. Occasionally he acted as president, and the minutes (not in his writing on this occasion) state that in that capacity he was "damned absolute." That he did not suffer fools, or even antagonists, gladly was admitted by himself in a naïve letter of this period to his friend Richard Shackleton, son of his old headmaster: "It is against my nature," he wrote, "to see people in an opinion I think wrong without endeavouring to undeceive 'em."[2]

Besides helping to found "The Club" (which still exists, under another name) he was prominent in the institution of a notable university magazine entitled *The Reformer*, of which thirteen numbers were issued between January and April 1748. The major part of the writing was from Burke's own pen. His contributions, the style of which was amazingly mature, show that at that time he was keenly interested in the morality of the theatre, the condition of the Irish peasantry, and the evidences of the Christian religion.[3]

In the last year of his college life (1748–49) he became involved in a furious controversy that convulsed not only the university, but the city of Dublin. It is known as the "Lucas Controversy." A certain Dr Charles Lucas made a fierce and sustained attack on the notorious corruption of the Dublin Corporation. The Corporation found a defender in the able but unscrupulous Sir Richard Cox, the honour of whose family was involved. Wigs were on the Green. Burke (aged nineteen) intervened "with holy glee" in the glorious hullabaloo,

---

[1] Not 1743, as is sometimes stated. The T.C.D. year began on July 9.

[2] Samuels' *Early Life of Edmund Burke*, p. 67.

[3] Samuels, *op. cit.*, pp. 161–177, and Appendix II, where all the thirteen numbers are reprinted *in extenso*.

contributing four pamphlets on the side of Lucas the reformer which served very materially to pour oil upon the fire of Hibernian passion.[1] Like most of Burke's later political writings, they show how, in a curious way, Burke combined essential moderation of view with extreme violence of expression. That strange combination is, perhaps, characteristic of Irish sanity.

III

In 1750 Burke was sent by his father to London in order that, by way of the Middle Temple, he might enter upon the career of the law. For this career he had long been marked out. In 1745, during one of his vacations, as we learn from a letter of his, he had assisted his father at the Cork Assizes. In 1747 his name had been entered at the Temple. Mr Richard Burke, recognising his son's brilliant abilities, anticipated for him a lucrative practice, culminating in silk and the Bench. But Edmund disappointed his father's expectations. Although in London he acquired a knowledge of law that stood him in good stead all his life, he soon decided that the Bar was no place for him. Anticipating the young Disraeli—whose course in many respects was strikingly similar to Burke's—he gradually deserted law for literature, and literature for politics.[2] The elder Burke did not regard his son's abandonment of his profession with equanimity. He, like Edmund, was "damned absolute"; and the clash of two equal and opposite "damned absolutenesses," of the intense Irish variety, led to electrical discharges which in 1755 fused all connections between them and left the young man penniless to his own resources.

For the next ten years (1755–65) Edmund Burke was adrift

---

[1] The pamphlets are printed in full by Samuels, *op. cit.*, pp. 331–395. In both thought and expression they are of an incomparably higher order than any other of the utterances of the controversialists.

[2] Not only did both Burke and Disraeli desert law for literature, and literature for politics, they both, before they entered Parliament, gained intimate acquaintance with its procedure by assiduous attendance in the Strangers' Gallery; both were outsiders who forced their way into the front rank of politics by sheer energy and ability; both were impecunious and harassed by debt all their days; both, in order to improve their status, bought landed estates that they could not pay for, and both in Buckinghamshire; both, when a peerage was offered to them, selected Beaconsfield as the seat of their dignity. So much for externals. In ideas and in political principles the parallel was still closer.

upon the surface of the world. It is not easy to follow his movements, or to discover how he managed to make a livelihood. He published anonymously his *Vindication of Natural Society* (1756); he refurbished and completed his essay on *The Origin of our Ideas of the Sublime and the Beautiful* (1757). Neither of these can have produced much cash. More lucrative was the *Annual Register*, a chronicle of the events of the preceding year, which he initiated in 1759 and continued to edit for nearly thirty years. Still more satisfactory, as a source of regular income, was a secretaryship which he secured that same year (1759). His employer was a member of Parliament, wealthy, and at the time well known, W. G. Hamilton by name. Secretary to Hamilton he remained for nearly six years, during three of which his duties took him back to Dublin, and renewed his acquaintance with the political and social problems of his native land.

Mr W. G. Hamilton, however, proved to be a hard master. He demanded the whole time and the undivided service of his servant. Hence Burke, who was seething with ideas—especially concerning Irish reform—and full of ambition, bade Hamilton a tempestuous farewell, early in 1765, and so once again, at the age of thirty-six, found himself at large.

IV

Burke had served a long and strenuous apprenticeship to politics. How different his fate from that of the favoured scions of the "governing class"! The younger Pitt, for instance, finished his apprenticeship in the nursery, entered Parliament while he was still legally an infant, and by the time he was thirty-six had already been Prime Minister for a dozen years. If, however, Burke's period of preparation was protracted, and his task of procuring an entry into the closed circle of official Whigdom one of prodigious difficulty, there can be no doubt that the experience in practical affairs which he gained under Hamilton, combined with the intimate acquaintance with current problems which his editorship of the *Annual Register* entailed, enabled him to embark on a public career in 1765 with an equipment of knowledge and wisdom such as none of his contemporaries possessed.

THINKERS OF THE REVOLUTIONARY ERA

In the summer of 1765 George III, yielding to painful necessity, had called to office his enemies, the oligarchic Whigs, under the Marquis of Rockingham. Rockingham possessed rank, wealth, and character, without knowledge, intelligence, or experience. In a moment fortunate for both Burke was introduced to him as possessing precisely those endowments which he himself lacked. He made Burke his secretary, and before the close of the year helped to secure for him a seat in Parliament. Burke at once became, what he remained to the end of his days—the brain of the Old Whig party. Within a few days of his entry into the House of Commons he made a speech on American affairs that, said his friend, Dr Samuel Johnson, who surveyed him with benevolent eyes from the Strangers' Gallery, gained for him "more reputation than any man at his first appearance had ever gained before." He showed a mastery of detail combined with a grasp of underlying principle such as had rarely been seen up to that date. In force of oratory and command of language, as well as in some of his leading ideas, he recalled Bolingbroke. But he had a diligence, a sense of duty, a consciousness of responsibility, a freedom from the taint of self-seeking, that placed him in a class wholly above that of his great Conservative predecessor.

Burke had been in Parliament but little more than six months when (July 1766) George III found means to get rid of the uncongenial Rockingham Whigs. The tool of the King's malignant unfriendliness was the elder Pitt, who became at this date Earl of Chatham. Burke never forgave Chatham for his refusal to support Rockingham in 1765, and for his readiness to subvert him in 1766. On all essential points of policy Chatham and the Old Whigs were at this time in agreement. In union they might easily have averted the revolt of the American colonies. But an insane conceit, combined with a dislike of the party system of government, prevented Chatham from consenting to serve under the Whig leader. Numerous and immeasurably evil were the consequences of Chatham's intransigeance and intractability at this date.

Burke's first work in an opposition which endured for sixteen years was to write a brief but conclusive apologia for the

Rockingham Government in his *Account of a Short Administration* (1766). More considerable was a detailed pamphlet, entitled *Observations on a Late Publication*, issued in 1769. The publication criticised was a dissertation by George Grenville, Rockingham's predecessor in office, on *The Present State of the Nation*, in which that disagreeable and disgruntled politician defended Lord Bute and himself, denounced both Rockingham and Chatham, proposed fresh schemes for taxing America (together with Ireland and the East India Company), and finally recommended various changes in the British Constitution. Burke fell upon Grenville's dissertation with devastating effect: exposed the errors and folly of Bute and his successor, defended the doings of the Rockingham Whigs, riddled with ridicule Grenville's financial proposals, and denounced his suggestions for laying impious hands upon the inviolable ark of the Constitution as set up by the Covenant of 1689. The *Observations* provide a magnificent example of Burke's encyclopædic knowledge, his complete comprehension of his theme, and his overwhelming mastery in argument. The crushed and abject Grenville could make no attempt at a rejoinder. The fact, however, that Burke in his *Observations* was compelled to follow the lead of the dissertation to which he was replying necessarily cramped his style and restricted his scope. In 1770, in a still finer utterance, unrestrained by any extraneous control, he let himself go. This new work was entitled *Thoughts on the Causes of the Present Discontents*. It began by describing the troubles that harassed the Government and the nation at that date—the dispute with America, the agitation that centred round Wilkes, the Radical programme propounded by the mysterious " Junius," and so on. It went on to examine and reject the explanations of these discontents advanced by the Ministry; the true cause, it contended, was the establishment of the " double-cabinet system " of the King—the system according to which the King and his friends exercised real control over affairs of State behind the backs of the nominal and responsible Parliamentary heads of the executive. It concluded by condemning as inadequate and undesirable such suggested remedies as a Triennial Bill or a Places Bill, and contended that the only effective corrective would be a frank and full return to the party system. No defence of the party system, or government by connection, has ever been more convincing than that with which Burke concludes this masterly treatise.[1]

Of all the discontents of that distressful time the most menacing was that which was driving the thirteen American colonies to the verge of rebellion. It had been generated by the oppressive enforcement of the British Navigation Acts, by the restrictions placed on colonial industry and commerce in the interests of home manufacturers and merchants, and by the misgovernment of British officials ; it had been raised to fever-heat by the attempt of the Mother Country to tax the dominions by means of the notorious Stamp Act (1765) and Imports Duties Act (1767); in 1774 it was rapidly passing beyond the sphere of argument into the sphere of war. The British Parliament, the American Congress, the Press and the Pulpit on both sides of the Atlantic—all were angrily debating the question of right : Had the Parliament the *right* to tax the colonies? Had the American settlers the *right* of resistance? and so on. In the midst of this juridical jangle Burke inter-vened with a superb speech which lifted the whole controversy on to a higher plane. Refusing so much as to consider the problem of abstract right, whether on the one side or on the other, he devoted himself to an unanswerable demonstration of the practical unwisdom of the policy which Lord North's Government was pursuing. Next year (March 22, 1775), in the same strain, in another inimitable oration, he urged a policy of conciliation. "The question will be," he remarked in ever-memorable words,

> not whether you have a right to render your people miserable, but whether it is not your interest to make them happy. It is not what a lawyer tells me I *may* do, but what humanity, reason, and justice tell me I *ought* to do.[2]

Burke's attempts at conciliation were, of course, unsuc-cessful. Passions on both sides of the ocean were roused to so intense a pitch of exasperation that nothing but blood-letting and separation could suffice to restore tranquillity. Nevertheless, even when the blood-letting had begun Burke still strove to avert separation. Very notable is the letter

[1] Burke's works, 1854-57, i, 372-381. [2] *Ibid.*, p. 475.

which he addressed in April 1777 to the Sheriffs of Bristol—
the city for which at that date he had his seat in Parliament.
This great letter is a passionate plea for pacification, a masterly
argument for the reconciliation and harmonisation of *imperium*
and *libertas*. In spite, however, of Burke's plea, and in spite
of the labours of many other men of good will, the dreadful
arbitrament of slaughter dragged on. In 1778 Britain's
European enemies began to intervene, and by 1780 it was
evident that the colonies were irrecoverably lost. Peace by
surrender became the only possible issue of the conflict. But
Lord North, the *bête noire* of the triumphant colonists, was not
the man to negotiate peace on these terms. The Whigs, who
under Burke's guidance had all along advocated moderation,
were the only people who could do it. Hence in 1782
Lord North resigned, and the Marquis of Rockingham
came back.

It is curious that when Lord Rockingham constructed his
second Cabinet Burke had no place in it. After all the
attempts of Lord Morley and others to explain the fact, it
remains a mystery. But though excluded from the responsible
inner-circle of the Government, Burke received the lucrative
appointment of paymaster-general of the forces—an office out
of which some of Burke's predecessors had managed to extract
more than £20,000 a year. One of Burke's most public-
spirited and self-sacrificing acts was to reduce the emoluments
of this office from fluctuating percentages, which could be
made to yield almost anything that avidity could desire,
to a fixed £4000 a year. This reduction he effected as
part of a big scheme of economic reform which, outlined
in a great speech on February 11, 1780, he was able partially to realise during Rockingham's brief tenure of power
in 1782.

Brief tenure! Rockingham lived but three months after
his recall to office in March 1782. His death bereft Burke
of a faithful and lavishly generous friend. One of his last
commands, as he lay dying at Wimbledon, was to order the
cancellation of bonds for some £30,000 which represented
Burke's indebtedness to him. After Rockingham's death
Burke attached himself to Fox and Sheridan, rather than to
Shelburne and the younger Pitt, who carried on the tradition

of Chatham. Thus Burke became involved with Fox in the disastrous coalition that overthrew Shelburne in the spring of 1783, but was itself overthrown by George III and Pitt in the December of the same year.

The specific measure that enabled George III to evict the Fox–North coalition, just before Christmas 1783, was an India Bill, every item of which bears the impress of Burke's moulding hand. Burke was furious at the loss of this Bill, and still more furious at the enactment, in the face of his terrific tirades, of Pitt's very different measure for the reform of the East India Company's administration (1784). From that time onward, for the next five years and (though less exclusively) for a second five, Indian affairs occupied his attention. He was interested in India, first, as a shareholder in the East India Company, and one who had lost a good deal of money in the famous slump of 1769; secondly, as an enemy of Parliamentary corruption who resented and dreaded the hold over the constituencies which the Indian 'nabobs' (retired servants of the East India Company) were securing by means of their wealth;[1] thirdly, as a humanitarian who realised that the fortunes which the 'nabobs' were bringing back to England were not made by way of legitimate trade, but by cruel extortion and diabolical intrigue. With fiery zeal, unwearying diligence, and consummate skill he tracked these ill-gotten fortunes to their sources, and exposed them to the execration of mankind in a series of masterly speeches and writings. He came to the conclusion that the East India Company was rotten to the core and that it was totally unfit to exercise any sort of political authority. Further, he thought that he saw in the Governor-General, Warren Hastings, the *fons et origo* of all the tyranny and corruption that he discovered and denounced. Hence, when Warren Hastings returned from India in 1785 Burke and his friends at once proclaimed their intention to impeach him. The impeachment, as is well known, duly took place, dragging on its dreary length from 1788 to 1795. Although in the end Warren Hastings was

---

[1] The most conspicuous of these 'nabobs,' Paul Benfield, who was said to have come back from India with wealth that yielded him £149,000 a year, purchased eight pocket-boroughs, the representation of which passed entirely under his control. See Burke's *Speech on the Nabob of Arcot's Debts* (works, 1854–57, iii, 174, 180–182, 185–189).

acquitted—his doubtful deeds being excused by difficult circumstances and to some extent atoned for by conspicuous
services—nevertheless, the damning exposure of the nefarious
practices of the East India Company's officials for ever prevented a repetition of their crimes.

V

The conduct of the later stages of the impeachment of
Warren Hastings was greatly complicated by the fact that
Burke and the other chief managers, Fox and Sheridan, had,
while co-operating in the attack on Hastings, come into violent
conflict respecting another matter of even greater magnitude
and importance. This other matter was nothing less than the
French Revolution and the attitude of the British Government
towards it. Fox and Sheridan welcomed the Revolution with
enthusiasm, rejoiced in the emancipation of the French people,
excused their little exuberances, and wished Great Britain to
proclaim itself whole-heartedly on their side in their struggle
against a despotic king, an effete nobility, and an obscurantist
Church. They saw in the French Revolution of 1789 an
exact replica of the glorious English Revolution of a hundred
years before.

Burke from the first took a wholly different view of the
situation. He had visited Paris in 1773, had been introduced
to some of the *salons*, and had come away from them profoundly perturbed by the anti-monarchic, equalitarian, and
atheistic sentiments which he found dominant in their midst.
He had predicted at the time that such sentiments, if persisted
in, must subvert society. When, therefore, he saw them
becoming operative in 1789 he realised that the movement
just commencing was one wholly different from the cautious
and conservative change of dynasty effected in England by
the Whig magnates and the Anglican bishops in 1688–89.
While still the movement was in its early and less violent
stages he compared it with the Jacquerie in France, the
Peasants' Revolt in England, and the Anabaptist eruption in
Germany. Later, as it progressed in sanguinary terrorism,
he realised that it was the manifestation of a more profound
social upheaval than even these portentous events; that it was

"a revolution of doctrine and theoretic dogma" comparable in its magnitude to nothing less epoch-making than the Reformation itself.

The sharp divergence of view respecting the French Revolution which separated Burke and Windham from Fox and Sheridan first openly displayed itself in a great speech which Burke delivered in the House of Commons in February 1790. But the final crash and definite breach did not come until May 6, 1791, when, as the sequel to a tremendous debate, Burke repudiated both his public association and his private friendship with Fox. He soon crossed the floor of the House, and took a seat near his old antagonist (henceforth his close ally), William Pitt. In 1794, under his inspiration, the leaders of the Old Whig group—Portland, Fitzwilliam, Windham— joined Pitt's Government, and thereby brought into existence the great Conservative Party. The foremost champion of party government wrecked the party to whose interests he had devoted the best energies of the major portion of his public career. In deliberately doing so, and in thus dooming himself to obloquy and impotence, he showed that to him, after all, party government was but a means to an end, and not an end in itself; that the supreme object of all government was the well-being of the nation as a whole; and that if party degenerated into faction and went astray it was necessary for the patriot to sever himself from it and by all means oppose it.

Whilst this gradual schism of the Whigs into 'Old,' or Conservative, and 'New,' or Radical, was taking place, Burke published the most famous of all his works—namely, his *Reflections on the Revolution in France* (November 1790). Taking into consideration the date at which it was written—the middle of the second year of the Revolution—it was an amazing work. We can, of course, now see that it had serious defects; for example, that it under-estimated the grievances of the Tiers État; that it over-appreciated the merits of the French monarchy, aristocracy, and ecclesiastical hierarchy; that it failed to recognise the number and complexity of the causes that made a revolutionary change in the administration of France (however effected) imperatively necessary. But, keenly as we may be aware of the inadequacy of Burke's *Reflections* as a scientific explanation of the epoch-making events which they surveyed, we are none the less impressed by the unerring instinct which detected the true and world-wide significance of the phenomena that seemed so petty and provincial to the limited intelligence and undeveloped imagination of Fox and his friends. He saw that the bases of society and the State were menaced; he perceived that an irremediable breach in the continuity of past and present was threatened; he realised that the very life of the French nation was at stake. With his profound insight went a penetrating foresight. He predicted with uncanny prescience the course of the Revolution, deducing the probable sequence of events from the nature of the principles by which the Revolutionists were inspired. While still the King was on the throne, and ere yet the Terror had begun, he foretold the republic, the proscription, the anarchy, the war, and the final military dictatorship.

Probably no work written in England ever had a more immediate or more profound effect upon public opinion. Defective as were some of its analyses, it supplied elements of important truth that were lacking equally in the enthusiastic eulogies of Fox and in the complacent neutralities of Pitt. It enabled men—nay, it forced them—to make up their minds whether to regard the Revolution as an anticipation of Paradise or as an emanation from the Bottomless Pit. It made them realise that it was either the one or the other, but certainly not a negligible half-and-half compound of the two. It caused all the vague current sentiments of approval or disapproval to crystallise into hard convictions of zealous support or determined hostility.

As the Revolution ran its predicted course Burke followed up his *Reflections* by writing a *Letter to a Member of the National Assembly* (January 1791), an *Appeal from the New to the Old Whigs* (August 1791), and some disquieting *Thoughts on French Affairs* (December 1791), in which the approach of war was clearly indicated. Finally, when the war had broken out, when the task of checking the spread of the Revolution had proved less easy than had been expected, and when the first coalition against the French showed signs of collapsing, Burke—rapidly declining to the grave—wrote, as a testamentary bequest, his tremendous *Letters on a Regicide Peace*

(1796). " I shall not," he said at the beginning of his first letter,

> live to behold the unravelling of the intricate plot which saddens and perplexes the awful drama of Providence, now acting on the moral theatre of the world. Whether for thought or for action, I am at the end of my career.

He did not, indeed, live to complete the fourth of these minatory epistles. Just when his country's fortunes touched the lowest ebb, on July 9, 1797—the year that saw the isolation of Britain by the French, saw the imminent prospect of invasion, saw the mutiny of the Fleet at the Nore and Spithead —in the midst of almost unrelieved despondency and gloom, the great spirit of Burke passed away.

VI

To estimate the character and the achievements of Burke lies outside our province. It must suffice to say that his was a nature of singular disinterestedness and nobility; that in him the flame of patriotism—first Irish and secondarily British —burned with consuming purity and luminous clarity; that closely associated with his patriotism, yet always subordinate to it, was his devotion to his party and his loyalty to its chief; that he possessed a superb courage which enabled him without perturbation or flinching to face his angry constituents at Bristol, the raging rioters of Gordon's rout in London, the sullen hostility of the King's Friends, and the resentful fury of the Radicals and Revolutionaries; that in his speeches and writings he displayed an intellectual power of the highest order—a power of accumulating and digesting vast masses of material, a power of classifying and arranging it with masterly lucidity, a power of presenting it with overwhelming effect in the light of general principles; and that he combined with his splendid mental capacities a keenly sensitive, high-strung, emotional disposition. Such qualities, of course, had their defects. His nobility was such that he did not always detect the ignobility of some of his associates; his patriotism occasionally took the negative shape of mere hostility to foreigners; his loyalty to his party sometimes led him (especially during the lustrum 1784–89) into excesses of factiousness; his courage tended to degenerate into insensate obstinacy; his emotional sensitiveness led him (especially in his later years) into displays of unbridled passion that alienated the sympathy of even his most devoted friends. He had plenty of wit, but he lacked the saving grace of humour. He showed a marvellous command of all the resources of language, yet he failed in that supreme art of the orator which consists in the adaptation of the theme to the capacity of the audience. As his friend Goldsmith said in lines that have become hackneyed, he,

> too deep for his hearers, still went on refining,
> And thought of convincing, while they thought of dining.

He was a fine conversationist, not inferior to his friend and rival in the Literary Club, Dr Samuel Johnson. He was at his best in addressing his fellowmen, and it is noteworthy that all his greatest works are cast in the form of either speeches or letters. Even when he was writing he was never wholly at ease unless he had in his mind's eye a specific correspondent whom he was endeavouring to convince or to refute. Thus, as we have already remarked, he composed no formal treatise on the science of politics or the theory of the State. He dealt with the current public affairs of the day. Most of his important utterances, whether of voice or of pen, grouped themselves round one or other of five great themes—namely, (1) Ireland, (2) the American colonies, (3) the British Constitution, (4) the East India Company, and (5) the French Revolution.

The most conspicuous general features of his political outpourings are, first, his avoidance of abstract political speculation and his denunciation of the metaphysical treatment of practical affairs; secondly, his insistence on the empirical nature of the art of government; thirdly, his appeal to history and experience as the only satisfactory guides in administrative matters; fourthly, his emphasis on considerations of expediency, rather than on arguments based on rights, in all debatable problems of policy; and, finally, the essential moderation of all his opinions, even when he expressed these opinions with extreme immoderation of language.

When Burke began his public career he found himself in

the midst of a furious battle of clashing ideologies. On the one side stood Rousseau and his followers vehemently proclaiming the dogmas of the original liberty and the primitive equality of man; the natural rights of the individual; the sovereignty of the people; and the supremacy of a universal law, entirely different from the laws of civilised society, known only to the anarchic conscience of the illuminated. Over against this revolutionary rout stood the serried forces of the more or less "benevolent despots." These forces were entrenched for the defence of the dogma of the divine right of kings, with all its appendant doctrines of the duty of passive obedience and the invariable wrongfulness of resistance to the Lord's anointed. Burke felt himself to be entirely out of sympathy with both sets of combatants. He realised that the theories of each party—benevolent despots or malevolent democrats—if carried to their logical conclusions would lead to intolerable consequences. Was there no way of escape for suffering man from horrible alternatives of the Scylla of tyranny and the Charybdis of chaos?

He believed that there *was* a way of escape, and that it lay along the road of compromise and common sense. The end of government, he held, was not the realisation of idealistic theories, but the welfare of the nation. To this extent he was, like David Hume, a utilitarian before Bentham—but not before Bolingbroke. Intensely as he detested Bolingbroke's theology, in politics he was undoubtedly his disciple, and the developer of his ideas. Striking as are the superficial differences between the *Patriot King* and the *Thoughts on the Present Discontents*, there is in them a fundamental identity in motive and a broad agreement as to means. Bolingbroke had said in 1738, in words the novelty of which was more evident to his contemporaries than it is to us, "The ultimate end of all Governments is the good of the people, for whose sake they were made, and without whose consent they could not have been made." [1] No sentiment could possibly have been more consonant with Whiggism, and Burke constantly echoed and re-echoed it. In his American speeches, his Indian addresses, his Irish letters, his French reflections—everywhere it occurs and recurs. "All political power," he said in supporting

[1] A. Hassall, *Bolingbroke on Patriotism*, p. 73.

Fox's India Bill in 1783, "which is set over men . . . ought to be some way or other exercised ultimately for their benefit." Again, in his *Reflections*: "Kings, in one sense, are undoubtedly the servants of the people, because their power has no other national end than that of the general advantage." So too in his letter to Sir Hercules Langrishe anent Ireland: "The good of the commonwealth is the rule which rides over the rest, and to this every other must completely submit." The application of this rule meant that measures were to be judged not by their accordance with systems antecedently constructed, but by their consequences as estimated by the standard of—not exactly felicity, and certainly not mere material comfort, but rather a real and comprehensive well-being that looked more to character and destiny than to circumstances and ephemeral pleasure. It was in this appreciation of spiritual values that Burke differed profoundly from the utilitarians of the schools of Hume, Helvétius, Bentham, and—low be it whispered respecting the venerable archdeacon—Paley.

Bolingbroke, then, was Burke's great forerunner and teacher. But, although Bolingbroke in his later political writings had propounded principles of (considering the writer's antecedents) astonishing Whiggishness, it was scarcely possible for a prominent member of the Whig Party during the reign of the son of Bolingbroke's model "patriot king" openly to avow himself a Bolingbrokian. "Who now reads Bolingbroke? Who ever read him through?" he asked in his *Reflections*; and a little later in the same work he remarked, "I do not often quote Bolingbroke, nor have his works in general left any permanent impression on my mind. He is a presumptuous and a superficial writer." These unkind observations recall the repudiations of Peter in the hall of the high-priest's house. For Burke, especially in his early and most impressionable years, was soaked in Bolingbroke; and his style never lost the form given to it by that Augustan master of resounding rhetoric.

Not Bolingbroke, however, but Locke was the oracle of the Whig Party. Locke was the philosopher of the "glorious revolution" of 1688, and upon the basis of that revolution, as interpreted and vindicated by Locke, the whole edifice of eighteenth-century Whiggism had been erected. Hence it followed that Burke, who in his fundamental political conceptions differed *toto cælo* from Locke, was compelled to render him life-service; just as the modern Labour M.P., however sensible an individualist he may be, is bound to speak respectfully of Marx. One of the most interesting tasks that a student of political theory is called upon to perform in his perusal of the writings of Burke is to observe the way in which his author, when he comes face to face with a distinctive Lockian idea, bows down to it and worships, circumvents it, knocks it over from behind, and then goes on his way rejoicing. What are the principal Lockian ideas in the sphere of political theory? They are, of course, (1) the conception of the State and Government as artificial creations, based on contract, and built up by means of a series of legal enactments; (2) the inherence in the individual, anterior to the formation of the State, of a number of natural rights—especially the rights to life, liberty, and property—the protection of which is the prime function of the State; (3) the superiority of natural law to all laws of human origin; and (4) the complete separation of the functions of Church and State.

Perhaps the best example of Burke's attitude to Locke is to be found in his treatment of the contract theory. This theory is fundamental to Locke; for the whole Whig defence of the expulsion of James II in 1688 was based on the assertion that the Stuart monarch had "endeavoured to subvert the constitution of the kingdom by breaking the original contract between King and people." [1] The contract theory was the Whig riposte to the Tory dogma of the divine hereditary right of the ruler. Burke, therefore, as a member of the Whig party, as secretary to the Whig Prime Minister, and as the vindicator of Whig policy in Parliament and Press, could not be disrespectful to contract. But it was wholly alien from his system of thought. This is how, in a famous passage, he saluted and destroyed it:

> Society is indeed a contract . . . but the State ought not to be considered as nothing better than a partnership agreement in a trade of pepper and coffee, calico or tobacco, or some other such low concern, to be taken up for a little temporary interest, and to be dissolved by the fancy of the parties. It is to be looked on with other reverence;

[1] Resolution of House of Commons, January 1689.

because it is not a partnership in things subservient only to the gross animal existence of a temporary and perishable nature. It is a partnership in all science; a partnership in all art; a partnership in every virtue, and in all perfection. As the ends of such a partnership cannot be obtained in many generations, it becomes a partnership not only between those who are living, but between those who are dead and those who are to be born. Each contract of each particular State is but a clause in the great primeval contract of eternal society, linking the lower with the higher natures, connecting the visible and invisible world, according to a fixed compact sanctioned by the inviolable oath which holds all physical and all moral natures each in their appointed place.[1]

If one asks what is the meaning of this sonorous passage, the answer is that as it stands it has none. It is resounding nonsense. In particular, the concluding sentence respecting "primeval contracts" and "inviolable oaths" is the emptiest verbiage. But its sheer vanity and vacuity has a profound significance; it sublimates Locke's contract theory into limbo. What could a sober lawyer make of an agreement between the dead and the unborn; from whom would he get his fee? What sort of an oath is that which holds the stars in their courses? Language has obviously lost its ordinary meaning. But, with the rest of the vocabulary, the term "contract" has virtually vanished away; that is to say, it has been so completely eviscerated and embalmed that it remains as a mere mummy of its Lockian self. With it has departed from the palace to the pyramid the whole attendant company of Locke's individualistic concepts. The way is made clear for the entry of the new (yet immemorially old) idea of society as an organism; of the State as arising from the will of God rather than from the wit of man; of the community as an entity claiming priority to each and all of its members. Burke, in short, was preparing the way for the transmutation of Old Whiggism into New Conservatism.

VII

Respecting the other Lockian fundamentals—that is, natural law, the inherent primeval rights of the individual, and the

[1] *Reflections on the Revolution*, Burke's works, 1854–57, i, 368–369.

complete separation of the spheres of Church and State—it is
not possible to quote quite so striking an example of formal
acceptance combined with substantial repudiation as in the
case of the contract theory. Nevertheless, they were all of
them, in effect, eliminated from his system. The only laws
that Burke in practice recognised were the laws of God and
the laws of civilised society. The *lex naturæ* or *jus naturale*,
which had played so large a part in juridical speculation from
the days of the Stoics and the early Christian Fathers down
to the days of Aquinas, Suarez, Hooker, Grotius, and Locke,
simply vanished ghostlike from the political stage. It was
playing too prominent a part in Rousseau's travelling mena-
gerie for Burke to have any place for it in his subsidised
theatre.

The inherent primeval rights of the individual—the right
to life, the right to liberty, the right to property—were in the
same case. Burke did not—could not as a good Whig—
definitely denounce them. Nay, he even appealed to them
now and again, when it suited him to do so, as, for example,
in his defence of the peoples of India against the tyranny of
Warren Hastings. But as a rule he ignored them, and, in the
case of the French Revolutionists, refused to allow them to be
employed as weapons to rebut the claims of the French
monarchy. The only rights that he commonly admitted as
valid were rights based on the civil laws of the State, provided
that civil laws accorded with the precepts of the eternal law
of God.

But the law of God, the will of Heaven, the Divine Providence, he regarded as supreme over all. It was, indeed, in
the eminent place that he assigned to religion that he differed
most widely from the philosophical and semi-secular Locke.
Locke's famous theory of toleration was based on the view
that the State has nothing to do with religion. The State,
he maintained, is wholly concerned with this world; religion
with the next. The function of the State is to defend man's
natural rights on earth; the function of the Church is to
convey his soul to heaven. Hence, unless the Church tres-
passes upon the sphere of the State by promulgating immoral,
anti-social, or anti-political doctrines, it should be left severely
alone—neither fostered nor persecuted. This attitude of

rather unfriendly aloofness was impossible for Burke. For he was profoundly religious, and he held that the very foundations of society were laid deep in the doctrines of God, free will, and immortality.

Thus, if we ask what was the system of thought that Burke instituted in place of the individualistic, conventional, legalistic, contractual, and semi-secular system of Locke, the answer will, I think, be in substance as follows. First and foremost he emphasised the religious basis of society. Professor John MacCunn so clearly and tersely summarises his views that I cannot do better than quote his words. "Burke's political religion," he says,

> has its roots deep in three convictions. The first is that civil society rests on spiritual foundations, being indeed nothing less than a product of divine will; the second, that this is a fact of significance so profound that the recognition of it is of vital moment, both for the corporate life of the State and for the lives of each and all of its members; and the third, that whilst all forms of religion within the nation may play their part in bearing witness to religion, this is peculiarly the function of an established Church in which the "consecration of the State" finds its appropriate symbol, expression, and support.[1]

It is in the *Reflections on the Revolution in France* that Burke most strongly expresses these views. He was horrified at the naked atheism that he saw rampant on the devastated fields of France. "We know," he cried, "and, what is better, we feel inwardly that religion is the basis of civil society, and the source of all good and of all comfort." Again: "We know, and it is our pride to know, that man is by his constitution a religious animal; that atheism is against not only our reason, but our instincts." The State, equally with society, is, he contends, of divine institution. God is its builder and maker. "He willed the State," he boldly asserts; "He willed its connection with the source and original archetype of all perfection." In another passage he adds: "All who administer in the government of men . . . stand in the person of God himself." Hence "the consecration of the State by a State religious establishment is necessary," and in England

> the majority of the people, far from thinking a religious national establishment unlawful, hardly think it lawful to be without one. . . .

[1] J. MacCunn, *Political Philosophy of Burke*, p. 122 (1913).

95

They do not consider their Church establishment as convenient, but as essential to their State. . . . They consider it as the foundation of their whole constitution, with which, and with every part of which, it holds an indissoluble union. Church and State are ideas inseparable in their minds, and scarcely is the one ever mentioned without mentioning the other.

An echo of the last sentiment occurs in the first letter to Langrishe:

There is no man on earth, I believe, more willing than I am to lay it down as a fundamental of the constitution that the Church of England should be united and even identified with it.

A thinker so convinced as was Burke of the divine origin of society, State, and government could not take a merely mechanistic view of human institutions. Just as "poeta nascitur non fit," so, in his opinion, was community more akin to an organism than to an organisation. It was created rather than constructed; its development was a growth rather than an elaboration; it had the unity and continuity of life rather than the fortuitous complexity of an invention. In other words, Burke lifted political theory out of the category of law in which it had wallowed for a couple of centuries into the category of biology, wherein it was to run riot during the next hundred years. He constantly used such metaphors as "The physician of the State, who, not satisfied with the cure of distempers, undertakes to regenerate constitutions, ought to show uncommon powers." Metaphors like this imply that the body politic is an organism in the full and proper sense of the term; but metaphors often imply more than their employer intends. And Burke never in his discreet moments went farther than to say that the State was closely akin to an organism. He never so completely divested himself of his Old Whig individualism as completely to merge man in the State, or as utterly to reduce the citizen to the rank of a mere cell in a larger entity. Indeed, in his first letter on *Regicide Peace* he went so far as to argue against those who pressed the biological analogy to the point of contending that States had necessarily the same stages of childhood, manhood, and old age as had the individual man. "Parallels of this sort," he said, rather furnish similitudes to illustrate or to adorn than supply analogies from whence to reason. The objects which are attempted to be forced into an analogy are not found in the same classes of existence. Individuals are physical beings, subject to laws universal and invariable . . . but commonwealths are not physical but moral essences. They are artificial combinations and, in their proximate efficient cause, the arbitrary productions of the human mind. We are not yet acquainted with the laws which necessarily influence the stability of that kind of work made by that kind of agent.

In this passage Burke, in the heat of argument, approaches nearer to the Lockian position than in any other passage that I recollect. Commonly, however, all his metaphors and similes indicate that he conceived of the State as an entity possessed of some kind of life—a life transmitted from bygone generations, and a life to be passed on undiminished in abundance to succeeding ages. So essential, in fact, was the biological analogy to his system of political thought that it gives us the key to his attitude toward all the great practical questions that he was called upon to discuss. He was a reformer in respect of Ireland, India, America, and the England of 1770, because he realised that circumstances constantly change, and that as they change old institutions become obsolete and need to be modified or removed. In the later language of evolution, he perceived the continual need for an organism that wishes to survive to adapt itself to its environment. On the other hand, in respect of the France and the England of 1790–97, he was an anti-revolutionary, because he was acutely conscious of the fact that Jacobinism menaced the national existence itself. The body politic might be sick and need a physician; but Jacobinism was not a medicine, but a deadly poison. The body politic might be diseased and require an operation; Jacobinism, however, did not connote a remedial amputation, but a fatal decapitation. In other words, he realised the vital necessity of preserving the continuity of the national life; the peril of making too complete a breach with the past; the mortal error of sweeping away the whole heritage of the past and trying to create all things new.

Burke as a conservative reformer was equally opposed to Jacobitism and Jacobinism. In the interest of progress he advocated the cautious improvement in the working of old-established institutions. In the interest of order he resisted irreverent innovations that paid no regard to venerable tradition, but, in contempt of historic antecedents, proceeded

> to build Jerusalem
> In England's green and pleasant land.

In the sphere of practical politics Burke was entirely consistent throughout his career: he was always a reformer and never a revolutionary; always a Conservative and never a Tory. In the sphere of political theory it is not so easy to assert and prove his undeviating consistency. For he always had Locke, like the Old Man of the Sea, on his shoulders. Sometimes he says what the Old Man tells him, and at other times he says what he himself thinks. And, as we have seen, concerning such matters as contracts, rights, law, and religion the two voices did not naturally accord. But considering the difference of spirit between the two, the divergence of language is not so great as might have been expected.

VIII

When Burke died Jacobinism seemed to be definitely in the ascendant in Europe. The "Regicide Directory" ruled in France; the Revolutionary armies, having broken up the great coalition formed against them, were sweeping victoriously over the Continent, and were menacing even England with invasion. In England itself sedition and treason, welcoming the expected Jacobin attack, threatened the total subversion of both throne and altar.

The very completeness, however, with which Burke's warnings had been justified, and his prophecies fulfilled, gave impressiveness to his reflections and appeals. His influence began to grow and to extend its range. Young statesmen, like George Canning, who for a moment had been carried away by the delusive hopes engendered by Jacobin enthusiasm, rallied to the defence of the old and tried constitution. Literary men, such as Wordsworth, Coleridge, and Southey, all of whom at one time or other had professed revolutionary principles, disillusioned by the excesses of the French, became avowed disciples of Burke, and in due course, as such, initiated

98

the Romantic Reaction, which did something to repair the damage done by the wanton destroyers of antiquity. And from that time onward the power of Burke has continued to increase and to spread the scope of its operation, until to-day the great Whig thinker and statesman lives and moves in the minds of all men throughout the wide world who wish to combine devotion to liberty with respect for authority ; hope for the future with reverence for the past ; support of party with service of the nation ; profound patriotism with sincere goodwill to all the "vicinage of mankind" ; essential moderation with zealous enthusiasm ; a sane conservatism with cautious reform.

THE EDITOR

BOOK LIST

A

BURKE, EDMUND :
1. Works. 8 vols. London, 1854–57.
2. *Speeches.* 4 vols. London, 1816.
3. *Correspondence.* 4 vols. London, 1844.

B

BAUMANN, A. A. : *Burke, the Founder of Conservatism.* 1929.
BISSET, R. : *Life of Edmund Burke.* 1798.
BURKE, PETER : *The Public and Domestic Life of Edmund Burke.* 1854.
COBBAN, A. : *Edmund Burke and the Revolt against the Eighteenth Century.* 1929.
CROLY, GEORGE : *A Memoir of the Political Life of Edmund Burke.* 1840.
HAZLITT, WILLIAM : *Political Essays.* 1819.
MACCUNN, JOHN : *Political Philosophy of Burke.* 1913.
MACKNIGHT, THOMAS : *History of the Life and Times of Edmund Burke.* 3 vols. 1858–60.
MORLEY, JOHN : *Burke, a Historical Study.* 1867.
MORLEY, JOHN : *Burke, a Biography.* 1879.
NAPIER, SIR JOSEPH : *Lecture on the Life of Burke.* 1862.
NEWMAN, BERTRAM : *Edmund Burke.* 1927.
PAYNE, E. J. : *Burke's Select Works.* 3 vols. 1874.
PRIOR, JAMES : *Life of Edmund Burke.* 1824.
ROSEBERY, EARL OF : *Appreciations and Addresses.* 1899.
SAMUELS, A. P. I. : *Early Life of Edmund Burke.* 1923.

THOMAS PAINE

IN the placid pages of an eighteenth-century English diarist, himself the incumbent of a Norfolk country parish, there occurs an interesting entry under the date January 11, 1793, Friday: "Yesterday afternoon at Lenewade Bridge the Effigy of Tom Paine and a fox's skin was hung on a Gibbet and afterwards burnt. A Barrel of Beer was given on the occasion."[1] This evidence of the disturbance created by the publication of *The Rights of Man* of Thomas Paine (the first part of which political treatise had appeared in February 1791, and the second in February 1792) is the more interesting because the diary of Parson Woodforde emphasises the remoteness of English rural society from the epoch-making events which had been happening in France since 1789. In its pages the references to the outbreak of the French Revolution are few at first, and of a date considerably later than the occurrence of its outstanding episodes, until the execution of Louis XVI shocked the conscience of Europe; nor did the incumbent of Weston Longeville concern himself with the activities of the English sympathisers with the French emancipation, beyond his hearing at archidiaconal visitations of an occasional "very good constitutional sermon preached . . . against the Seditious writings that have been and now are daily published by the Dissenters, Atheists and ill-designing Men."[2] The holocaust of effigies of Paine which was provoked throughout England by the widespread dissemination of *The Rights of Man* helped to prepare for the outburst of indignation which greeted the execution of the French monarch and for the popular enthusiasm in support of the declaration of war by Pitt against the French republic. Within less than a fortnight of the incident recorded by Parson Woodforde Louis XVI was guillotined, on January 21, and on February 1

[1] James Woodforde, *The Diary of a Country Parson*, ed. John Beresford (1929), iv, 2.
[2] *Ibid.*, iii, 379–380.

France declared war upon Holland, the prelude to hostilities with England. In the preceding December Thomas Paine, the chief representative and champion of republican and revolutionary propaganda in this country, had left its shores to escape imminent prosecution and to take a more direct part in the development of French politics by assuming the place in the National Convention to which he had been elected in the autumn by no fewer than four electoral departments.

In many respects the career of Paine was characteristic of the age in which he lived. During the threescore and twelve years of his life many revolutions occurred, in the spheres of thought and industry no less than of politics and government. It is difficult to realise that he was born into an England still enjoying the peace and plenty of Walpole's *régime*, with the second Jacobite rebellion still eight years ahead, and with the stormcloud which was to result in the conflict with France for the control of India and North America appearing as yet but the size of a man's hand upon a distant horizon. Even more difficult is it to conceive that the great economic revolution, which changed the entire face of England and the conditions both of agricultural and industrial operations, was yet unperceived, and that John Wesley had not experienced that conversion which was to mark a turning-point in the religious history not only of these islands, but of the continent of North America. The fortunes of Paine were cast in no unheroic age ; nor was he of such character as to be indifferent or unimpressed by its manifold activities. The eighteenth century was the age of Chatham and of his greater son ; it was an epoch of scientific and philosophic discovery, distinguished by the names of Cavendish, Priestley, and Hume ; its restless questioning of traditional opinions led to the vogue of deism and rationalism, whilst in historical composition its fame was established by the immortal work of Gibbon. Not less worthy of mention were the speculations of Adam Smith, and the doctrines of the French encyclopædist philosophers. Further, in reaction against the principles of the enlightenment and of common sense, came the religious revival associated alike with the rigid Calvinism of George Whitefield, and with the less exclusive and more benign Arminianism of John Wesley ; and this movement gave a noteworthy impetus to the humanitarian sentiment which in the early part of the century had found expression in the foundation of hospitals, and in the later was to turn to schemes of social philanthropy which mitigated the hardships incident upon the Industrial Revolution. Correspondent with this mental activity went an abounding physical energy, which maintained a difficult intercourse between England and the New World no less than with India, which drove Whitefield to cross the Atlantic thirteen times, and Wesley to accomplish incredible labours and itineraries of travel throughout these islands. From such an age the active mind of Paine could not fail to receive stimulus and inspiration, and of many of its activities he was a typical representative. In particular he embodied the flamboyant optimism of the early decades of the century, translating it into the political republicanism of *The Rights of Man*, and the deistic democracy of *The Age of Reason*. The external circumstances of his life are worthy of a brief survey to illustrate and elucidate the ideas of his writings and their relation to the spirit of his age.

II

Thomas Paine was born at Thetford on January 29, 1737, of a Quaker father and an Anglican mother. His education was received at the Grammar School, where he did not learn Latin—according to his own relation—"not only because he had no inclination to learn languages, but because of the objections the Quakers had against the books in which the language was taught." His natural bent was toward science and poetry, the latter of which was not encouraged, "as leading too much into the field of imagination," though his scientific interest was always acute and penetrating. The general result of this pedagogic discipline was that he " had an exceedingly good moral education and a tolerable stock of useful learning," a combination which may help to explain his convinced deism (for he loved to argue from the analogy of the watch and watchmaker) and his assurance that all men were by nature of good and beneficent moral disposition. At the age of thirteen he was apprenticed to learn his father's trade of staymaking, but after three years ran away to sea. From this adventure he returned to his trade, but not to

Thetford, and after a series of vicissitudes secured appointment as an excise officer, from which he was first dismissed for alleged neglect of duty, then restored, and finally dismissed again upon the failure of an agitation of which he had been leader to secure an increase in the remuneration of excisemen. During this period he had married twice, losing his first wife by death after a year and parting from the second by mutual consent and separation after three years' connection. He had also contracted a variety of acquaintances, including the friendship of Thomas Rickman, his subsequent biographer, and of Benjamin Franklin, the agent in London for various American states. It was by the latter's advice and with a letter of commendation to Franklin's son-in-law in Philadelphia that he determined to seek adventure and experience in North America, where he landed on November 30, 1774.

The succeeding thirteen years of Paine's life in that continent were full of pregnant events, important alike for the history of the Old and New Worlds, and for the public career of the English political agitator. He could not remain long unmoved or inactive in prospect of the series of incidents which exasperated the colonists against the home country and led finally to the expansion of sporadic outbursts of hostility into the public declaration of war. Within a year of his arrival he had contributed, under the pseudonym of "Humanus," an article to the *Pennsylvania Magazine* of October 18, 1775, which expressed his conviction "that the Almighty will finally separate America from Britain"; and this assurance developed into the dominant theme of the two-shilling pamphlet *Common Sense*, which he published on January 10, 1776. The purpose of this public profession of political faith was to sound a resounding call to the American people to fight for independence; its circulation was estimated at half a million copies, and it was followed on July 4 by the Declaration of Independence of the united provinces. The enterprise thus undertaken was to prove difficult of achievement; and in "the times that tried men's souls" of the ensuing years Paine's pen was employed with frequent recurrence in a series of hortatory pamphlets, of increasing denunciation of England and insistence that only by complete independence could the liberty of America be ensured. In all his writings Paine was the unrelenting foe of compromise or pacification without emancipation from the allegiance of the British Crown. Nor were his services limited to the power of his pen; he enlisted in the army, and acted also as secretary to a Committee of Foreign Affairs set up by the states. He remained to see the victory won, and to receive official recognition of his meritorious efforts in the shape of the grant of a house, estate, and revenue from a grateful President and administration. But he could not endure to remain in the tranquillity of hardly won victory; his spirit was moved with desire to return to England in order to propagate there the principles of liberty and republicanism which had won such a resounding triumph in America. Accordingly, in the spring of 1787, he returned to Europe.

During the first months after his arrival Paine moved to and fro between England and France, renewing the friendships of his earlier years and making the acquaintance of the American ambassador Jefferson in Paris. From September 1789 to March 1790 he was resident in the French capital, a first-hand spectator of the stirring events of the French Revolution, which had already kindled the hopes and fears of many of his own fellow-countrymen. Burke, indeed, had written already, and Paine had read, his *Reflections on the Revolution in France*, which represented the reaction of the conservative-minded. Paine belonged naturally to the more optimistic company of those who hailed with joy the emancipation of France and counted their times fortunate, since

> Bliss was it in that dawn to be alive,
> But to be young was very heaven.

Inevitably he set his hand to the composition of a reply to Burke which should correct that writer's misrepresentation of fact concerning the events of the Revolution by a recital of his own experiences as an eye-witness, and demonstrate the falsity of the political philosophy of monarchical conservatism by an exposition of the principles of the American constitution. The first part of *The Rights of Man* was published, with a dedicatory epistle to George Washington, in February 1791, after which Paine returned to Paris to help in the agitation for a republic, and resumed his frequent journeys between

London and the French capital. In London he became the centre of an active company of reformers, which included Horne Tooke, Rickman, Priestley, Mary Wollstonecraft, and Romney, and after the lapse of a year, in February 1792, appeared the second part of *The Rights of Man*, dedicated to the Marquis de la Fayette. Both in France and England it circulated widely; and in the latter country provoked the popular bonfires of Paine in effigy, and the official decision of Pitt's Cabinet to prosecute the author which led to Paine's final departure from his native land. On June 8, 1792, he actually appeared before the Court of King's Bench, which appointed the trial of his case for December 18 following. Before this date he deemed prudence the better part of valour, and, having been elected by four French departments to membership of the National Convention, sailed for Calais to honour that town by representing it in the Convention. He arrived in Paris on September 19, having fortunately escaped the September Massacres which had begun the darker history of the Revolutionary movement, and still optimistic concerning the immediate possibility of establishing in France that scheme of democratic republicanism which had inspired his political writings.

Disillusionment was to follow speedily. On January 15, 1793, the Convention voted for the execution of Louis XVI, Paine being numbered with the minority, which had no taste for regicide or bloodshed. Within a month the declaration of war by France against Holland had succeeded, and Great Britain was drawn into the incipient conflict. The quick intelligence of Paine perceived the impossibility of controlling revolution within the narrow bounds of the abolition of monarchy. To those who had not the benefit of his own "exceedingly good moral education" liberty could degenerate easily into licence; it was one thing to unleash the tides, another to ordain the limits of the flood. Paine, though friendly with the Girondist leaders, began to lose confidence in their ability to restrain the devotees of violence. He ceased to attend the meetings of the Convention after June 2, and devoted himself instead to the composition of *The Age of Reason*, designed as a constructive essay to preserve the essentials of religion, theology, and morals from subversion in the confusion which followed the proscription of Roman Catholicism in France. Not even the liberty of quiet abstention from the tumult of public debate was long allowed to him. His absence was construed aright as a lack of sympathy with the proceedings of the Convention—for he himself in private was "cursing with hearty good-will the authors of that terrible system that had turned the character of the Revolution he had been proud to defend"—and he was arrested and carried off to the Luxembourg prison on December 28, 1793. There his life was darkened by occasional reports from the outside world—of the executions of Danton on April 5 and of Robespierre on July 28—and by the more terrible disappearance of his companions within the prison to provide victims for the bloodlust of the Reign of Terror. Apprehension of a similar sudden fate for himself was never absent, throwing him into a severe fever, to which circumstance and to happy accident he probably owed his own escape from the guillotine. On November 4, 1794, he was released by the good offices of James Monroe, the American Ambassador, who claimed him as a citizen of the United States, and lodged him for eighteen months in his own house. There Paine recovered his health and spirits, until in the calmer days of January 1795 he was readmitted into the ranks of the chastened Convention, which was to be dissolved in the following autumn by Napoleon's whiff of grapeshot. The recovery of energy and strength was signalised by a vigorous denunciation of Washington, as "treacherous in private friendship . . . and a hypocrite in public life," since his attitude toward the European conflict was entirely unintelligible to Paine; and by a plea in the Convention in July 1795 in favour of universal suffrage against the proposed restriction of the franchise. Even at this late hour Paine cherished the belief in the essential virtue of the French administration and the fundamental corruption of the English Government. He could even discuss with Napoleon, the apostle of despotism, the project for a naval attack upon the English coast from the Thames to the Wash as an instrument for the liberation of the English people from the oppressive tyranny of their rulers. But the stars in their courses fought against French republicanism; and as the career of Napoleon proceeded from strength to strength the English philosopher, realising the logic of events, resolved to forsake the shores of the country which had betrayed the cause of liberty. When absolutism and superstition were reconciled in a pact of formal alliance by the *Concordat* of Napoleon and the Papacy Paine sailed, on September 1, 1802, from Le Havre with the sad confession : "This is not a country for an honest man to live in ; they do not understand anything at all of the principles of free government. . . . I know of no republic in the world except America."

Even in the United States, where he landed at Baltimore on October 30, 1802, and proceeded directly to Washington, the face of liberty was veiled in part. Paine had left that continent in 1787 in full enthusiasm for the republican constitution recently established, and in confident expectation of persuading Europe to follow its bright example. Yet, as he informed his fellow-citizens,

> while he beheld with pleasure the rising dawn of liberty in Europe, he saw with regret the lustre of it fading in America. In less than two years from the time of his departure some distant symptoms painfully suggested the idea that the principles of the revolution were expiring on the soil that had produced them.

But the young prophet who had laboured so earnestly for the establishment of freedom in the New World had been sobered by the experiences he had encountered meantime in the Old. Of the French Revolution he wrote the simple epitaph : "The principles of it were good ; they were copied from America, and the men who conducted it were honest. But the fury of faction soon extinguished the one and sent the other to the scaffold." It is interesting to read Paine's strictures in the light of the most recent study of the leaders of the French Revolution by M. Louis Madelin, who admits their sincerity, whilst exposing their incompetence, and finds in their earnestness and inexperience alike the cause of the failure of the initial ideas of the movement and its degeneracy through murder into tyranny. For Paine, however, the storms and tempests of revolution were overpast. The last six and a half years of his life were passed in circumstances of external tranquillity. He was received kindly by Jefferson, now President of the United States, and settled again in 1804 on the estate at New Rochelle, which had been the gift of the grateful revolutionary Government after the recognition of American independence. His mind was still vigorous, fertile, and inventive, and his pen active in denunciation of the slave-trade. Surviving a severe illness in 1806, he removed to New York in 1808, where he died on June 8, 1809. At the time of his death the issue of the European conflict was still unsettled. The Napoleonic *régime* had led away France still farther from the dreams of universal suffrage, of representative democracy, and of complete freedom of thought and conscience which Paine had sketched in *The Rights of Man*. It had developed further into a dynastic empire; and the struggle for liberty against the imperial conqueror was being led still by the native country of Paine, the champion not of despotism, but of freedom. Such were the strangely contradictory and ironic circumstances of Europe in the year of Paine's death.

III

From a biographical survey of Paine's career the close relation between his political writings and the events of contemporary international affairs may be perceived readily. A great deal of the argument of *The Rights of Man* was concerned with the vindication of the character of the French Revolution against the aspersions of Burke, with a scornful examination of the origins of English political institutions, and with a confident proclamation of the advent of the millennium. In this regard the facts of history—more especially of the subsequent history of the French Revolution—have judged between Burke and his antagonist. So much of Paine's political thought as depended upon his historical knowledge or prophetic capacity must be pronounced ephemeral and transitory. In truth he was ill-equipped with the information necessary to meet Burke upon the ground of historical argument. Possessed by a flaming zeal for the abstract rights of man, he could not endure the imperfections and (still worse) the incredible inertia of existing political societies when tested by the ideal of human government. He could not conceive that any man could hinder the immediate realisation of the millennium unless his natural honesty were perverted by self-interest. Even less could he understand the hiatus between the dream of a perfect

108

social structure and the fashioning of a practical mundane counterpart of the pattern laid up in the heavens. In part this defect was not surprising, nor in anywise culpable. Paine lived in an age which lacked understanding of the concept of evolution as the universal law of life, and which had not been schooled to acquiesce in political matters in the principle of the inevitability of gradualness. In his haste to establish an uncorrupt republican democracy, itself but the prelude to international peace and disarmament, he could perceive no difference between the constitutional monarchy of England and the Bourbon absolutism of France as instruments of this purpose. So far as he did distinguish between them he preferred the naked tyranny of France, which because of its unqualified character had provoked an egalitarian revolt, to the mixed constitution of his own country which embodied a sufficient appearance of popular control to deceive the unwise and the unsuspecting. Notwithstanding, the admission must be made that Paine's knowledge of British history was wholly inadequate, as his references to the British Crown and Parliament were uniformly derogatory. His historical survey began with, and continually reverted to, the Norman Conquest, in which he found the origin of that military oppression and arbitrary prerogative which remained characteristic of its government in his own day. For such a tradition no denunciation could be too strong. William of Normandy himself was but "the son of a prostitute and the plunderer of the English nation," and the government which he established was "originally a tyranny, founded on an invasion and conquest of the country." Even the supposed constitutional glories of English history, Magna Carta and the Bill of Rights, were no more than attempts to soften the harsher features of this dictatorship whilst leaving its essential character intact. For the former was "no more than compelling the government to renounce a part of its assumptions," whilst the latter was "more properly a bill of wrongs and of insult." Such equivocal contrivances were truly "of the nature of a reconquest, and not of a constitution," which could not be secured until the nation had expelled entirely the usurping monarchy. Few eighteenth-century historians possessed either the insight or information necessary to understand the Middle Age, much less to evince sympathy for its institutions and ideas; but Paine could see nothing praiseworthy in the entire histories of France and England until the enlightened subjects of the former and the rebellious colonists of the latter resolved to lay aside the times of ignorance and inaugurate the era of freedom. His attitude toward the Tudors, Stuarts, and even to William III and the Hanoverians was equally censorious with his opinion of the Middle Ages. For the squabbles concerning the Revolution Settlement of 1689 and the Protestant Succession as its necessary corollary he had an unrelieved contempt, concluding the entire proceeding to be that of "a cabal of courtiers" in order to "send for a Dutch stadtholder or a German elector." The fruits of such folly he found to have been reaped abundantly in the Wars of Devolution and of the Spanish Succession occasioned by the interests of Holland, and those of the Hanoverian monarchs undertaken on behalf of their petty German principality. Accordingly the supposed struggles of the English nation for liberty and constitutional government were illusory; they had at best curtailed the despotism of their kings, and at worst had changed the form rather than the substance of the tyranny, resulting in the contemporary chaos of electoral misrepresentation and corruption which maintained "a despotic legislation."

It would be as easy as unprofitable to demonstrate the fallacies of Paine's interpretation of the development of English political institutions. The historical sense and the reverence for tradition which inspired the writings of Burke were entirely foreign to his temperament. *Stare super vias antiquas* was for him the greatest treason against humanity. Nor were his impassioned predictions of the dawn of a new age, heralded by the revolutions of America and France, and his insistence upon the impossibility of a counter-revolution in France of any greater value. Unhappily his own experiences disproved the truth of the latter, whilst the conversion of Washington the leader of rebellion into Washington the President of the United States involved actions which Paine denounced as apostasy and betrayal of the cause of humanity. In 1776 he had assured the citizens of America that

they had it in their power to begin the world over again. A situation similar to the present had not happened since the days of Noah. The birthday of a new world was at hand and a race of men, perhaps as numerous as all Europe contained, were to receive their portion of freedom from the events of a few months.

The promise of *Common Sense* was repeated in *The Rights of Man*; for the intervening period had demonstrated that the New World would regenerate the Old; and that in very truth

> not favoured spots alone but the whole earth
> the beauty wore of promise.

Therefore Paine insisted in 1791 that

> those who talked of a counter-revolution in France showed how little they understood of Man. There did not exist in the compass of language an arrangement of words to express so much as the means of effecting a counter-revolution. The means must be an obliteration of knowledge; and it had never yet been discovered how to make a man unknow his knowledge or unthink his thoughts.

Such exuberant optimism and the strange foreshortening of the time which must elapse before the existing order of society could be transformed into the perfect commonwealth have been characteristic of the prophets of humanity. Impatience and over-confidence have often marked their utterance. Of this prophetic fellowship Paine was numbered, alike in his denunciation of vice and oppression and in his prediction of a speedy revolution. But if he misunderstood the past and misread the immediate future, his diagnosis of the social evils of the present was full of penetration, and his prescription of remedies characterised by sapient and constructive suggestion.

It is important to emphasise this constructive and positive aspect of Paine's political writings. The failure of the French Revolution to realise the hopes of liberty, equality, and fraternity did not disprove the excellence of these ideals; nor did the inability of many of the English revolutionaries to perceive the sober benefits of the constitution of their own country detract from the truth of their exposure of its weaknesses. Much of Paine's political philosophy was of his own day and generation; but some was also of the future. Upon his readers who are possessed of the advantage of a knowledge of the actual history of nineteenth-century England there must rest the obligation gratefully to differentiate and acknowledge the element in his thought which has borne fruit since his death.

M. Halévy has observed that the proud discovery of the school of writers on economics in the eighteenth century was the idea of the essential difference and separability of the terms, society and the State.

> Les deux notions de société et de gouvernement sont séparables: sans contrainte une société commerciale résulte du jeu spontané de l'échange et de la division du travail. Dès lors pourquoi restreindre au domaine économique, pourquoi ne pas étendre aux choses de la politique le principe de l'identité des intérêts? [1]

This extension and application was the work of Paine, who preached in season and out of season the principle of *laissez-faire* in its political aspect, demanding that civil government should be as cheap and as restricted as possible. At the outset of his first political treatise *Common Sense*, and again in the first part of *The Rights of Man*, he emphasised the separation of society and government. "They are not only different," he wrote in 1776,

> but have different origins. Society is produced by our wants and government by our wickedness. The former promotes our happiness positively by uniting our affections; the latter negatively by restraining our vices. The one encourages intercourse, the other creates distinctions; the first is a patron, the last a punisher. Society in every state is a blessing, but government even in its best state is but a necessary evil, in its worst state an intolerable one. . . . Government like dress is the badge of lost innocence; the palaces of kings are built on the ruins of the powers of Paradise.[2]

Accordingly the institution of government, arising from "the inability of moral virtue to govern the world," had as its object and end freedom and security. The same doctrine was enunciated in 1791, when Paine chided Burke for appealing to historical precedents of comparatively recent date instead of prosecuting his inquiry to its foundation in the original condition of man in society. " It may be worth observing that the genealogy of Christ is traced to Adam"—one of the few complimentary references to the Bible—" why then not trace the Rights of Man to the creation of Man?" By this standard of reference it would be perceived that "all men are of one

---

[1] É. Halévy, *La Formation du radicalisme philosophique*, i, 237.
[2] *Common Sense*, I.

degree and consequently that all men are born equal and with equal natural right." The only original distinction was that of sex and the sole ultimate differentia would be that of good or evil. In the State of Nature, however, men lacked the power to enforce all their rights, and therefore entered into a condition of civil government "not to have fewer rights than they had before, but to have those rights better secured." Even within the framework of constituted government the forces which held the State together were those of identity of interest, not of legal coercion. In the second part of *The Rights of Man* Paine asserted that the "great part of that order which reigned among mankind was not the effect of government. It had its origin in the principles of society and the natural constitution of man. It existed prior to government and would exist if the formality of government were abolished." As proof of this minimising of the province and functions of government he appealed to the organisations for trade, commerce, and exchange which were sustained solely by such bonds without the intervention of organised government.

> As Nature created man for social life, she fitted him for the station she intended. In all cases she made his natural wants greater than his individual powers. No one man was capable without the aid of society of supplying his own wants; and these wants, acting upon every individual, impelled the whole of them into society as naturally as gravitation acts to a centre.

From his sparse amount of historical knowledge Paine adduced a few instances to support his contention that the abolition of formal government in a country would lead not to chaos, but to the resuscitation of social forces.

> The instant formal government is abolished, society begins to act. A general association takes place and common interest produces common security. So far is it from being true, as has been pretended, that the abolition of any formal government is the dissolution of society that it acts by a contrary impulse and brings the latter the closer together.

The common principle of these passages is that of the restriction of the functions of organised government. The best political society will be that in which the civil government is least in evidence. When called into operation its duty will embrace the protection of the individual in the enjoyment of life and property and the assurance of those rights which, though possessed by nature, could not be enforced by his individual power. In the field of the spontaneous and creative activity of its citizens the State could have no place ; it would serve to control and restrain, not to initiate or originate.

From this conception of the authority of civil government it followed that the natural rights of man, translated into civil rights by the acceptance of government, were inviolable and sacrosanct. "Man did not enter into society to become worse than he was before, not to have fewer rights than he had before, but to have those rights better secured. His natural rights were the foundation of all civil rights." The individual surrendered nothing by his creation of civil government, save the authority to use private force in the defence of his rights ; and since this force was admittedly inadequate to the end designed, he was wholly the beneficiary by the change. In return for the surrender he was ensured in the enjoyment of all his rights. "Society grants him nothing ; every man is a proprietor in society and draws on the capital as a matter of right." From these premises Paine deduced

> three cardinal and certain conclusions: first, that every civil right grows out of natural right; or in other words is a natural right exchanged; secondly, that civil power, properly considered, as such, is made up of the aggregate of that class of natural rights of man which becomes defective in the individual in point of power, and answers not his purpose; but when collected to a focus, becomes competent to the purpose of every one; and thirdly, that the power produced from the aggregate of natural rights, imperfect in power in the individual, cannot be applied to invade the natural rights which are retained in the individual and in which the power to execute is as perfect as the right itself.

It was not sufficient, however, that the restriction of the powers of government should be accepted as a point of theoretical agreement. The exact and detailed definition of its authority must be embodied in a constitution. Paine became the champion, therefore, of written constitutions. The inviolability of the natural rights of man would be ill-observed unless precise specification were accorded. Otherwise the king or the aristocracy would persuade or bribe the people to forgo them; and if once forgone, they would be forgotten and obliterated. The only safeguard of popular liberties lay in the commitment of them to imperishable letters. *Littera scripta manet* was the theme of Paine's discourse on this point, as it was the testimony of such historical episodes as the framing of the Licinian laws or the Mosaic tables of stone. Only by a written constitution could the insatiable appetite of all civil government for the extension of its authority be corrected; and by this means the principle of the superiority of the constitution to the established administration was secured.

> A constitution is not a thing in name only, but in fact. It has not an ideal but a real existence; and whenever it cannot be produced in a visible form there is none. A constitution is a thing antecedent to a government; and a government is only the creature of a constitution. The constitution of a country is not the act of its government, but of the people constituting a government.

Nor could a constitution properly so called be confined to the enunciation of general principles. Though founded upon the natural rights of man it must safeguard them by a detailed interpretation of their relation to constituted government. It must be a document " to which you can refer and quote article by article "; and it must embrace " in fine everything that relates to the complete organisation of a civil government, and the principles on which it shall act and by which it shall be bound." Herein lay one of the fundamental differences between England on the one hand and both America and France on the other; and, still more important, it pointed to the substance of the conflict between the political schemes of Burke and Paine. Upon his own principles Paine had no difficulty in demonstrating that the English Constitution was non-existent. The East India Company had a charter, and so had a host of smaller societies. But as for the nation, it was without such defence. " The country has never yet regenerated itself and is therefore without a constitution." Of such a people Burke was the natural champion, with his rhetorical effusion rather than logical argument and his sense of the mystery of government instead of a prosaic analysis of its constituent parts. For, as Paine observed of his antagonist in a gentle *jeu d'esprit*, " even his genius is without a constitution; it is a genius at random and not a genius constituted."

The difference between the two writers, and between the types of constitution which they defended, was of deeper import than a variation of words or of literary style. Burke's political outlook was inspired by a profound reverence for the intangible social tradition of the past. Written forms were for him but a secondary and imperfect expression of the great formative ideas which had operated secretly and silently throughout the generations of past experience. The present was only a fraction of a wider whole, articulate by reason of its heritage from the past. Accordingly he considered the body politic to be a complex organism, incapable of being reduced to the few simple formulas of the Rights of Man, and he regarded it with a sense of awe as a sublime mystery, the product of centuries of corporate life in society. In such an organism anomalies were natural ; they were part of the endless process of change and becoming, but their resolution into the political forms necessary and adequate to the future circumstances of the people was to be effected by the slow process of adaptation to environment, not by the drastic surgery of a levelling revolution. To the direct and simple mind of Paine such subtleties and distinctions were unintelligible. The heritage of the past, with its inconsistent and illogical elements of compromise, was to him but a cumbrous agglomeration of futile expedients to bolster up tyranny. He desired to make a new start; and he believed implicitly in the possibility of political *tabulæ rasæ*. Once the oppressed majority of citizens was relieved from the burden of existing political machinery, the natural intelligence and virtue of mankind would construct new and perfect forms of government. The demolition of the bulwarks of tyranny would obliterate the traditions and even the memory of ancient government associated with them, just as the fall of the Bastille was symbolic of the emancipation of the French people from despotism to freedom. Paine from his own standpoint complained justly that Burke allowed the present no rights against the past; to his mind the past was dead, the future unborn, and the present alone had real existence. Here his essential individualism found full scope. He was concerned only with the present hour, which needed neither to justify itself according to the ideas of the past nor to attempt to win the suffrages of the future. "Paine néglige cette solidarité des générations que Burke considérait comme le fait social fondamental," observes M. Halévy ; and from this it followed that the gulf between them was impassable. With Paine's depreciatory view of the entire constitutional development of England, such a neglect of its social experience was inevitable. In his reply to Burke he compared the British and French constitutions entirely to the advantage of the latter. In the French Revolution he saw the promise of complete democracy, of international fraternity (for wars were solely due to the dynastic ambitions of the old monarchies), and of complete religious toleration and freedom of thought. Of the alliance of Church and State which was so pleasing to his antagonist he would have none. The very idea was anathema. "By engendering the Church with the State a sort of mule animal, capable only of destroying and not of breeding up, is produced called 'the Church established by law.'" This confusion of principles also produced evil results politically. "The union of Church and State has impoverished Spain. The revoking the Edict of Nantes drove the silk manufacture from that country to England ; and Church and State are now driving the cotton manufacture from England to America and France."

But Paine was no apostle of abstract principles unapplied to the practical details of constitution-making. Boldly he proceeded to examine the various types of existing government in order to discover the form best adapted to modern nations. Defying the cautious doctrine of Aristotle, he pronounced an unequivocal condemnation of "mixed governments," on the ground of the impossibility of fixing responsibility upon any definite element in the constitution. "What is supposed to be the king in a mixed government is the Cabinet ; and the Cabinet is always a part of the Parliament, and the members justifying in one character what they advise and act in another, a mixed government becomes a continual enigma." Accordingly the English Constitution was "a pantomimical contrivance," in which "the advisers, the actors, the approvers, the justifiers, the persons responsible and the persons not responsible are the same persons." Such a Government was the natural parent of corruption, in addition to being the *reductio ad absurdum* of scientific administration. But despite

117

external differences all existing Governments could be traced ultimately only to two sources; they were either hereditary Governments, founded upon conquest, or representative, based on consent. The futility of all hereditary Government was self-evident, for political ability was no prerogative of one or even a majority of families. To suppose that the art of government descended by heredity was as foolish as to suppose that a poet's son would necessarily inherit his father's genius. Representative government alone was consonant with reason and liberty. In his championship of the representative form of government Paine showed a sound political insight. Despite his admiration for Athens he was no follower of Rousseau, who desired to reduce the nation-state to the parochial proportions of the ancient Hellenic city. For the achievement of Athens Paine had unreserved praise. "We see more to admire," he wrote, "and less to condemn in that great extraordinary people than in anything which history affords." But he realised that the direct democracy of Periclean Athens was no longer practicable, and his suffrage was cast for a republican constitution, functioning by means of elected representatives. "By ingrafting representation upon democracy we arrive at a system of government capable of embracing and confederating all the various interests and every extent of territory and population." America had pointed the way toward this new form of political organisation; and in his judgment "what Athens was in miniature, America will be in magnitude."

Upon this foundation of representative democracy Paine constructed the edifice of practical administration. Repelled by the English theory of the Crown as the executive element in the constitution, he refused to recognise the customary distinction of the legislative, judicial, and executive powers.

> It has been customary to consider government under three distinct general heads: the legislative, the executive, and the judicial. But if we permit our judgment to act unencumbered by the habit of multiplied terms we can perceive no more than two divisions of power, that of legislating or enacting laws and that of executing or administering them. Everything therefore appertaining to civil government classes itself under one or other of these two divisions. So far as regards the execution of the laws that which is called the judicial power is strictly and properly the executive power of every country.

The problem of the nature of the executive power was perplexing, and he returned again to the task of elucidating its character. He desired

> to examine with more precision the nature and business of that department which is called the executive. What the legislative and judicial departments are, every one can see; but with respect to what in Europe is called the executive as distinct from these two, it is either a political superfluity or a chaos of unknown things. Some kind of official department to which report shall be made from the different parts of the nation or from abroad, to be laid before the national representatives, is all that is necessary; but there is no consistency in calling this the executive; neither can it be considered in any other light than as inferior to the legislative. The sovereign authority in any country is in the power of making laws, and everything else is an official department.

This studied depreciation of the executive was the result of the example of the French Constituent Assembly and of Paine's doctrine of the supremacy of the legislature. Accordingly he considered with much care the constitution of the legislative body, weighing the arguments and advantages of single- and dual-chamber government respectively. He admitted that "experience was yet wanting to determine many particulars," but had confidence in the smooth working of any government based upon a detailed and specific constitution "defining the power and establishing the principles within which a legislature should act." The necessity of such restriction was seen from the English Septennial Act, by which the Whig House of Commons had prolonged arbitrarily its legal term of existence and had thereby asserted its irresponsibility and tyranny over the people. It was the example of the English House of Lords which inclined Paine to favour a single legislative chamber, with the practical provision that it might be subdivided by lot into two or three sections, debating proposed measures in turn and voting finally as one body. "Every proposed Bill should be first debated in those parts by succession, that they may become hearers of each other, but without taking any vote; after which the whole representation to assemble for a general debate and determination by vote." In order to ensure the closest correspondence between the legislature and the electorate, one-third of the delegates should retire each year, thereby keeping "the representation in a state of constant renovation." These matters were a subject of detailed arrangement; the one essential and inviolable principle of government was that of representation. "There is one general principle that distinguishes freedom from slavery, which is, that all hereditary government over a people is to them a species of slavery, and representative government is freedom."

Thus far the political philosophy of Paine had been based on a thoroughgoing individualism. Suspicious of the expense of contemporary Governments of the *ancien régime*, and captivated by the notion of the competence of society to discharge the greater part of their functions, he had enunciated the axiom that civil government should be as restricted in scope and costliness as possible. "Le gouvernement démocratique, étant un minimum de gouvernement, est un gouvernement à bon marché." In the fifth chapter of the second part of *The Rights of Man*, however, he forsook the straitness of individualist doctrine, or at least clothed it in the semblance of what modern theorists have denominated socialism. In this last section of his chief political treatise he passed from experiments in political carpentry to the sphere of social reform. His survey of the existing governments of Europe had convinced him that their rapacity was due chiefly to their insatiable appetite for military adventures. The obnoxious system of National Debts had made this process of war and taxation interminable; deliverance could be found only in a subversive revolution to abolish entirely hereditary dynasties. On the other hand, despite the burden of taxes and the discouragement of the arts of peace, the social instincts of men had built up a flourishing trade and commerce, the profits of which were perverted to finance the wars of monarchs. To Paine the flourishing state of trade was a perpetual, almost miraculous monument of the essentially social and civilised nature of man. Provoked by the spectacle of the poverty and degradation of the majority of the subjects of oppressive Governments, he resolved to frame a utopian scheme for relieving their necessities out of the surplus taxation devoted to military and naval preparations, and at the same time to encourage the development of international amity by the reduction of armies and navies and the extension of trading facilities. M. Halévy has emphasised the importance of this aspect of his philosophy. " C'est probablement Paine qui doit être considéré comme le premier auteur, avant Buckle, avant Spencer de la distinction des deux régimes, militaire ou gouvernemental, et commercial."[1] Of the international policy of the old Governments no condemnation could be too severe. " All the European Governments (France now excepted) are constructed not on the principles of universal civilisation, but on the reverse of it. So far as those Governments relate to each other, they are in the same condition as we conceive of savage, uncivilised life." Their aims were selfish and aggressive, and they endeavoured to control trade in the interests of their political projects. But trade should be free and without restriction. " If commerce were permitted to act to the universal extent it is capable, it would extirpate the system of war and produce a revolution in the uncivilised state of government." It is important to remember this eulogy of the beneficent and pacificatory results of commercial intercourse, for it exercised a considerable influence upon the practical ordering of Paine's schemes of social reform.

Fundamentally, however, these projects sprang from the spectacle of misery and want among the subjects of European States. Wherever his eye fell he saw " age going to the workhouse and youth to the gallows " ; and the prospect convinced him that the so-called civilised Governments were in fact the enemies of civilisation and anti-social. " Civil government does not consist in executions, but in making that provision for the instruction of youth and the support of age as to exclude as much as possible, profligacy from the one and despair from the other." To provide the means for raising the position of the young and the infirm without additional taxation he proposed a drastic reorganisation of national expenditure. Accepting the estimate of £17,000,000 as the average annual income from taxation in England, and setting aside the necessary sum to pay interest on the National Debt, he believed that an extensive provision could be made for social amelioration and yet that the current expenditure could be reduced considerably. At the outset he insisted on a radical reform of the salaries of

[1] Halévy, *op. cit.*, ii, 69.

the chief officers of State. "Public money ought to be touched with the most scrupulous consciousness of honour. It is not the produce of riches only, but of the hard earnings of labour and poverty. It is drawn even from the bitterness of want and misery. Not a beggar passes in the street whose mite is not in that mass." A beginning of reform could be made by fixing the maximum salary of any public officer at £10,000 per year ; three such salaries could be allowed, with ten at £5000, twenty at £2000, and thus in a graduated scale. Even if the three hundred legislative representatives were allowed a salary of £500 per year each, with deductions for non-attendance, Paine calculated that a total expenditure of £1,500,000 would be "a sufficient peace establishment for all the honest purposes of government," of which only half a million would be devoted to the ordinary expenses exclusive of armies and navies. Out of the surplus of £6,000,000 a progressive programme of remission of taxes could be fashioned. Into the details of the scheme it is not necessary to enter ; a brief survey will suffice. First came the total abolition of the poor rate and a grant of £4,000,000 for the benefit of the poor. This sum was to be disbursed in the form of family allowances at the rate of £4 per year for each child, and old-age pensions, beginning at the age of fifty and increasing in amount after the age of sixty. Further educational grants were to be given to parents who found their incomes barely adequate to the education of their children, together with maternity benefits and a bonus to newly married couples, or a grant toward the cost of funeral expenses in certain cases. Special provision was to be made to cope with the problem of temporary and casual unemployment in the capital, in order to protect the victims from temptation to vice or crime. Since Paine's scheme included the effecting of substantial reductions in the military and naval forces, pensions must be provided for the discharged soldiers and sailors ; and finally, if the window-tax were abolished, any loss to the Exchequer might be met by a graduated land-tax of increasing severity with the extent of the landed property possessed. The limitation of armies and navies was to be effected by a tripartite alliance of France, Holland, and England, to which it was hoped that America would accede, thereby making possible the liberation of South America from the control of Spain and "the opening of those countries of immense extent and wealth to the general commerce of the world."

Such a programme was revolutionary at the time of its proclamation, but singularly prophetic of the future development of paternal government. More remarkable than its detailed provisions were the principles upon which their adoption was urged and by which the scheme was defended. Paine enunciated clearly the axiom of the duty of the State to care for the indigent and the young. He declared that at the age of sixty a man's labour "ought to be over, at least from direct necessity," whilst ten years before that limit there would be many persons who, having suffered from the ill-effects of their occupation on their physical health, desired "to be better supported than they could support themselves," and that "not as a matter of grace and favour but as a right." His provision of old-age pensions, paid for in part by those taxes to which every one contributed and in part by further exactions "from those whose circumstances did not require them to draw such support," he defended as "not of the nature of a charity but of a right." Such expenditure was far better employed in this way than in the support of effete royalty. "Is it then better," he asked, "that the lives of 144,000 aged persons be rendered comfortable or that one million a year of public money be expended on any one individual, and him often of the most worthless or insignificant character?" Similarly his project for the establishment of hostels to provide lodging and work for the casual unemployed of London and Westminster, capable of helping six thousand persons, was justified on the ground that "hunger is not amongst the postponable wants, and a day, even a few hours, in such a condition is often the crisis of a life of ruin." The money for the experiment was to be contributed in part by the tax on coals; and there is a distinct anticipation of much contemporary political argument in the indignant denunciation of this tax "so iniquitously and wantonly applied to the support of the Duke of Richmond. It is horrid that any man, more especially at the price coals now are, should live on the distress of a community; and any Government permitting such an abuse deserves to be dismissed." Paine's inveterate opposition to

123

the English landed aristocracy, with their virtual monopoly of the House of Lords and their control even of the Commons by their influence in the elections for boroughs and counties, found expression in his resolve to readjust the incidence of taxation so that the heaviest burden fell upon owners of large landed property. He confessed the principle of his graduated land-tax. "Its object is not so much the produce of the tax as the justice of the measure. The aristocracy has screened itself too much and this serves to restore part of the lost equilibrium." Nor would its good effects be confined to this result. It would help to break down the law of primogeniture, which he regarded as anti-social and inhuman. He rejoiced that it would go far "to extirpate the overgrown influence arising from the unnatural law of primogeniture, which is one of the principal sources of corruption at elections." But if the Crown and the hereditary peerage were objects of especial detestation, the industrial and commercial interests were proper to be encouraged and assisted. In this regard Paine was an apostle of free trade, believing that unrestricted and extended commerce was profitable to all countries and a strong agent of international amity. Not less interesting was his demand for the removal of all restrictions on the association of workmen. "Several laws are in existence for regulating and limiting workmen's wages. Why not leave them as free to make their own bargains as the lawmakers are to let their farms and houses? Personal labour is all the property they have. Why is that little and the little freedom they enjoy to be infringed?" The publication of such a programme of reform, combined with the demand for the abolition of charters to corporations, of the monarchy, and of the House of Lords, and the insistence upon the remodelling of the House of Commons, was sufficiently alarming to Paine's contemporaries apart from his fervent championship of the French Revolution. It needed but the sequel of *The Age of Reason* to convert the revolutionary into an atheist according to the opinion of the vulgar, and to earn for him a discredit which the lapse of more than a century has scarcely succeeded in modifying.

IV

The eighteenth century is not accorded usually a place of honour in the catalogue of the Ages of Faith. The general verdict upon its character ascribes to it the unpleasing title of an age of unbelief. But, though it may not be regarded as a century of orthodoxy, it was certainly interested in religion. The fact that this interest found expression in peculiar forms has tended to obscure its religious aspect and to hinder appreciation of the real value of its contribution to scientific theology. For in truth the most characteristic eighteenth-century writers were severely critical of the orthodox Christian apologetic, often (albeit unconsciously) rationalist and sceptical in their philosophical presuppositions, and, above all, devotees of natural religion as distinct from revealed. For their defence of natural religion and their attempts to find a satisfactory justification for religion in the constitution of human nature as they understood it they received scant appreciation from contemporaries, since their theories were associated with attacks upon what were generally believed to be the foundations of the Christian revelation. Modern critical study, which conceives the postulates of revealed religion differently, may do more justice to the deists. Deism, indeed, is a just and proper title, fitting better the characteristics of these exponents of natural religion than the term theism, which has been invested with particular associations by Christian theology. Dr Tennant has described the deist movement as " the beginning of modernity in English theology "; and since the creed of Paine was the purest deism, the approach to a study of *The Age of Reason* must lie through a consideration of the historical antecedents of that eighteenth-century fashion.

The various forces which influenced the deist tradition had one characteristic in common—their naïve interest in man. The text of the movement was furnished by the famous line of Pope's, " The proper study of mankind is Man." Hobbes had set the fashion by his endeavour to explain all human action, whether political or religious, by an examination of the psychology of the individual. At an earlier date Lord Herbert of Cherbury in his *De Veritate* had enunciated five fundamental propositions of natural religion which he believed to be provable by the exercise of reason. Upon this basis the philosopher Locke had, in his essays on *The Human Understanding* and on *The Reasonableness of Christianity*, built up a scheme of apologetic which appealed as much to the deists as to the defenders of the Christian revelation. These tendencies of philosophical speculation were reinforced especially by the new scientific discoveries of the latter part of the seventeenth century, in reaction against its theological development. The history of the Reformed Churches, indeed, had been full of disappointment. Against the rigid definitions of the Council of Trent there had been set the new scholasticism of Calvin. The Protestant sects had shown an alarming tendency to subdivision, and a distressing incapacity to restrain the excesses of the extremists of their society, whose eccentric experiments had fathered upon the Spirit a scene not of order, but of confusion. Europe and England had suffered the ravages of war in consequence of disputes between Lutheran and Calvinist, Presbyterian and Independent. In particular the appeal to the authority of the Bible, originally launched by the Reformers as a weapon against Rome, had become a two-edged sword in the hands of its holders. The air was filled with the clamant preachings of divines, each confident of the inerrancy of his private exegesis of Holy Writ. Against the unseemliness and shame of these quarrels of the sects there stood the new sense of the harmony and order of the universe as revealed by the telescope to earnest scientific discoverers. Creation testified with a convincing authority to the wisdom and majesty of its Creator. The realisation of the unfailing regularity of the universe gave men a joyful appreciation of the character of God as no longer arbitrary and capricious, but rational and reliable. Thus deist theology was characterised by a sentiment of relief and optimism; chaos was giving place to order, and all dark corners in the universe were being understood; a 'mystery' was but something formerly obscure but now in process of explanation; the very order and reliability of the universe was a further testimony of the divine beneficence; and man's self-esteem was flattered immeasurably by the persuasion that the Creator had fashioned all these wonders for the especial delectation of the human race. For a brief space under the influence of this benign creed of optimism men became literally as little children, rejoicing in the novelty and variety of creation, and engaged

> in tireless play
> attentively occupied with a world of wonders,
> so rich in toys and playthings that naked Nature
> were enough without the marvellous inventory of man.

From this sentiment there sprang inevitably the vogue of natural religion. The contemplation of nature revealed its Creator as beneficent, orderly, and omnipotent. Such a God could not be the author of the confusion and quarrels of the various Churches and sects. Nor, if theological disputes derived from a diverse exegesis of the text of Holy Scripture, could He be truly the author of the Bible, which had become the parent of such disorder. A pretended revelation which did not clarify but rather intensified obscurity could not proceed from the Deity, Whose law was plainly written in the order of nature. From a study of creation the attributes of the Creator could be deduced by every man; but for the understanding of the Christian Scriptures a knowledge of ancient tongues was necessary, and even this qualification did not produce unanimity of conclusion. Further, the actual state of the text of the Bible was marred by many corruptions; its transmission had been effected by fallible men, who had often perverted its meaning by interpolation or deletion, sometimes unwittingly, at other times perhaps with intent to defraud; and the result of this process was that certainty in regard to correctness of text was unattainable. From these arguments it was a short step to the conclusion that the Bible itself was an invention of the priesthood in order to enhance its own prestige as the custodian of such a mysterious volume and to prevent the ordinary layman, unskilled in letters, from attempting his own private interpretation. Thus the whole idea of revelation was believed to be a pious fraud. For how could the credentials of such a revelation be attested? Locke's contention that Jesus was the Messiah because He fulfilled the prophecies and performed miracles was ridiculed by opponents who disbelieved in the predictive character of the Old Testament prophetic writings, and argued that miracles (if they had actually happened) could only serve as proof to eye-witnesses of their occurrence.

This line of argument was not intended to leave the majority of men without a religion. Rather it was designed to enable them to fashion their own creed. By its substitution of the clear ideas of God deducible from His works in the universe for the beliefs about His nature handed down from the pre-scientific age of the Jews it endeavoured to afford certainty and individual conviction in the place of complete uncertainty and the acceptance of indirect tradition. Natural religion was believed by its apostles to be more immediate, convincing, and specific than revelation. The beneficence of the Creator was itself an example to His creatures; men could imitate in their social relations His disinterested favour; and the testimony of human reason was sufficient ground for assurance of immortality. Deism was the true religion of democracy, making every man his own divine; the enemy of democracy was revelation, which required an official priestly caste to expound its doctrine and administer its sacraments. In its democratic aspect the deistic movement allied itself naturally with the republican and revolutionary strand in political speculation. Both in the pages of Burke's writings and in the practical affairs of contemporary France the established Churches were defenders of the *ancien régime* of aristocracy and hereditary privilege. To Burke the close connection of Church and State in England was a valuable bulwark against revolution, whilst the higher clergy of France were on the side of oppression and prerogative. The apostles of equality could not escape this challenge; and in deism they found a useful counterpart to the political doctrines which they were proclaiming.

The interest which Paine displayed in religion was therefore an essential part of his political thought. Its importance consists precisely in the circumstance that he was an almost perfect representative of the deist school. At this distance of time it should be unnecessary to labour the point that charges of atheism made against him are mere abuse. In a famous passage of his *Sentiments of a Church of England Man with Respect to Religion and Government* Swift had contended that "whoever professes himself a member of the Church of England ought to believe a God and His providence, together with revealed religion and the divinity of Christ." There can be no doubt that Paine's rejection of the last two articles of this succinct creed would prevent his acceptance as a Church of England man; but there should be equal assurance that his profession of faith in God and in immortality may give him a place amongst the religious deists. In this regard he belonged to the early eighteenth century, not to the later atheistic school of political republicans, as M. Halévy has insisted.

> L'individualisme de Paine est un individualisme spiritualiste, fondé sur une théologie; tous les hommes sont égaux en sortant des mains du Créateur, et la seule inégalité qui ne soit pas artificielle, c'est l'inégalité qui sépare le bon d'avec le méchant. A Paris en 1792 comme à New York en 1776 Thomas Paine reste toujours, même lorsqu'il renonce à l'orthodoxie chrétienne, un quaker; et par son intermédiaire le christianisme révolutionnaire des Protestants anglais d'Amérique rejoint l'athéisme révolutionnaire des sans-culottes français. L'individualisme de Bentham ou d'Adam Smith reposait sur un principe tout différent.

Paine's interest in religion had a twofold aspect; it was native to his own genius and character, and it was necessary also to the completion of his political philosophy. In the first regard he had two important qualifications for his self-chosen *rôle* of the prophet of deism: the sound moral education received from his parents and his natural aptitude for scientific study and mechanical experiment; whilst in relation to the second problem of the relation of religion to political organisation he perceived clearly the perils of antinomianism inherent in the collapse of the established Churches, and desired to prevent their realisation by allying republican democracy with an individualist deism, which in its turn could inculcate the complementary truths of individual freedom and personal responsibility.

The Age of Reason was therefore *un livre de circonstance*, and was designed as a constructive and steadying force. This statement may seem almost perversely paradoxical in view of the destructive criticism which Paine launched against the doctrines of orthodox Christianity, and it was inevitable that to defenders of orthodoxy, even of the liberal and latitudinarian character of Bishop Watson of Llandaff, its negative and destructive aspects should assume large proportions.

Notwithstanding, the essential purpose of the volume was edificatory, since Paine regarded his criticism of orthodoxy as a strict parallel to his exposure of hereditary Governments, being necessary to liberate the human mind from bondage in order to prepare it for the freedom of republicanism and deism. In *The Rights of Man* Paine had already attacked the notion of established Churches defended by Burke, pouring scorn upon the very theory which his antagonist expounded. "As to what are called national religions we may, with as much propriety, talk of national gods. It is either political craft, or the remains of the pagan system when every nation had its separate and particular deity." The difference between them, however, went deeper, for Paine denounced the idea of 'toleration,' contending that every man had a natural and inalienable right to freedom of thought and conscience, which needed no recognition from Governments to establish its validity. Toleration implied the authority of Government to refuse to any man this right of freedom of worship, and was itself in consequence a symbol of tyranny. Variety of belief and practice was correspondent with the character of nature, and therefore agreeable to the Creator Himself.

> If we suppose a large family of children who, on any particular day or particular circumstance, made it a custom to present to their parent some token of their affection and gratitude, each of them would make a different offering and most probably in a different manner. . . . The parent would be more gratified by such variety than if the whole had acted on a concerted plan and each had made exactly the same offering. . . . Why may we not suppose that the great Father of all is pleased with variety of devotion; and that the greatest offence we can act is that by which we seek to torment and render each other miserable?

The development of the hints thus thrown out as *obiter dicta* in *The Rights of Man* was reserved for a future occasion, when leisure and opportunity should combine to create a proper time for the work. Actually the rapidity with which the French Revolution proceeded necessitated an anticipation of the season. As Paine wrote in his introduction to the first part of *The Age of Reason*:

> The circumstance that has now taken place in France of the total abolition of the whole national order of priesthood, and of everything

appertaining to compulsive systems of religion and compulsive articles of faith, has not only precipitated my intention, but rendered a work of this kind exceedingly necessary; lest in the general wreck of superstition, of false systems of government and false theology, we lose sight of morality, of humanity, and of the theology that is true.

The contrast between the intended time of composition—at an advanced period of the author's life, and as his last offering to his fellow-citizens of all nations—and the actual circumstances of writing was tragic; for Paine took up pen to write the hurried first part during the disorders of French politics, when "the tribunals styled revolutionary supplied the place of an Inquisition, and the guillotine of the State outdid the fire and faggot of the Church," and as the threat of imprisonment closed in upon himself, "conceiving that he had but a few days of liberty, he sat down and brought the work to a close as speedily as possible." The manuscript of this first part was written without a copy of the Bible for reference, and was lodged with Joel Barlow whilst Paine was actually on his way to prison. It was not until after his release and recovery of health that he embarked in the second part on the detailed justification of the principles laid down in the first by full reference to and quotations from the Old and New Testaments.

The first part opened with a *confessio fidei*—sincere and individualistic, as were all Paine's opinions. His creed embraced two positive articles : belief in one God and no more, and the hope for happiness beyond this life. He rejected the claims of all Churches to prescribe their official creeds for the acceptance of all men, basing his religion upon the postulate "my own mind is my own Church." The remainder of the slender volume was devoted to an argument for the superiority of natural religion over revealed. Its interest lay, as has been suggested before, in its almost perfect reproduction of the principles of deism of the early eighteenth century. The qualification is necessary because the early optimism of the deist movement provoked a reaction which led in turn to a depressing pessimism, reflected in the sombre temper of the writings of Butler and in the appearance of a literature of the tomb and the charnel-house. From this tinge of darkness Paine was wholly free; his religion retained always the undoubted inspiration of optimism. His apologia for deism was certain and convinced. "The word of God is the creation we behold; and it is in this word, which no human invention can counterfeit or alter, that God speaketh universally to man." Here the emphasis is on the universality of natural religion. All men may apprehend the character of God as revealed in creation: "it is only in creation that all our ideas and conceptions of a word of God can unite. The creation speaketh an universal language, independently of human speech or human language, multiplied and various as they be." To Paine in particular, with his keen scientific interest and his mechanical genius, the universe seemed a singular proof of the beneficence of God:

> The Almighty Lecturer, by displaying the principles of science in the structure of the universe, has invited man to study and to imitation. It is as if He had said to the inhabitants of this globe we call ours: I have made an earth for man to dwell upon, and I have rendered the starry heavens visible, to teach him science and the arts. He can now provide for his own comfort, and learn from my munificence to all to be kind to each other.

The true theology was thus the study of creation, which was far superior in value to that devotion to ancient languages necessary to understand the classical authors. "That which is now called natural philosophy, embracing the whole circle of science, of which astronomy occupies the chief place, is the study of the works of God and of the power and wisdom of God in His works and is the true theology." The prominence of astronomy in this catalogue of the theological sciences may account in part for Paine's resolute optimism. The *Analogy* of Butler, published in 1736, had endeavoured to turn the flank of the deist position by pointing out that natural religion itself was not unembarrassed by the problems of evil, obscurity, and imperfection which were alleged against revelation. The sombre picture which he painted of the darker aspect of nature and of the deficiencies of natural religion helped considerably to induce the feeling of pessimism which succeeded to the optimism of the early deists. Although Paine's *Age of Reason* was written more than half a century after the *Analogy*, he retained the buoyant confidence of the early years of the century. His argument appears to have been unaffected by the conclusions of Butler, since to his mind all was still open and clear in natural religion, all dark and uncertain in revealed. From the realisation of the infinity of the universe, which chilled the faith of many, his mind drew renewed inspiration.

> Our ideas, not only of the almightiness of the Creator, but of His wisdom and His beneficence, become enlarged in proportion as we contemplate the extent and structure of the universe. The solitary idea of a solitary world rolling or at rest in the immense ocean of space gives place to the cheerful idea of a society of worlds so happily contrived as to administer even by their motion instruction to man.

In his defence of natural religion Paine was an optimist *sans peur et sans reproche.* Astronomy revealed little of the harsher aspect of nature, and to his mind creation seemed indeed, as in the poet's vision, to be a pæan of praise to the beneficence of its Maker.

In contradiction to this idealised picture of natural religion stood the confusion and uncertainty of revelation when subjected to the criticism of human reason. Herein also Paine was an individualist. "It is only by the exercise of reason that man can discover God," and he proceeded therefore to examine the credentials of Christianity by the test of his own vigorous and penetrating reason. The chief difficulty of a pretended revelation was that its power of conviction was limited to the individual who was its recipient. If he communicated its content to other men, how were they to judge of its authenticity? The simple assertion of the receiver could not be sufficient, for he might be a wilful deceiver, or mistaken in his conclusions. Others could accept his communication only in so far as it commended itself to their sense of truth and moral fitness. Revelation therefore could not embrace the record of historical events, such as the crucifixion of Jesus, for they were matters of ordinary experience. It could include only the direct instruction of men by God upon matters supernatural, the nature of which could not be arrived at by the exercise of natural reason. So far as this information did not contradict reason it might be accepted; when it became contradictory it ceased to have any claim to be believed. Judged by this criterion, the greater part of the written record of the Bible did not partake of the nature of revelation, more especially in its historical books. Other portions were unedifying or even repellent, and therefore could not be ascribed to divine authorship. Since revelation had need of external props to maintain its credit with the unreflecting, it fell back upon miracle, mystery, and prophecy. Of mystery Paine adopted the usual deist view. The word either signified something which the ignorance of former ages had not understood, but which was now in process of clarification, or else it was an attempt of priests to confuse the ordinary layman by the invention of supposedly secret traditions. "The God in Whom we believe is a God of moral truth and not a God of mystery or obscurity. Mystery is the antagonist of truth. It is a fog of human invention that obscures truth and represents it in distortion." Any pretence to mystery was a sign not of authenticity, but of fraudulent intention. Nor was the case different with regard to miracle. Paine pointed out that a miracle could be convincing only to the immediate percipient, and that even so its strictly miraculous character could be established only when the full knowledge of all natural laws had been vouchsafed to mankind. During the interval events which seemed miraculous to one generation might be part of the normal experience of its successor. To base belief in religion upon the credibility of miracles was to increase still further its uncertainty, and such action could not be predicated of God. If the content of a revelation could only be authenticated thus its moral value was exceedingly doubtful. "It is more difficult to obtain belief to a miracle than to a principle evidently moral without any miracle. Moral principle speaks universally for itself. Miracle could be but a thing of the moment and seen but by a few." With mystery and miracle thus dismissed there remained of the threefold strand of evidence only that of prophecy. The predictive character of the writings of the Old Testament prophets was wholly denied by Paine. He hit upon the origin of prophecy in the mantic exercises of such companies as that amongst which Saul found himself, and therefore refused to regard the prophetic books as other than poetic and rhetorical compositions.

Revelation, thus stripped of its accessories, compared unfavourably with the simplicity and universality of natural religion. In order to retain a semblance of prestige it affected to despise the study of natural science and to confine education to the learning of ancient languages. Nothing daunted, Paine proceeded to attack this citadel. He insisted that true education consisted in the new studies of natural philosophy, especially astronomy, which had a practical relation and value. " It would be advantageous to the state of learning to abolish the study of the dead languages and to make learning to consist, as it originally did, in scientific knowledge." The chief opponent of this reconstruction of education was the Christian Church, and the fittest commentary upon its ideal of public learning was the character of the Middle Ages: "The Christian system laid all waste; and if we take our stand about the middle of the sixteenth century we look back through that long chasm to the times of the ancients as over a vast sandy desert in which not a shrub appears to intercept the vision of the fertile hills beyond." The specifically Christian centuries, the Ages of Faith, were sterile and barren of true intellectual discovery, and only with the Renaissance did the sciences revive, being helped thereto by the break up of the Papal Church. "This was the only public good the Reformation did; for with respect to religious good it might as well not have taken place." In no respect was Paine more characteristically a child of the age of enlightenment than in his contempt for the Christian Middle Age and all its works.

The second part of *The Age of Reason* did but illustrate the principles enunciated in the first. In the meantime the author had furnished himself with a Bible and Testament, and had found them much worse than he had conceived. Accordingly he exposed with satirical pen the cruelties, immoralities, and absurdities of the Old Testament; he argued on critical grounds against the Mosaic authorship of the Pentateuch; he ridiculed the miracles and pointed out the self-contradictory statements of the historical books; he found deistic sentiments in the books of Job, Proverbs, and Psalms, but little more than a farrago of nonsense in the prophetical writings; and in particular he insisted upon the composite authorship of Isaiah. In the New Testament he dealt similarly with the discrepancies between the various evangelists, especially in regard to the Virgin Birth and Resurrection of Christ; he ascribed St Paul's experience on the road to Damascus to his being struck by lightning, and embarked upon an original and interesting discussion of the problem of immortality with reference to the fifteenth chapter of the first epistle to the Corinthians. The details of this survey are often striking, and always indicative of a virile intelligence, but their real importance lies in their relation to the principles expounded in the first part of the book. The historical Founder of Christianity emerged from Paine's survey shorn of all supernatural elements. Of His historicity Paine had no doubt, nor of His crucifixion. Nor did he design to write disrespectfully of His teaching.

> Nothing that is here said can apply, even with the most distant disrespect, to the real character of Jesus Christ. He was a virtuous and amiable man. The morality that he preached and practised was of the most benevolent kind, and though similar systems of morality had been preached by Confucius and by some of the Greek philosophers many years before, by the Quakers since, and by many good men in all ages, it has not been exceeded by any.

Indeed, the religion of Christ Himself was deism. "He founded no new system. He called men to the practice of moral virtues and the belief of one God. The great trait in His character is philanthropy." This was the essence of Christianity. All things else—doctrines of an Incarnation, Atonement, and Trinity—were the relics of pagan mythology. When prophecy should be done away, miracles should have ceased and mystery be made clear, the pure religion of deism would remain in its perfection.

> The only religion that has not been invented, and that has in it every evidence of divine originality, is pure and simple deism. It must have been the first and will probably be the last that man believes. . . . Were a man impressed as fully and as strongly as he ought to be with the belief of a God, his moral life would be regulated by the force of this belief, he would stand in awe of God and of himself, and would not do the thing that could not be concealed from either. To give this belief the full opportunity of force it is necessary that it acts alone. This is deism.

V

Of the impact of Paine upon his generation there can be no doubt. It was perhaps as inevitable as regrettable that the destructive and negative part of his political and religious writings should have impressed the imagination of contemporaries more powerfully than his constructive proposals and genuine zeal for social reform. It must be granted that the tone of his references to George III and the British Constitution could not create a disposition of impartial or favourable consideration of his views. Nor was it possible for his own generation to divorce his optimistic eulogy of the French Revolution from his republican democracy and his apostolate of deism. The decline of the Revolution besmirched the character of its disciple. Admittedly also his historical knowledge was inadequate and his sense of the character of the political organism too superficial to meet the philosophy of Burke. Yet apart from these shortcomings the political writings of Paine are of real importance. His individualism struck a new note in English political philosophy, as did also his concern for the condition of the people. M. Halévy has insisted that in this regard his ideas were not consistent; that he tended to vacillate between an extreme depreciation of the scope of government and a summons to it to assume a paternal regard for the young and the infirm. In the first part of *The Rights of Man* he was the defender of society against the State. Men found in society a means of meeting their natural wants, driven thereto by their needs and the insufficiency of each individual apart from the help of his fellows. Their commercial companies were built upon this principle of the need of co-operation, and these voluntary associations were the fruitful, creative, and civilised institutions of social life. Whence, then, arose the need for civil government? Paine sought its origin in the element of evil in man's constitution, which prevented him from living according to the perfect law of liberty. But was this imperfection limited to his political activities? Did it not vitiate also his commercial and trading relations? Could any voluntary society escape the consequences of man's imperfection and anti-social actions? If not, then government must extend, not contract, its functions to embrace the supervision of all societies within the State. Otherwise, if the root of evil in mankind found expression only in political organisations, in the tendencies to oppression and corruption of hereditary Governments, and not in its voluntary associations, what was the necessity of government?

This contradiction was not resolved, and Paine remains at once the champion of *laissez-faire* and the prophet of paternal government.

Of the two strands, his socialism was probably more important than his individualism. In his demand for old-age pensions and for other social services to be undertaken by the Government he was the father of those who looked forward, and the history of the nineteenth and twentieth centuries has justified his prognostication. In his *Agrarian Justice*, published in 1796, he carried farther his scheme of State provision for the poor by suggesting a means for the prevention of poverty. Briefly he proposed that the State should endow each citizen who attained the age of twenty-one with £15, in order to furnish him with a small capital to embark upon his career as a farmer. Such projects were far in advance of his own time; but the principles of taxation and of the distribution of pensions laid down in the fifth chapter of the second part of *The Rights of Man* have inspired not a little modern legislation. Even in this regard, however, Paine had singular limitations. His taxation was directed against the hereditary land-owning peerage. Although he lived in the age of industrialism he did not propose to tax the industrial magnates, nor did he perceive the evils of *laissez-faire* in the field of industrial development. Perhaps the most striking developments of paternal legislation in the nineteenth century were those in which successive administrations intervened to protect employees against their employers in the chief industries of the country. This possibility lay outside the range of Paine's vision, but in his resolute association of social responsibility with the art of government he stated the principle which has found such a varied and widespread application.

In his deistic writings Paine achieved a striking modernity, an achievement all the more remarkable in view of his own ignorance of ancient languages. The correspondence between many of the guesses of *The Age of Reason* and the agreed conclusions of modern critical Biblical scholarship is surprising. Nor have the general lines of his negative criticism failed to secure acceptance by Christian apologists. The predictive character of Old Testament prophecy is no longer stressed; miracles rarely form the bulwark of apologetic defences of

Christianity; whilst mystery in the sense that *omnia exeunt in mysterium* would have been as freely admitted by Paine as by modern students of natural philosophy. Against this must be set the fact that Paine undoubtedly misconceived the nature of revelation, but this misunderstanding, which was shared by orthodox divines, was not resolved until the science of historical criticism had made possible the application of the principle of evolution to the study of historical theology. Natural religion was not so simple or convincing as the deists supposed. Therein Butler was assuredly in the right. But it would be unfair to censure Paine for his failure to restate the idea of an historical revelation in the light of an historical criticism which lay still below the horizon of thought. The most conservative student of philosophy and theology must admit that, though Butler riddled the arguments in favour of the clarity and perfection of natural religion, the deist movement exercised a profound and very salutary influence upon the orthodox interpretation of revelation. Paine was a prophet of deism, but a good many of his conclusions form part of the armoury of modern defenders of Christian theism.

So far as Paine's personal character is revealed in his writings his sincerity and also his unbounded confidence are everywhere apparent. Nor did he lack a proper self-esteem, arising at times to conceit. Of the value of his achievement he had no doubt.

> From such a beginning and with all the inconveniences of early life against me I am proud to say that with a perseverance undismayed by difficulties and a disinterestedness that compelled respect I have not only contributed to raise a new Empire in the world, founded on a new system of government, but I have arrived at an eminence in political literature, the most difficult of all lines to succeed and excel in, which aristocracy with all its aids has not been able to reach or rival.

Such an adversary had no fear of the rounded periods and rhetorical arts of Burke. His own style was vigorous, terse, and direct, and he scored not a few direct hits against the Tory philosopher, of which two examples may be given. "Nature has been kinder to Mr Burke than he is to her. He is not affected by the reality of distress touching his heart, but by the showy resemblance of it striking his imagination. He pities the plumage, but forgets the dying bird." Or again:

139

THINKERS OF THE REVOLUTIONARY ERA

"The farce of monarchy and aristocracy in all countries is following that of chivalry, and Mr Burke is dressing for the funeral. Let it then pass quietly to the tomb of all other follies and the mourners be comforted." In regard to Paine himself, it is impossible to withhold admiration for his sincerity, his endurance, and his unfaltering belief in the goodness of humanity. He was the prophet of democracy and of deism, and he fulfilled his apostolate with abundance of journeyings, perils, and discomforts. To the end he remained a knight-errant, and as such he would be content with this epitaph of the late Poet Laureate:

> In his revel of knowledge
> all the world is his own : all the hope of mankind
> is sharpen'd to a spearpoint in his bright confidence,
> as he rideth forth to do battle, a Chevalier
> in the joyous travail of the everlasting dawn.

NORMAN SYKES

BOOK LIST

Works of Thomas Paine, edited by M. D. Conway. 4 vols. 1894–96.
CONWAY, M. D.: *Life of Thomas Paine*. London, 1909.
HALÉVY, É.: *La Formation du radicalisme philosophique*. 3 vols. Paris, 1901–1904.
STEPHEN, SIR LESLIE: *English Thought in the Eighteenth Century*. 2 vols. London, 3rd edition, 1902.

VI

WILLIAM GODWIN

GODWIN'S long life spans the period from the opening of the Seven Years War to the year before the accession of Queen Victoria. Yet he was essentially the man of a single book. Throughout those eighty years his mind moved along one undeviating line with an uncompromising consistency. Once his ideas were systematised he allowed neither criticisms nor experience to modify them in any essentials. A French writer has said that his career presents the simplicity of a triptych. In the period before the French Revolution he was amassing his learning; in the period during the Revolution he systematised it and presented it to the world; in the remainder of his life he moved no farther forward intellectually, but occupied himself in trivial undertakings in an attempt to cope with his enormous financial embarrassments. Had the French Revolution not occurred his name would probably have been entirely unknown, and his life might have been that of a mere journalist and hack-writer. The Revolution gave him his chance by presenting him with a focus for his multifarious reading and the occasion for a synthesis. When it passed Godwin's fame and power passed with it, and the very nature of his character and his thinking prevented him from so learning from experience as to retain his place as a major prophet of his age.

Born in 1756, son and grandson of a Nonconformist minister, he was brought up with great strictness in an atmosphere of dissent and of hostility to the Established Church. His early training seems only to have enhanced his own marked disposition. A typical introvert, intellectually precocious, he found himself starved of affection in that austere family. Early in life a craving for fame and a longing to teach others seems to have shown itself in him. He was always arrogant and bitterly resentful of any criticism; and as he

141

developed he became obsessed with an overweening self-confidence, which never left him. Under the influence of a Norwich tutor he became a Sandemanian—one of the strictest sects of Calvinism, denying the necessity for a national Church, opposing all coercion, and teaching an apostolic communism. It was as a Sandemanian that he entered Hoxton Academy in 1773 to study for the ministry. At the age of twenty-two he began his pastorate, but it lasted only five years. During that time, reading avidly the while, he was captivated by the leading French thinkers of the century. Under the influence of Helvétius and Holbach, Rousseau, Voltaire, and Mably, his ideas, both political and religious, changed. From Calvinism he passed into deism and then agnosticism; from Toryism he passed to Whiggery, then Radicalism, and finally anarchism.

He therefore abandoned his Church, and after a futile attempt to open a school entered upon a period of laborious journalism in London. For some time he lived in abject poverty; but gradually he established contacts which enabled him to gain an adequate livelihood. He contributed to various Whig journals, met some of the party leaders, and in 1787 was entrusted by them with the editorship of the *New Annual Register*, which was their reply to Burke's production. It was this miscellaneous political journalism which brought him into touch with the other famous Radicals of his generation, such as Holcroft, Hollis, and Priestley. The French Revolution evoked in him almost as much enthusiasm as it did in the rest of that circle. He, along with Hollis and Holcroft, arranged for the publication of Paine's *Rights of Man* in March 1791; but his own viewpoint differed considerably from that of the rest of the group, and he would never participate in any of the activities of the Radical societies for reasons which he sets forth in his works.

It was two months after the publication of Paine's book that the idea of *Political Justice* occurred to Godwin. He secured an advance from the publisher, and then spent the next nineteen months in executing his plan by slow and methodical work. During the writing of it the report of his book spread, and his name was already well known before it actually appeared in February 1793, under the title *An Enquiry concerning the Principles of Political Justice, and its Influence on General Virtue and Happiness.* It met with instantaneous success. In spite of its size—it was over 200,000 words in length, and only slightly shorter than Mr Shaw's *Intelligent Woman's Guide to Socialism*—it was read by all classes. Pirated copies began to appear, and workmen's groups clubbed together to buy and discuss it. The Cabinet on one occasion actually contemplated the prosecution of the author for sedition, and was deterred from doing so only by Pitt's observation that a book of three guineas could not cause a revolution. For two years Godwin's popularity remained at its zenith before the reaction began.

Meanwhile two different enterprises occupied his pen. He wrote his first novel, *Caleb Williams*, in 1794 in order to make money, and in the process increased his reputation still further. This psychological study of the criminal mind, written to show the influence of environment on character, had an enormous success. It was extensively copied, translated into five languages, dramatised, and pirated. In the same year Godwin produced his first political pamphlet, *Cursory Strictures on Lord Chief Justice Eyre's Charge to the Grand Jury.* This pamphlet had wide repercussions, and coming just before the famous trial of the leading members of the London Corresponding Society, no doubt helped materially to secure the acquittal of the prisoners. Another anonymous pamphlet of the following year, *Considerations on Lord Grenville's and Mr Pitt's Bills*, was less popular. While attacking the Government for its policy of suppressing meetings it also criticised the physical force party among the Radicals, and thereby led to a permanent breach with their leader, Thelwall. The second edition of *Political Justice* appeared, with slight modifications, that same year.

Thereafter the reaction against Godwin's teaching began. It increased in intensity as the public attitude toward the French war changed and as Revolutionary sympathies cooled over here. It reached its climax in the vitriolic abuse hurled at Godwin in the years 1797–98, especially in the *Anti-Jacobin*. It was just at this turn in his reputation that Godwin's association with Mary Wollstonecraft occurred. Had that continued Godwin's character might have been considerably modified; but their life together lasted only a twelvemonth, and Mary Wollstonecraft died in September 1797. A steady deterioration in his character is marked from this time forward. His *Memoir* of his wife, written immediately after her death, is in some respects his finest literary achievement, and marks the passing of an epoch in his life.

His second novel, *St Leon* (1799), was also a success, and added to his reputation with the story-reading public. Hazlitt even said, " It was ' another morn risen on mid-noon.' " Its only importance to the student of Godwin's political theory is that in the preface Godwin recants his teaching in *Political Justice* concerning affection, and now allows that it is not to be excised, since it is "inseparable from the nature of man." But in the twelve months following this announcement Godwin found himself losing more and more of his friends, for both political and personal reasons. Mackintosh attacked him in public in 1799, and Dr Parr followed in the annual Spital sermon in 1800. Slowly what his future son-in-law was to call "the contagion of the world's slow stain" spread over his life. He married again in 1801, and started a publishing enterprise. He steadily became more and more entangled in debt, sank to amazing depths of pusillanimity and double-dealing, and sponged upon all his friends. Four years of effort by Francis Place failed to establish his finances on a firm basis, and even Place gave him up in disgust. Meanwhile the young Shelley had sought out Godwin in 1812 and had soon become involved in the financial tangle. This is not the place to tell once again the story of that extraordinary association, and of Shelley's elopement with Mary Wollstonecraft Godwin. Two years after Shelley's death Godwin was declared bankrupt and gave up business. The last years of his life were spent in undisturbed seclusion, and he died in 1836, the holder of a sinecure office presented to him by the Whig Government three years before. It was an ironical end for the arch-priest of anarchism.

During the last thirty-five years of his life Godwin never gave up writing. His works are of an extremely miscellaneous nature: biography, novels, children's history books, text-books, and essays. Only two of these productions need be named. The first is his essay *Of Population* (1820). This was a long-deferred reply to Malthus, whose *Essay on Population* (1798) was itself provoked by Godwin's volume of essays *The Enquirer*, published in 1797. But the later volume, though not without some worth, contributed nothing of permanent value to the controversy. The second was his volume of essays entitled *Thoughts on Man* (1833), which reproduced the leading ideas of *Political Justice*, though with less emphasis on reason than formerly. The *Gentleman's Magazine* considered it as bad as all his other political writings —"full as irreverent, and almost equally as noxious, like the serpent, venomous but enticing." It contained nothing new.

Godwin's whole career was academic in every sense. His disposition and his training had produced in him a strange fondness for abstract ideas, and mere analytical speculation fascinated him to the end. His own introversion and resentment of criticism enhanced this characteristic. He had no practical sense; and he avoided all associations which might possibly have modified his character. He saw life in simple outlines, and he sought in his reading and his own writings a philosophy which presented the issues sharply, and drew all lines of doctrine with an unqualified logical distinctness. He was quite incapable of appreciating emotional subtlety and the complexity of human contacts. Complexity was the very antithesis of his nature, and he always ignored it if perchance he caught sight of it. He had, to the end of his days, an extraordinary capacity for converting the richness of life into the simplicity of a formula.

In this essay we shall concentrate our attention on *Political Justice* alone. That was not only his most important and most influential work, but it embodied the whole of his ideas. Relatively minor points were subsequently modified by him, but the edifice itself remained untouched.

II

Political Justice is a work which holds a unique place in the history of English political theory; it is unique in doctrine and in scope. Before examining Godwin's teaching in detail it is necessary as a preliminary to stress two general features of his treatise which may help us the better to appreciate the nature of its teaching—namely, that it was written during a period of very rapid transition, wherein were mingled ideas and forces both new and old; and that its author intended it to be a comprehensive system embracing every aspect of society and essentially valid for all time. Godwin sought for the permanent beneath the flux, and found cause for unbounded hope as a result of his quest.

This book is essentially the product of the epoch which separates the old world from the new, the agricultural from the industrial. Much of the interest it has for us lies in the fact that it is thus symbolical, being both retrospective and prospective in its reference. Godwin confronts the problems of the future with intellectual preconceptions derived from the past. His work, on the one hand, is in a very real sense a synthesis of the speculation of the previous century, possessing all the general features of that speculation both as to attitude and as to method. On the other hand, it states for the future its major problems and provides the starting-point for much of its speculation.

Godwin was not an original thinker. His book is definitely the product of extensive reading (frequently acknowledged in footnotes), the results of which have been organised and integrated by a man of marked intellectual characteristics and of striking personal temperament. He sets out to build a Temple of Reason, and it is always easy to see whence he has quarried his materials; but he remains his own architect. It has been said that no single idea in *Political Justice* is original, and this is probably true. From Locke and the empiricists he borrowed his ideas of the nature and structure of mind; from Rousseau, Helvétius, and Holbach he learnt the effects which education and political institutions have on the formation of character; from Mably and others he accepted the idea of the uniformity of truth; Paine taught him the distinction between society and government; and from all these writers he took over the criticisms of monarchy and aristocracy. His criticism of private property is obviously inspired by Mably and by Wallace, and to a less extent by Plato and Sir Thomas More. Such a statement of his indebtedness could be extended to cover practically every page of his writing, but it would avail little. No catalogue of sources can explain a man. His origin-

ality is rather to be sought in the logical unity of his scheme
and the intrepidity with which he pushed his system to its
logical extreme, as no English philosopher had done before.

Being thus eclectic, *Political Justice* possesses all the main
features associated with that line of Enlightenment speculation
which derives chiefly from the Cartesian outlook. It is individualistic and atomistic in its attitude to society, regarding
society as "nothing more than an aggregate of individuals."[1]
Moreover, it is uncompromisingly intellectualistic in tone, as
examination of the doctrine reveals, and is completely lacking in that emotional driving power of romanticism which
Rousseau introduced into political theory. If Rousseau stood
for the idyllic imagination, according to Irving Babbitt's
interpretation, and Burke for the moral imagination, then
Godwin above all stood for the rational imagination and its
concomitants—the idea of progress and of human perfectibility—which resulted from the confluence of the Baconian
and Cartesian influences. That rational imagination underlies
all his writing, and is revealed at the beginning of *Political
Justice*. One of the earliest chapters (dealing with the theorem
that "human inventions are capable of perpetual improvement") opens with the assertion that "there is no characteristic
of man which seems at present, at least, so eminently to distinguish him, or to be of so much importance in every branch
of moral science, as his perfectibility"; and it ends by clearly
stating his attitude:

> Is it possible for us to contemplate what he has already done,
> without being impressed with a strong presentiment of the improve-
> ments he has yet to accomplish? There is no science that is not
> capable of additions; there is no art that may not be carried to a still
> higher perfection. If this be true of all other sciences, why not of
> morals? If this be true of all other arts, why not of social institutions?
> The very conception of this as possible, is in the highest degree en-
> couraging. If we can still farther demonstrate it to be a part of the
> natural and regular progress of mind, our confidence and our hopes will
> then be complete. This is the temper with which we ought to engage
> in the study of political truth. Let us look back, that we may profit by
> the experience of mankind; but let us not look back, as if the wisdom
> of our ancestors was such as to leave no room for future improvement.[2]

[1] *Political Justice*, p. 90. (The references throughout are to the first, 1793, edition.)
[2] *Op. cit.*, p. 50.

If history for Burke was the "known march of the ordinary providence of God," for Godwin it was the "course of progressive improvement" in the emancipation of man's reason.

Another characteristic of Godwin's work, which is derived from the preceding century, and which is an inevitable accompaniment of his rationalism, is its *a priori* method. Analysis will show how rigidly Godwin bases the whole of his political teaching on his doctrine of an immutable moral law from which particular deductions to meet particular exigencies can be made. He presents his method unequivocally:

> There are two modes, according to which we may enquire into the origin of society and government. We may either examine them historically, that is, consider in what manner they have or ought to have begun, as Mr Locke has done; or we may examine them philosophically, that is, consider the moral principles upon which they depend. The first of these subjects is not without its use; but the second is of a higher order and more essential importance. The first is a question of form; the second of substance. It would be of trivial consequence, practically considered, from what source any form of society flowed, and by what mode its principles were sanctioned, could we be always secure of their conformity to the dictates of truth and justice.[1]

Politics was therefore to be regarded as a science much like mathematics.

All this represents familiar ground to students of the Enlightenment epoch of the seventeenth and eighteenth centuries. The importance of Godwin's work lies in the fact that he it was who first disclosed in England the essentially radical spirit inherent in the outlook of the Enlightenment. This was undoubtedly due to the influence of the French thinkers acting upon his own uncompromising Nonconformist dispositions. He turned these doctrines to account, not to make a plea for the enlightened despot who should remedy the abuses of organised society by purifying it and levelling it up through his wisdom, but to destroy social organisation entirely as something inevitably evil and opposed to reason.

But although Godwin's work is backward-looking so far as its intellectualism and its method are concerned, yet it has features which gave it marked significance for the future. For

[1] *Op. cit.*, p. 78.

instance, his insistence on the doctrine of progress involved
a *purposive* attitude to social phenomena, and that attitude—
coming as it did at the beginning of the mightiest epoch of
social change in our history—was destined to spread and to
modify political life to an incalculable extent.   It was an age,
says Dr Knowles, in which " it was difficult to convince people
that ' something ought to be done.' . . . There was a fatalistic
attitude abroad." [1]   Godwin's entire work is a protest against
such an attitude and a vehement denunciation of the doctrine
of indifference.   The fact that he sought a remedy in exactly
the opposite direction to that in which later generations have
gone—in abolition of all restraint, instead of increasing social
control—need not blind us to the essential significance of this
protest.   He had a keen sense of prevailing social misery and
of the appalling waste of human life involved in the social
system around him ; vivid paragraphs scattered throughout
his work make this obvious.   Consequently his soul revolts
against the cry that " nothing can be done."

> There is no mistake more thoroughly to be deplored on this subject
> than that of persons, sitting at their ease and surrounded with all the
> conveniences of life, who are apt to explain, "We find things very
> well as they are "; and to inveigh bitterly against all projects of reform
> as " the romances of visionary men, and the declamations of those who
> are never to be satisfied."   Is it well, that so large a part of the
> community should be kept in abject penury, rendered stupid with
> ignorance and disgustful with vice, perpetuated in nakedness and
> hunger, goaded to the commission of crimes, and made victims to the
> merciless laws which the rich have instituted to oppress them?   Is it
> sedition to enquire whether this state of things may not be exchanged
> for a better?   Or can there be any thing more disgraceful to ourselves
> than to exclaim that " All is well," merely because we are at our ease,
> regardless of the misery, degradation and vice that may be occasioned
> in others? [2]

In the next century such an attitude of social purposiveness
was to become general, instead of being the exception ; and
the dissemination of such an attitude was the prelude to
democracy.

[1] Dr L. C. A. Knowles, *The Industrial and Commercial Revolutions in Great Britain
during the Nineteenth Century*, pp. 105–106.
[2] *Political Justice*, p. 487.

In a second respect, however, Godwin's work has a bearing on the future—in his realisation that the idea of property is the fundamental problem of human society. He alone of all the English thinkers dealt with in this book gave that issue any serious consideration or saw the problem with anything like clarity. Few other political philosophers in England had for a century considered it as the paramount *practical problem*; but such it was for Godwin.[1] In this respect he shows greater detachment and more insight than most of the revolutionaries with whom he was associated. He says plainly that republicanism will not solve the social problems. Only a redistribution of property can do that. This issue had been raised during the Commonwealth period, but from the Restoration onward had fallen into the background of political speculation this side of the Channel. Godwin it was who restored the primacy of the whole question. Many post-Waterloo critics of society learnt their first lessons on the subject from him; and from that time onward the problems touching the justification and distribution of private property increasingly came to take their place as the central issue of social speculation and reforming activity. It is in this respect that his influence on the early English socialists was marked, and for this reason that Dr Anton Menger credits Godwin with being, in a sense, the first scientific socialist.

Apart from the attribute of social purposiveness and the question of property, there is another sense in which Godwin has significance for the century that followed, and that is in his emphasis on the necessity for leisure and education as the indispensable bases for the erection of democracy. This point of view—the complete antithesis of Burke's idea of the " swinish multitude "—follows from Godwin's conception of the perfectibility of man. He has a thoroughly evangelical regard for the intrinsic worth of every human being; his moral ideal involves the development of the reason latent in all men; and for him we fall short of this moral ideal so long as there remain any undeveloped potentialities in the soul of

---

[1] In a footnote Godwin cites Ogilvie (*Essay on the Right of Property in Land*), Plato, More, Swift, Mably, and Wallace (*Various Prospects of Mankind, Nature, and Providence*). But he complains that, although they see the truth, they either " quit the subject in despair," or do not go to the root of the evil.

man. Adopting as he did the Socratic position that knowledge is virtue, Godwin sees in the extension of education the only medium of progress and reform. It was this fact which made him distrust violence and any form of collective endeavour such as leagues, societies, and unions; it was this fact which led him to break with Thelwall and the physical force men; and it was this fact also that led him to imply in many places in *Political Justice* that reform must come relatively slowly through the propaganda work of a small intellectual aristocracy.

Besides this double aspect of *Political Justice* as both retrospective and prospective there is another general feature of the work which needs emphasising, and that is its comprehensiveness. In one sense Godwin's book is misnamed; it is far more extensive in scope than its title at first glance would imply. But Godwin is careful to explain in what sense he is using his terms. For him politics does not mean merely the machinery of government and its construction; nor does justice mean merely a legal ideal. By politics he means rather the general science of human virtue and happiness. Politics is really a general ethical study. He tells us in the preface that he "conceived politics to be the proper vehicle of a liberal morality"; and in his first chapter he criticises the generally accepted meaning of the word 'politics.' He says that it has been used in too narrow a sense by writers hitherto, for they have not displayed "a consciousness of the intimate connection of the different parts of the social system, whether it relates to the intercourse of individuals or to the maxims and institutes of states and nations." These remarks, he tells us, apply to the English writers upon politics in general, from Sidney and Locke to the author of the *Rights of Man*; while the more comprehensive view "has been perspicuously treated by Rousseau and Helvétius." Godwin is accordingly at pains to show that "government is still more considerable in its incidental effects than in those intended to be produced." It is all-pervading in its influence; it "insinuates itself into our personal dispositions and insensibly communicates its own spirit to our private transactions"; it is the ever-present but invisible environment, controlling the life of every single member of the community by compelling the adaptation of the individual to itself, unconsciously, but none the less completely. No other English writer had conceived his subject in such a comprehensive way, although since Godwin's time the complexity of the issues involved in the problems of politics has been increasingly realised.

Since he adopted this viewpoint, it is not surprising that Godwin made his own work 'perspicuous.' It is not so much a treatise on politics as on sociology. Besides being what he himself calls a "political science," it is a treatise on ethics, on philosophy, and on individual and social psychology. It treats of education and religion ; it roams from the problem of free will to the question of immortality. He definitely intended it to supersede all else written on the subject, especially "after the great change that has been produced in men's minds . . . and the light that has been thrown upon it by the recent discussions of America and France." Above all, he wrote with a practical intention. He clearly wanted to modify public opinion and to hasten the coming of the day of enlightenment. This was to be no mere academic treatise, but a work "from the perusal of which no man should rise without being strengthened in habits of sincerity, fortitude, and justice."[1]

This last remark reveals another general trait of *Political Justice*. It was comprehensive not only in the sense that a large variety of subjects was dealt with, but also in the sense that its author was trying to look at the issues *sub specie æternitatis*. He writes on cosmic problems with a consummate self-confidence, and his political theory is in a direct sense the by-product of his cosmology. From beginning to end he is always asking what are the "general principles," not what are the facts ; and he entertains no doubt in his own mind that once these general principles are found they can be applied to all concrete problems with ease. Godwin's outlook is religious, in much the same sense in which Mr J. M. Keynes has called Bolshevism a religion. He is completely convinced of the truth of his general principles ; he is quite confident that they alone embody the entire truth ; he is assured that his teaching is in perfect harmony with "the general scheme of things," so that even though the adventitious sin of man may postpone

[1] *Political Justice*, p. vii.

the coming of the reign of reason, yet that reign must come sooner or later, and neither principalities nor powers will be able ultimately to prevent it. Godwin had dropped the specific tenets of the Calvinist creed; but his book is Calvinistic in spirit throughout, and a realisation of this fact helps us the better to appraise his teaching. For a discoverable God he substituted a discoverable universe. For grace working silently in the heart of man he substituted reason. Instead of righteousness as the principle of conduct he pleaded for enlightenment, since the mind—once awakened to the sublimity of eternal truth—must of necessity act in conformity with it. Lastly, and as a corollary of what has been said, for the need of conversion he substituted the need for education; man could attain his true status only by turning away from the intellectual errors into which he had fallen, and by contemplating the immutable laws of the universe. Godwin in more than one place seems to think that this awakening of the soul may happen suddenly, though he hopes the process may not be too sudden in the community as a whole. He prefers that the awakening should first occur among the spiritual *élite*, who should be, as it were, missionaries to their fellows. When the enlightenment has become general, then the whole political and social problem will be solved. The awakening to the truth means automatically that the calm period of reason will succeed, since " in reality the chains fall off themselves when the magic of opinion is dissolved." [1] It is the old doctrine that the truth would make men free.

III

A man's political theory when he sets out to construct a system is to a large extent determined by his basic conceptions (be they held consciously or unconsciously) concerning the nature of man and the nature of the general world-process. The more, for instance, a writer adopts the view that man is essentially good, the closer will his political theory approach towards anarchism. Conversely the more a writer emphasises the inherent evil in man, the more he is driven toward some

[1] *Op. cit.*, p. 64.

kind of absolutism and seeks to assign the seat of ultimate sovereignty in society whereby that evil can be held in check. The accepted world-view is no less influential in shaping a thinker's political ideas. Dante's outlook in politics is as clearly influenced by his Christian cosmology as Herbert Spencer's is by his doctrine of evolution, or as T. H. Green's is by his doctrine of reality. These basic ideas may not always be clearly stated; they may be only implicit, and accepted tacitly. But they are none the less of great influence in determining the trend of thought, as the analytic work of Pareto, of Vaihinger, and of others has proved to us in our own day. It is essential, therefore, in any exposition of a writer's political philosophy to make clear to begin with just what are his basic assumptions. In the case of Godwin we are dealing with a man who consciously and deliberately deduced the whole of his political ideas from these assumptions, and who makes that fact clear beyond a doubt in almost every one of his eighty chapters. He reiterates his position to an almost wearisome degree, and recurs to his " first principles " with every specific problem. We will examine first, therefore, his theory of man; and next his conception of the universe, so far as he presents that as determining political theory.

His theory of man is fundamental. All men, whatever their colour and wherever they are born, are made in the same way. "All men are conscious that man is a being of one common nature, and feel the propriety of the treatment they receive from one another being measured by a common standard." [1] The points in which human beings are alike "are infinitely more considerable than those in which they differ." [2] This common nature has several marked features. First, all minds at birth are a *tabula rasa*, and we bring into the world with us no innate principles.[3] Consequently at birth there is " no essential difference between the child of the lord and the porter." But in the second place man is born endowed with reason, or at least the potentiality of reason. " All men are partakers of the common faculty reason, and may be supposed to have some communication with the common preceptor truth." [4] Godwin is always saying that man is an

---

[1] *Op. cit.*, p. 808.   [2] *Op. cit.*, p. 182.
[3] *Op. cit.*, p. 12.   [4] *Op. cit.*, p. 158.

intellectual being; but he nowhere tells us clearly exactly what he means by reason. He appears to mean by that term the capacity, or the faculty, for discerning cause and effect in phenomena. But the strangest aspect of Godwin's doctrine is his contention that reason exerts a compulsive power over its possessor. Man always acts in accordance with such reason as he has, even though that may not be fully developed. No other faculty intervenes in action; indeed, given the perception of one or more causal relationships, action follows automatically in accordance with that perception. Hence it follows that "Man being, as we have now found him to be, a simple substance, governed by the apprehensions of his understanding, nothing further is requisite but the improvement of his reasoning faculty to make him virtuous and happy." [1] So there can be no such thing as free will. Godwin devotes twenty pages [2] to destroying the case for free will, and to showing that if there is to be a science of mind it must be based on the necessitarian hypothesis. The mind is itself built up of associated sequences of ideas derived from the perceptions of reason. Thus the inner world of mind, like the outer world of matter, is a causal system. Therefore "man is in reality a passive and not an active being"; [3] "considered in himself he is merely a being capable of impression, a recipient of perceptions." [4] This doctrine Godwin uses at almost every stage of his argument, and especially in connection with treatment of crime and punishment. Paradoxically enough, also, it is this doctrine which is going to give him his chief reason for optimism for the future.

Four important consequences follow from this conception of human beings as passive creatures without innate ideas, but endowed with a potential reasoning faculty. The first is that there is no distinction between will and intellect; action is automatic, for it is impossible to imagine, in the light of the above teaching,

> that, in the case of an intellectual faculty placed in an aptly organised body, preference can exist together with a consciousness (gained from experience) of our power to obtain the object preferred, without a certain motion of the animal frame being the necessary result. We

[1] *Op. cit.*, pp. 303–304. [2] *Op. cit.*, pp. 283–304.
[3] *Op. cit.*, p. 310. [4] *Op. cit.*, p. 452.

need only attend to the obvious meaning of the terms in order to perceive that the will is merely, as it has been happily termed, the last act of the understanding.[1]

The second consequence is the moral and intellectual equality of all human beings, at least potentially :

> From these simple principles we may deduce the moral equality of mankind. We are partakers of a common nature, and the same causes that contribute to the benefit of one contribute to the benefit of another. Our senses and faculties are of the same denomination. Our pleasures and pains will therefore be the same. We are all of us endowed with reason, able to compare, to judge, and to infer. The improvement therefore which is to be desired for the one, is to be desired for the other.[2]

The third consequence, which again is utilised throughout *Political Justice*, is the doctrine that character is determined by environment, and by environment only :

> From these reasonings it sufficiently appears, that the moral qualities of men are the produce of the impressions made upon them, and that there is no instance of an original propensity to evil. Our virtues and vices may be traced to the incidents which make the history of our lives, and if these incidents could be divested of every improper tendency, vice would be extirpated from the world.[3]

The fourth consequence which Godwin deduces from his view of the capacities of man is "the doctrine of benevolence." Man does not act from the impulse of self-love, for the understanding of virtue is itself a motive exciting to action ; and by virtue he means conformity with the moral law, which commands the consideration of other people's needs as much as one's own.[4] "Man is not originally vicious."

When we turn from Godwin's theories of the nature of man to his theories of the nature of the universe we find him no less explicit, and from the combination of the two doctrines the whole of his political theory is derived. We may summarise his teaching under this head by the theorem that he conceived of the universe as a system of cause and effect, working by immutable laws, and implying a code of moral

---

[1] *Op. cit.*, p. 303.
[2] *Op. cit.*, pp. 106–107.
[3] *Op. cit.*, p. 18.
[4] *Op. cit.*, pp. 441 *et seq.*

principles which are themselves rational and discernible by the human reason.

To begin with, it is a *system*; and the main purpose of *Political Justice* is to delineate that system. "I am myself part of a great whole," he says; and it is this whole that he means by the word 'truth.' Literally scores of times throughout his nine hundred pages Godwin refers to this "system."

> Human beings are placed in the midst of a system of things all the parts of which are strictly connected with each other, and exhibit a sympathy and unison by means of which the whole is rendered intelligible and, as it were, palpable to the mind.[1]

But it is a system which works by the immutable laws of cause and effect. He speaks of "the great chain of causes from which every event in the universe takes its rise."[2] Human affairs themselves "through every link of the great chain of necessity are admirably harmonised and adapted to each other."[3] All things past, present, and to come are "links of an indissoluble chain," and "it is by general principles that the business of the universe is carried on."[4]

> This view of things presents us with an idea of the universe as connected and cemented in all its parts, nothing in the boundless progress of things being capable of happening otherwise than it has actually happened. In the life of every human being there is a chain of causes, generated in that eternity which preceded his birth, and going on in regular procession through the whole period of his existence, in consequence of which it was impossible for him to act in any instance otherwise than he has acted.[5]

These immutable laws involve a code of moral principles. Godwin is a utilitarian, and for him virtue and happiness are interchangeable terms. Virtue is thus organic to nature, in the sense that nature has ordained that all men shall pursue their own happiness; and in the attainment of that complete harmony which is real happiness they help to promote the happiness of others also. It is this harmony ordained by nature which constitutes the moral code, and which Godwin calls justice. "If truth be one," he says, "there must be one code of truths on the subject of our reciprocal duties,"[6] for

---

[1] *Op. cit.*, p. 502. [2] *Op. cit.*, p. 281. [3] *Op. cit.*, p. 207.
[4] *Op. cit.*, p. 246. [5] *Op. cit.*, p. 305. [6] *Op. cit.*, p. 237.

157

"the course of nature and the course of perfect theory are the same."[1]

There is no situation in which we can be placed, no alternative that can be presented to our choice respecting which duty is silent. "What is the standard of morality and duty?" Justice. Not the arbitrary decrees that are enforced in a particular climate; but those laws of eternal reason that are equally obligatory wherever man is to be found.[2]

And there is "no criterion of duty to any man but in the exercise of his private judgement." Since the universe is "palpable to mind," and since man is endowed with reason, each man can discover for himself what his duty is in any particular set of circumstances. It is not a question of commands, either human or divine, for "I perceive that these things, and a certain conduct intending them, are connected in the visible system of the world, and not by the supernatural interposition of an invisible director."[3] The only general statement we can make about justice, therefore, is that it means "I should contribute everything in my power to the benefit of the whole."[4] In any given case this must involve a calculation as to what actually does benefit the whole; and in one place Godwin says "the decision of the question is in reality an affair of arithmetic." The value of a man is his usefulness, and our conduct should so be determined as to promote the maximum of usefulness in the world. Godwin's famous example regarding Fénelon shocked contemporaries, but at least it logically conformed to his own definitions. "The illustrious Archbishop of Cambrai was of more worth than his chambermaid, and there are few of us who would hesitate to pronounce, if his palace were in flames, and the life of only one of them could be preserved, which of the two ought to be preserved."[5] If the chambermaid had been my wife, mother, or benefactor that would not alter the truth of the proposition, for "justice, pure unadulterated justice, would still have preferred that which was most valuable. . . . What magic is there in the pronoun 'my' to overturn the decisions of everlasting truth?"[6]

Such are Godwin's basic theories of man and the universe.

[1] *Op. cit.*, p. 773.   [2] *Op. cit.*, p. 699.   [3] *Op. cit.*, p. 502.
[4] *Op. cit.*, p. 81.   [5] *Op. cit.*, p. 82.   [6] *Op. cit.*, p. 83.

Man is of one nature ; the universe is one system ; the moral law is one code ; and necessity reigns everywhere. There follow certain consequences of great importance for politics, "leading to a bold and comprehensive view of man in society." Five such consequences have in particular to be noted.

In the first place, all doctrine of rights in the political sense completely disappears. The moral law prescribes what duty the individual owes to his neighbours and what duty they owe to him, and nothing more is necessary. The argument is simple. "By right . . . has always been understood discretion, that is, full and complete power of either doing a thing or omitting it, without the person's becoming liable to animadversion or censure from another." But

> the rights of one man cannot clash with, or be destructive of, the rights of another; for this, instead of rendering the subject an important branch of truth and morality (as the advocates of the rights of man certainly understand it to be), would be to reduce it to a heap of unintelligible jargon and inconsistency. If one man have a right to be free another man cannot have the right to make him a slave.

Nobody has a right to omit what his duty prescribes: "from hence it inevitably follows that men have no rights."[1] Nothing is more surprising, says Godwin, than that two ideas so incompatible as man and rights should have been associated together, since either term "must be utterly exclusive and annihilatory of the other." Once posit that man is an intellectual being, it follows that he can learn from immutable justice what his duties are, and thereby all talk of rights becomes meaningless. Both Godwin and Bentham denied the existence of inherent rights, which was so popular a doctrine during the revolutionary epoch, but for exactly opposite reasons. To Bentham the doctrine was "nonsense on stilts," because it implied some immutable and universal principle, and ignored the simple hedonistic calculus. To Godwin the doctrine was "conspicuous by its immoral tendency," because it implied a negation of "the grand and simple system" of immutable justice. Society cannot change eternal truth.[2] It can require of me everything that it is my duty to do, and no more (hence it cannot compel me to go to war on its behalf).

[1] *Op. cit.*, p. 111.   [2] *Op. cit.*, p. 90.

Conversely, society is bound to do for its members everything that can contribute to their welfare (and on the strength of this Godwin later denies any absolute right to property).

A second consequence, no less important than the denial of inherent rights, follows from Godwin's views of man and his world, and this is the fact that there can be no such thing as legislation in any real sense. Law cannot be made, for it simply *is*; and the most venerable Senate "can only interpret and announce the law which derives its real validity from a higher and less mutable authority." And, again, legislation is

a term not applicable to human society. Men cannot do more than declare and interpret law; nor can there be an authority so paramount as to have the prerogative of making that to be law which abstract and immutable justice had not made to be law previously to that interposition— [1]

though he admits that as a temporary expedient it might be found necessary to have an authority empowered to declare those general principles.

The third consequence is that no obedience is due to government as such. The object of government is the exertion of force; and the duty of man is the exercise of his reason. I am bound to submit to justice and truth, because they approve themselves to my judgment; but I submit to erroneous government only because there is no alternative.

The compliance I yield to government independently of my approbation of its measures is of the same species as my compliance with a wild beast that forces me to run north when my judgment and inclination prompt me to go south.[2]

So it follows that "no Government ought pertinaciously to resist the change of its own institutions," or to hinder the fullest possible discussion. The individual judgment is the only valid tribunal, and man is in all cases

obliged to consult that judgement before he can determine whether the matter in question be of the sort provided for or no. So that from this reasoning it ultimately appears that no man is obliged to conform to any rule of conduct farther than the rule is consistent with justice.[3]

The contrary doctrine has been the source of more calamities to mankind than all the other errors of the human understanding. "Depravity would have gained little ground in the world, if every man had been in the exercise of his independent judgement."[1]

A fourth consequence of Godwin's general philosophical outlook is that there is one best form of government. Truth is one; and truth "cannot be so variable as to change its nature by crossing an arm of the sea"; it is at all times and in all places the same. Man's nature is everywhere the same in essentials also; therefore he always needs the same things. Hence "there must in the nature of things be one best form of government which all intellects sufficiently roused from the slumber of savage ignorance will be irresistibly incited to approve."[2] Difference in climate need not modify political theory.

Such are the general premises of Godwin's political thinking, and such are the consequences which these premises involve for him. But if the living of a social life is part of the general problem of morality, and if on the other hand man is born morally neutral, but endowed with the potentialities of reason, the question then arises: What are the causes of moral improvement? The general nature of the answer to this question has already been implied, but Godwin examines it with considerable fullness.

There are three principal sources of moral improvement: literature, education, and political organisation. The first two are limited in their scope. Literature, although it has already "reconciled the whole thinking world respecting the great principles of the system of the universe," appeals only to a few. The bulk of the community has neither the time nor the capacity to devote to it, because of the inequitable distribution of wealth. Education, although in some respects a more powerful instrument, is also circumscribed in its influence; partly because of the difficulty of finding the sagacious and disinterested teacher, but mainly because its benefits will be neutralised by the evil environment when the youth passes into the world. The environment must first be altered before the other two instruments can be fully utilised. That is why political organisation is of such overwhelming importance. If that organisation be based on the true laws

[1] *Op. cit.*, p. 174.   [2] *Op. cit.*, p. 182.

of morality, then man, being a creature passive to his environment, will himself grow moral. By creating the invisible but omnipresent social environment government has an incalculable power of suggestion, entering into every action and every thought of man.

All the effects that any principle adopted into the practice of a community may produce, it produces upon a comprehensive scale. It creates a similar bias in the whole, or a considerable part of the society. The motive it exhibits, the stimulus it begets, are operative because they are fitted to produce effect upon mind. They will therefore inevitably influence all to whom they are equally addressed. Virtue, where virtue is the result, will cease to be a task of perpetual watchfulness and contention. It will neither be, nor appear to be, a sacrifice of our personal advantage to disinterested considerations. It will render those the confederates, support and security of our rectitude, who were before its most formidable enemies.[1]

The first duty of the thinker must accordingly be to examine existing institutions in the light of his first principles. When that is done the nature of the ideal community will more clearly be seen.

IV

A very large proportion of *Political Justice* is taken up with expounding the deleterious effects of existing institutions and with pointing out the evils of the prevailing social environment. There are six institutions that Godwin particularly denounces ; three concern the external organisation of society, and three concern social tradition and the more personal life of the individual. The external institutions are government, law, and property ; the social traditions are sentiment, promises, and marriage.

Before dealing with the traditional forms of government Godwin makes a preliminary examination of the doctrines of previous writers concerning the basis of political authority. Three such doctrines he rejects outright, and two of them with the scantiest treatment. To the question What are the foundations of political government? he finds that four answers can be given : force, divine sanction, contract, and

---

[1] *Op. cit.*, p. 28.

" common deliberation." The doctrine that force is the basis of government is a total negation of abstract justice, and therefore " puts a violent termination upon all political science; and seems intended to persuade men to sit down quietly under their present disadvantages . . . and not to exert themselves to discover a remedy for the evils they suffer." [1] The hypothesis of divine right is rejected as " equivocal"; either it is identical with the first theory or it is without any criterion whatever. For if the argument on its behalf be made from the idea of patriarchal descent, Godwin replies that this is not discoverable; and if the argument be made from the idea of divine justice, Godwin answers that this involves the unfettered use of reason, and therefore the doctrine is superfluous. The contract hypothesis is examined much more fully, but this too is rejected, mainly by arguments taken from Hume.[2] He asks the thinkers of the contractarian school certain leading questions: Who are the parties to the contract, and how can they bind subsequent generations? To how great a variety of propositions does assent apply? (e.g., to the laws of England in fifty folio volumes?) Is the contract but the result of a majority vote? Godwin finds the answers to each of these questions wholly unsatisfactory. Therefore he concludes that common deliberation is the only true foundation of government, and in support of that conclusion he pleads the equal needs of mankind, the equal endowment of mankind with reason, the common object of mankind—viz., security—and the effects that common deliberation has on men by making them equally "conscious of their own importance."

It is in the light of such conclusions that Godwin examines the existing structure of government. He makes a preliminary statement of his position:

> Under each of these heads it will be our business, in proportion as we adhere to the great and comprehensive principles already established, rather to clear away abuses than to recommend farther and more precise regulations, rather to simplify than to complicate. Above all we should not forget that government is an evil, an usurpation upon the private judgement and individual conscience of mankind; and that, however we may be obliged to admit it as a necessary evil for the present, it behoves us, as the friends of reason and the human

---

[1] *Op. cit.*, p. 141.   [2] Hume, *Essays*, Part II, Essay 12.

species, to admit as little of it as possible, and carefully to observe whether, in consequence of the gradual illumination of the human mind, that little may not hereafter be diminished.[1]

Three general lines of criticism keep recurring in Godwin's attacks on the various kinds of government. Each form, even in its purest examples, is shown to be ineffective owing to its limited composition and to the fact that no general form of government can possibly cope adequately with the multiplicity of particular cases in any community; each form corrupts by its example, because it introduces a false scheme of social values conflicting with the dictates of reason; lastly, each form sooner or later comes to seek some other purpose than the development of the mind of man, and comes to resort to coercion in achieving that purpose—and all forms of coercion are evil.

Monarchy in all its varieties is to be utterly condemned. A king, after all, is only a man; therefore he is limited both in his knowledge and in his sympathy. He is educated in pernicious circumstances, being neither disciplined nor contradicted, and is always surrounded by flatterers. The very nature of his luxurious environment prevents his having contact with the poverty and effort of ordinary men; and the host of servants which surrounds him obviates all necessity for work on his part. When he comes to the throne he continues to be surrounded by sycophants and to be insulated from the realities of life by the insincerities of his associates. Above all, monarchy is evil because it vilifies its subjects. They become deluded by the pomps and mysteries of regal show, and come to accept a false social valuation, regarding kings and courtiers as beings superior to themselves. They regard riches and birth as the criteria of well-being, instead of listening to the dictates of their own conscience; and the monarchic system is so organised as to perpetuate this state of ignorance and moral depravity, for it is based on a deep fear of the lower classes. A limited monarchy is, if anything, even worse than a despotic one, because in addition to the vices already enumerated it involves the pernicious fiction that "the king can do no wrong"; and such a fiction is based on the utmost hypocrisy.

[1] *Political Justice*, p. 380.

Aristocracy is to be condemned for similar reasons, though in this case each evil is multiplied, since it attaches not to a single man, but to a group. Even more than monarchy does aristocracy mean the monopolisation of an undue amount of the wealth of the community. Moreover, the king may at least be accessible, whereas an aristocracy never can be. In his writings (though not in his life) Godwin has nothing but bitter scorn for all forms of social distinction and of titles, which he dismisses as "stuffed feudalism."

What of democracy? Here we have to emphasise a feature of *Political Justice* which has not been hitherto apparent in our discussion of it—the fact that it is not completely consistent. In his first volume, after analysing the various hypotheses as to the foundation of government, Godwin had come to the conclusion that "common deliberation" was the only satisfactory explanation. Such deliberation, he found, could be rendered practicable only by a system of representation; and he spent six pages vindicating such a system even against Rousseau. He realised that it had dangers, but said that "within certain limits, however, the beauty of the spectacle must be acknowledged." He had even come near to justifying the doctrine of majority rule.[1] Three hundred pages farther on he was saying much the same thing. One of the reasons for the breakdown of the democracies of the ancient world was that the ancients were unacquainted with the idea of representation.

> By this happy expedient we secure many of the pretended benefits of aristocracy, as well as the real benefits of democracy. We are to conceive of the representatives not only as the appointed medium of the sentiments of their constituents, but as authorised upon certain occasions to act on their part, in the same manner as an unlearned parent delegates his authority over his child to a preceptor of greater accomplishments than himself.[2]

Indeed, it is a principle "in which the sound political philosopher will rest with the most perfect satisfaction."

But although in these two separate sections of the book Godwin has given representative institutions his definite approval, yet seventy pages later he is criticising the scheme of national assemblies vehemently. They produce "a fictitious

[1] *Op. cit.*, pp. 164–165. [2] *Op. cit.*, p. 497.

unanimity," since the dogma of majority rule means that the minority will always be overridden, and than this "nothing can more directly contribute to the depravation of the human understanding and character," for it renders a man timid, dissembling, and corrupt. The system of decision by votes means that desire for success will take the place of desire for truth, and that parties, with all the evils of the party system, will be organised. There will thence follow the perversion of reason by mere oratory, contentious disputes, and the triumph of ignorance and vice. Godwin has thus come to approximate closely to Rousseau's position, which he had so vigorously criticised in the first volume. The conclusion he draws from these facts is that national assemblies are to meet as infrequently as possible, elected either for emergencies (which he prefers) or for a single appointed day each year.

What is the explanation of this change in Godwin's position? It is probably to be found in the preface to the whole work. There he tells us that the printing of the book was begun long before the composition of it was finished. The result is that

> some disadvantages have arisen from this circumstance. The ideas of the author became more perspicuous and digested, as his enquiries advanced. The longer he considered the subject, the more accurately he seemed to understand it. This circumstance has led him into a few contradictions. . . . He did not enter upon the work without being aware that government by its very nature counteracts the improvements of individual mind; but he understood the full meaning of this proposition more completely as he proceeded, and saw more distinctly into the nature of the remedy.[1]

Enough has been said to show Godwin's opinion on "the quackery of government." But if government in all its forms is an evil, the whole legal and police system and the entire idea of punishment and restraint are no less so.

Law is harmful for numerous reasons. In the first place, once the process of law-making has begun, it goes on endlessly. It is an attempt to make a generalisation fit a concrete case, and this, by the nature of the case, is bound to prove impossible, for every case should have a rule to itself; hence laws have constantly to be remade or stretched by legal fictions, since the rigid legal classifications are always breaking down. Laws

[1] *Op. cit.*, pp. ix–x.

in their very nature "pretend to foretell events," because they claim a finality valid for all future circumstances; therefore they tend to stagnation, and, like every form of creed, become a hindrance to progress by attempting to define a single standard of action and belief. Moreover, laws are uncertain. Their volume is vast, unmanageable, and contradictory; they can be quoted on both sides of a case, and nobody in any given instance can possibly know what the result of a lawsuit is going to be; so that recourse to legal process is just a gamble. Lawyers, from the nature of their situation, are bound to be dishonest; indeed, an honest lawyer may do more harm than good by modifying the effects of this institution and preventing its evils from becoming manifest. Law is only necessitated by, and relative to, the exercise of political force. It is evil, as all use of force is evil, since it involves another standard than the individual's free and unfettered judgment; and it will perish when the necessity for such force ceases.

But if the making of laws is bad, the enforcement of them by a system of punishment is worse. Perhaps the most brilliant and penetrating of all the sections of *Political Justice* are those that deal with this subject. Even to-day they possess a significance which is more than historical, and embody lessons which society is still in the stage of learning. Godwin's own thinking on the subject has been supplemented by the influence of Beccaria, from whom he borrows extensively, and the result is one of the finest pleas ever written in English for the rational consideration of the problem of punishment and the treatment of the criminal. No writer in English political theory had given the subject fuller and more lucid considera-tion, or had seen more clearly the implications of the problem.

To Godwin the subject is "perhaps the most fundamental in the science of politics." [1] What is punishment? he asks. It is the deliberate infliction of evil upon the vicious for one or both of two reasons: because public advantage demands it, and because there is a "certain fitness in the nature of things" in so doing. But both these reasons presuppose the doctrine of free will; they assume the criminal might have done other than he did, and that if sufficiently painful sanctions are attached to given actions, members of the community will

[1] *Op. cit.*, p. 687.

voluntarily refrain from committing those acts. But Godwin has already been at pains to destroy the doctrine of free will, and he refers his readers to the argument for necessity once again. "Mind," he tells us once more, "is an agent in no other sense than matter is an agent." The criminal is impelled by irresistible forces derived from his past life, so that "the assassin cannot help the murder he commits any more than the dagger." It is apparent, moreover, from the nature of Godwin's general philosophical position that there is no such thing as an absolute and independent *retributive* justice, which can be vindicated from the system of nature, for nature cannot be thought of as arbitrary and as adjusted by a designing mind. Such an argument from "the nature of things," says Godwin, was that used to justify religious persecution in the past. The idea of retribution must therefore be swept entirely out of our minds, and unqualified necessitarianism must be accepted instead. There can be no such thing as desert; so it must always be unjust to inflict suffering except it tend to good; "the only measure of equity is utility." Consequently it is useless to punish a man for that which is past; he must be considered as innocent at the time of its infliction.

On what grounds can coercion be defended? As self-defence? This certainly is "the most innocent of all the classes of coercion," and may be at times necessary. But even here mere passive resistance might be adequate, for "who shall say how far the whole species might be improved, were they accustomed to despise force in others, and did they refuse to employ it for themselves?" This is the only concession to the defenders of coercion that Godwin will make, though even here he qualifies it by a rhetorical and nebulous possibility. Certainly all other grounds of coercion are to be condemned outright. The argument that coercion is necessary for restraint—*i.e.*, punishment on account of suspicion regarding a man's future conduct—is arbitrary and abhorrent to reason. The argument that punishment may be necessary to effect a reformation of the man at first appears to have more plausibility; but in reality this is just as weak a case as the others. Coercion has nothing whatever in common with reason, and so it cannot possibly generate virtue. Adversity is not the best way of awakening latent reason; it only sours the mind.

WILLIAM GODWIN

Worst of all is the argument that coercion is necessary as an example. This involves the futile and silly doctrine that vicarious punishment can do good to others; it leads to the devising of newer and crueller barbarities, which soon cease to provoke terror; and it "supersedes argument, reason, and conviction, and requires us to think such a species of conduct our duty because such is the good pleasure of our superiors." Underlying all Godwin's treatment of the subject is his doctrine of the power of environment, his belief in reason, and his profound conviction that "my propensities are the fruit of the impressions that have been made upon me, the good always preponderating, because the inherent nature of things is more powerful than any human institutions."[1] Lastly, quite apart from the general justification of punishment, there is the practical difficulty of applying it. How is the degree of punishment to be measured? No standard of crime is discoverable, and anyway delinquency and coercion are incommensurable quantities. For instance, the question arises whether punishment shall be proportioned to the action or the motive. Beccaria says to the action and its result. Yet this may present great difficulties; not only the actual difficulty of fact—*e.g.*, did the blow cause death, or was death due to the shock imposed on an already weak heart?—but also the difficulty of motive, for righteous and justified indignation might rouse the temper to commit a crime as much as a perverted moral sense. But even if we take motive as our basis of calculation we are confronted with the inscrutable, both as to motive itself and as to the criminal's future conduct. Above all, the whole issue is rendered still more complicated by the problems of evidence.

What conclusions are to be drawn from all this? It is taken as axiomatic that coercion can never make men better. The only true remedy is to change the entire system of society by establishing political justice forthwith—a state of society "which by the mere simplicity of its structure, will infallibly lead to the extermination of offence." The moment men can be persuaded to form such a society coercion should be dropped. A second and curious conclusion is that coercion as a temporary expedient may have to be admitted; but only individuals may coerce, not the community. Coercion of an offender hardened

[1] *Op. cit.*, p. 713.

169

in guilt is analogous to war against a despot invading one's country; it is a painful necessity for the time being. The wise man, until he can help introduce that form of society which his reason approves, will contribute to the support of so much coercion as is necessary to prevent a worse state of affairs than the existing one. He must be quite clear, however, that temporary restraint is his only motive, not retribution or reform. Consequently torture and death are never justified. Corporal punishment will be regarded as absurd and atrocious, as violating all the principles of reason. And the method of restraint also must be given careful consideration. Existing prison systems are denounced. Solitary confinement, such as Howard was advocating, met with Godwin's disapproval, for reasons which have long since become obvious. Slavery is an unqualified evil. The best method, if properly organised, is to banish the miscreant and settle him in one of the colonies, there to work out his own salvation.

Property is the third of the existing major social institutions which Godwin denounces. Nothing, he says, so much distorts our judgment as erroneous views about property.

> And here with grief it must be confessed that, however great and extensive are the evils that are produced by monarchies and courts, by the imposture of priests and the iniquity of criminal laws, all these are imbecile and impotent compared with the evils that arise out of the established system of property.[1]

The existing system is to be condemned on five counts. First, because of the sense of dependence that is engendered among the less wealthy citizens through the inequality of possessions. The pauper fawning upon his benefactor, the servant obeying his master's every word, the tradesmen studying his whims, and the masses generally showing obsequiousness are all symptoms of the same disease; and it is absurd to expect any general improvement while the cause remains untouched and while all the members of the community are thus subjected to hourly corruption.

Second, because the perpetual spectacle of injustice before their eyes corrupts the moral sense of men. It inflames their acquisitive instincts, and "perpetually goads the spectator to the desire of opulence"; and it distorts the integrity of their

---

[1] *Op. cit.*, p. 799.

judgment by introducing a false scheme of social values, making men callous and insensible to virtue. The wealthy are merely the pensioners of society, and "the rent-roll of the lands of England is a much more formidable pension list than that which is supposed to be employed in the purchase of ministerial majorities."

Third, because it involves a discouragement of intellectual attainments by perverting the motives of the wealthy and compelling the masses to endure crushing toil.

> Accumulated property treads the powers of thought in the dust, extinguishes the sparks of genius, and reduces the great mass of mankind to be immersed in sordid cares, besides depriving the rich of the most salubrious and effectual motives to activity.[1]

As a result of all this we have the fourth count in the indictment of property—the fact that it multiplies vice. "The first offence must have been his who began a monopoly"; and the crimes of the poor are but so many attempts to rectify inequality. Force has therefore to be used by the wealthy to meet force. Thus a class war springs up. But worse develops, for the passions of the wealthy themselves proliferate; ambition and desire consume them and lead to war. Like all the later socialists, Godwin sees in the institution of private property the basic cause of war. "As long as this source of jealousy and corruption shall remain it is visionary to talk of universal peace."[2] Were this impediment removed each man could be united to his neighbour the world over "in love and mutual kindness."

The fifth consequence of property is the maintenance of a state of under-population. Godwin quotes Ogilvie's calculations that the cultivation of the country could be so improved as to maintain a population five times greater than its present one. But since it is a principle of human society that population is always kept down to the level of subsistence, private ownership of land means "strangling a considerable portion of our children in their cradle."

Obsequiousness, class war, moral and intellectual degradation, ill-distributed leisure: in the name of these colossal evils Godwin demands the abolition of all private property, the third of the monsters of social iniquity.

[1] *Op. cit.*, p. 806.   [2] *Op. cit.*, p. 812.

But there are three other social traditions which Godwin wants abolished, but which are not comparable in the magnitude of their consequences with those just treated. He rules out of consideration as a harmful factor every form of sentiment, whether it be family sentiment or the sentiment of friendship. The wise man will eliminate it from his life without more ado, since it merely befogs his reason, and thus distorts his judgment. The majesty of cold, clear reason alone must be reverenced by the man who pursues the ideal of justice. This denial of any place for sentiment in life was only a deduction from Godwin's own philosophical presuppositions. A man who thought of human beings as essentially intellectual animals, who thought of emotion as an intellectual process, and who could say that desire is only opinion maturing for action, could scarcely be expected to find room in his system for affection. Yet although Godwin adopted such a rigid position in the first edition of his work, he did not maintain it later. His own love affair with Mary Wollstonecraft and his contacts with the children modified his position considerably. The modifications are stated both in the subsequent editions of *Political Justice* and in the later novels. It was in the preface to *St Leon* that he made his fullest recantation.

If his attitude to the sentiment of affection shocked contemporaries, his attitude to marriage gave the more unscrupulous of his opponents a splendid weapon to use against him. But here again his theories are only a logical development of his philosophy. The institution of marriage, according to Godwin, is but "a system of fraud." It retards individual development; it is inimical to happiness, since the wishes of no two people can ever coincide even approximately, owing to the differences of their earlier training. It means a degrading economic dependence for the woman, and thereby entails her complete moral perversion. Marriage is thus only a branch of the prevailing system of property. It was these doctrines which were the main object of attack in those virulent diatribes against Godwin which appeared in the *Anti-Jacobin*. They gave ample scope for misrepresentation and scurrilous abuse, especially by the righteous, whose indignation had prevented their reading *Political Justice*; and this attack was undoubtedly one of the chief factors which not only wrought a subtle change in Godwin's own spirit, but which was largely responsible for the oblivion into which *Political Justice* itself very soon fell.

The third minor item in the contemporary moral code of which Godwin disapproved was the idea of promises. He considers that promises are always immoral, and his argument has the naïve simplicity of his first principles. The thing promised is either right or wrong : it either conforms to the immutable laws of reason or it does not. If it does, if the action is right, it should be performed in any case, and the promise is unnecessary. If it does not, if the action is wrong, then it means that a pledge has been given deliberately to violate the principles of justice, and this is obviously immoral. Consequently promises are never in any circumstances justifiable, be they the promises of the marriage ceremony or the promises of international treaties. No promise will ever be made in a rationally organised society.

This completes Godwin's destructive survey of existing institutions. What of the future? His analysis, of course, implied throughout the existence in his own mind of a definite political ideal. This is alluded to in passing at various points of his argument, but, curiously enough, is never anywhere presented at much length or in any systematic form. We may, however, piece together the fragmentary hints he gives us, and make a fairly coherent picture of his ideal community.

V

There is only one road to freedom, though there are numerous false roads ; and even along the right road there is a half-way house which, it appears, man has to aim at first.

The false roads and the false methods have already been implied in what has gone before. All government is bad, as we have seen. Thus it follows that monarchy, aristocracy, and presidential government are ruled out of consideration. Democracy, in the sense of a large community governing itself by the representative system and working through houses of assembly meeting frequently and exercising sovereign power, is likewise an evil. So also is co-operative endeavour and group communism.

There is no need of common labour, common meals, or common magazines. These are feeble and mistaken instruments for restraining the conduct without making conquest of the judgement. . . . Such a system was well enough adapted to the military constitution of Sparta; but it is wholly unworthy of men who are enlisted in no cause but that of reason and justice. Beware of reducing men to the state of machines. Govern them through nò medium but that of inclination and conviction.[1]

To understand the provisional ideal which Godwin approves it is important to remember his ideas about legislation. Properly speaking, as we have already noted, there can be no legislation.

Legislation, that is, the authoritative enunciation of abstract or general propositions, is a function of equivocal nature, and will never be exercised in a pure state of society or a state approaching to purity, but with great caution and unwillingness. It is the most absolute of the functions of government, and government itself is a remedy that inevitably brings its own evils along with it. Administration on the other hand is a principle of perpetual application. So long as men shall see reason to act in a corporate capacity, they will always have occasions of temporary emergency for which to provide. In proportion as they advance in social improvement, executive will, comparatively speaking, become everything, and legislative nothing.[2]

Godwin therefore disapproves of any governmental system needing two houses, and of the idea of checks and balances. If there is to be a national assembly at all, the only check necessary is to ensure slow and deliberate proceedings, so that no proceeding should have the force of a general regulation until it has undergone five or six discussions. Nor should there be any distinction between legislature and executive, since the real purpose of the two is identical. If national assemblies meet but rarely, Godwin thinks that this will eliminate most of the objections against democracy.

The usual objects of government are the maintenance of national glory and the pursuit of international rivalry. These should be ignored, and it would follow that all the "complications of government," such as ambassadors, treaties, and complex organisation, would disappear also. This would cut down expenses enormously. Extensive territorial possessions

[1] *Op. cit.*, p. 842.   [2] *Op. cit.*, p. 555.

would become superfluous in a rationally organised community. Godwin visualises the steady break-up of the nation-state into smaller and ever smaller self-governing communities, all organised (so far as there is any organisation at all) in the same way, "because we have all the same faculties and the same wants." He wants the idea of secession to become familiar; the whole human species thus "would constitute, in one sense, one great republic."

What amount of organisation would be necessary? Godwin wants to see the large community divided up into small parish units. The only real purpose of organisation is its police purpose—*i.e.*, the suppression of injustice. So the only necessary criterion of the size of each independent community is that it should be large enough to provide a jury to decide on offences committed within its boundaries. In a unit of such a size public opinion would be far more effective than it is at present. No individual would be vicious enough to defy the "general consent and sober opinion that would surround him." Appeals to reason would be much more effective in such a simple community than they are at present, and most juries would have only to recommend, and the offender would readily submit; otherwise he would feel "so uneasy under the unequivocal disapprobation and observant eye of public judgement, as willingly to remove to a society more congenial to his errors." Co-operation between contiguous parishes might at first be necessary for police purposes or for self-defence; this could be secured by means of delegates from the parishes sent to a national assembly. But such assemblies would become steadily rarer.

But, after all, it is not the police and political organisation which is of paramount importance. It is the new system of property which will ensure rational felicity and the stability of the new organisation. We have seen how Godwin condemns the system of absolute individual ownership. Under that system the peasant himself consumes only one-twentieth of the produce of his own labour, whereas the rich man consumes the produce of twenty peasants. All this must be swept away. There must be only one criterion of property—justice. Godwin, like the early socialists, who wrote in the next forty years, seems to hesitate at times between the two contradictory standards—to each according to his needs, and to each the produce of his labour. But on the whole he follows the first of these two principles. Each man should have that which he wants; if want can be proved, no other right to property can bar that claim. In one passage he says clearly that no amount of labour can justify the possession of unwanted excess. No monopoly of any kind can be tolerated, and the land must be open to him who wishes to cultivate it. Until this kind of complete economic equality is established, other reforms will be partial and ineffective; and even republicanism will be useless.

The country will thus be far more productive; waste will be eliminated, leisure will allow the faculties of man to develop. He calculates that half an hour's work a day by every able-bodied citizen would be sufficient to supply all the needs of the community; and who would shrink from this? No regulations would be necessary once the system were established, for it would so completely commend itself to the reason of men. Even accumulation would not be forbidden, for men would realise its absurdity. Bolts and locks would be unknown. There would not even be any organised system of exchange; wants would be supplied immediately.

Ultimately all organisation, even the attenuated form of the parish, will disappear. Each man will become a sovereign arbiter of his own concerns. No kind of co-operation will be tolerated, education will be purely an individual affair; actors will never commit the insincerity of allowing themselves to speak the words of other men; nor will musicians allow themselves to co-operate in orchestras. The untrammelled reason of man will reign supreme. As Godwin contemplates the remote future his imagination expands freely. He has visions of mind becoming supreme over matter; of automatic machines doing the manual work of men; of propagation ceasing to be necessary. For in the long last man will achieve immortality and the fully developed reason will have produced a race of men like gods.

On the transition from existing society to communistic anarchism Godwin is very vague. It is to be achieved only by the dissemination of truth. Let the truths he has proclaimed be studied, and the result is inevitable. Meanwhile the wise must "wait till the harvest of opinion is ripe." The task which the friend of man must set himself is inquiry, instruction, and discussion, but "the time may come when his task shall be of another sort." The transition may be a silent and almost imperceptible affair ; but it may also come with violence. Much depends on the extent to which reasoning and inquiry have preceded the event. The longer the day of reckoning can be postponed, the better for all concerned, for the shorter-lived will be the agony. Godwin is deliberately nebulous about this transition ; he casts a thick fog of optimism over that day, and blurs all the outlines, consoling himself repeatedly with the reflection that however painful the event may be, its evils cannot be worse than the despotism which it supplants.

VI

What shall we say, in conclusion, of the value and influence of this strange work, which is the longest and most systematic vindication of anarchism produced by an Englishman ? Godwin ranks with Auguste Comte as one of the great optimists in the history of political theory ; yet he was completely wrong in his vision of the future. To dismiss him thus summarily, however, is not only to be insufficiently appreciative of what he did, but is also to fail in explaining the influence he undoubtedly exercised in the first third of the nineteenth century. We must therefore distinguish between Godwin's judgments of fact and his judgments of value. He was undoubtedly a man with a keen intellectual sense of moral values. He forced all questions down to first principles in a logical fashion rare among English political writers, but in a way which his rigid and extreme Nonconformist upbringing, as well as his study of the French thinkers, had made habitual. In his analysis he found only compromises—or worse—established where he thought abstract principles should reign. And an impartial reading of his work can scarcely lead one to deny that his moral values were largely and amazingly right. Nevertheless, his schemes for shaping the facts to achieve those values were glaringly wrong. This was due to various causes.

Foremost, it was due to his false psychology—both individual and social—and especially to his denial of an adequate place to emotion in human life. He failed to see that to live rationally does not mean to live by reason alone; and the development of both biology and psychology since his day has made his treatment of human nature look strange and childish. There has also to be named his now *démodé* philosophy of the mechanical universe discoverable by unaided reason. The evolutionary hypothesis has smashed his philosophical outlook as completely as the Vienna and Zurich schools have destroyed his psychology. Thirdly we have to remark upon his inadequate data for the construction of such a vast system, and his use of the *a priori* instead of the scientific method. He sweeps aside the problems of heredity with a naïve simplicity, and his abstract treatment prevents his even glimpsing the possibilities of a science of anthropology such as Montesquieu had guessed at. After all, his work was but an exercise in the phantasy of Utopia construction. He had a weak sense of institutions, and hence was ludicrously weak when it came to precise plans for the transition period and for the future. He completely failed to grasp the nature of the industrial changes going on around him. He was blind to the fact that, so far from scientific large-scale industry making men more isolated, it would integrate their activities and interests to an extent undreamed of before.

Yet he wrote a Utopia of great significance, for the denunciations it embodied were a clear challenge to the accepted principles of society. Every evil of which his denunciations were most vigorous has remained to some degree even to our own day, a problem which the democratic experiment has not yet solved adequately. The problems of property, of education, of crime and punishment, of the deficiencies and limitations of representative government, and, above all, the problem of war—these are issues as living to-day as when Godwin first discerned them. Many of his judgments on these topics were uncannily right, even though his proposals may have been futile. And in the generation after Waterloo his teachings, but most of all his questionings, were revived. The history of the movement of ideas among the middle and lower classes during that epoch has yet to be written; but when it is written the influence of Godwin will assuredly be shown. Owen's teaching about the influence of environment, as Hazlitt said in a memorable article, is only a restatement of part of Godwin's system. Thomas Hodgskin similarly revived his doctrine of extreme individualism in another form. Thomas Rowe Edmonds, in his *Practical, Moral, and Political Economy* (1828), reveals his reading of Godwin in almost every chapter. Many Radical societies studied *Political Justice* in discussion circles. And so the list could be continued. But undoubtedly the greatest channel of his later influence was Shelley. We cannot here examine the poet's debt to his father-in-law, for that has often been done. In *Queen Mab, Prometheus Unbound,* and *Hellas* (though to a decreasing extent in that order) the influence is patent. Shelley gave the intellectual analysis an emotional significance, and turned the philosophical system into a religious mythology. Nobody can estimate in any satisfactory way the influence which Shelley may have had on Radicals and reformers during the nineteenth century. Certainly it was far from negligible; we have it on the authority of Eleanor Marx Aveling, for instance, that his influence on the Chartists was marked. But the Godwinian teaching, as a system, very soon failed to satisfy; and by the time of Peterloo had ceased to have intellectual validity for most of the practical reformers of the new age. Godwin was a Calvin who never found his Knox.

Shelley's own poems give clear hints of the fate of the "New Philosophy." By the time he wrote *Hellas* the simple faith of the men of 1793 had gone, and the Holy Alliance was the mockery of their hopes. Holcroft, on the day that Paine's *Rights of Man* was published, had ended a note to Godwin with a jubilant "Heigh-ho for the New Jerusalem!" That was nearly thirty years since; and the last lyric of *Hellas* betrays the fate of that dream. It opens with an echo of Godwin:

> The world's great age begins anew.

But it closes with that doubt which was now gnawing at Shelley's heart:

> Oh, cease! must hate and death return?

The Revolutionary apocalyptic could make little appeal to a generation that had passed through the Napoleonic wars and was distraught with the post-war depression. Yet Godwin's influence was of the kind that is more likely to be overlooked than to be over-estimated by later times. He had bequeathed to the new age his Testament of Rationalism, his critical method, and his unresolved problems. Above all, he had bequeathed to a generation predominantly fatalistic in its attitude to social problems his ardent belief that "what the heart of man is able to conceive, the hand of man is strong enough to perform."

C. H. DRIVER

BOOK LIST

ORIGINAL SOURCES

The following represent Godwin's principal works dealing with political and social theory :

An Enquiry into the Principles of Political Justice ; and its Influence on General Virtue and Happiness. 2 vols. London, 1793. 2nd edition, corrected, London, 1796.

The Adventures of Caleb Williams ; or, Things as they are. London, 1794.

Cursory Strictures on Lord Chief Justice Eyre's Charge to the Grand Jury. (Anonymous pamphlet.) London, 1794.

Considerations on Lord Grenville's and Mr Pitt's Bills, by "A Lover of Order." London, 1795.

The Enquirer: Reflections on Education, Manners, and Literature. London, 1797.

Thoughts occasioned by Dr Parr's Spital Sermon. London, 1801.

Of Population, etc. London, 1820.

Thoughts on Man, his Nature, Productions, and Discoveries. London, 1831.

BIOGRAPHIES AND STUDIES

The standard biography is by C. Kegan Paul, *William Godwin : his Friends and Contemporaries* (London, 1876).

A more recent work, largely based on Kegan Paul's, is by Ford K. Brown, *The Life of William Godwin* (London, 1926).

There are two useful French studies, *William Godwin*, by R. Gourg (Paris, 1908), and *William Godwin*, by H. Roussin (Paris, 1913). The latter is the more valuable ; both contain full bibliographies.

Shelley, Godwin, and their Circle, by H. N. Brailsford, is an admirable sketch of the epoch, while H. Foxwell's edition (with introduction) of Anton Menger's *Right to the Whole Produce of Labour* is helpful on Godwin's influence on economic speculation.

For the general background the two following are indispensable :

HALÉVY, ÉLIE : *The Rise of Philosophic Radicalism.* London, 1928.

STEPHEN, SIR LESLIE : *History of English Thought in the Eighteenth Century.* London, 1902.

VII

JEREMY BENTHAM

IT is fortunate that Bentham is not one of those writers whose every word should be read before we begin to write about them. That is, indeed, very fortunate, because to do so in his case would require, I think, a superhuman endurance. His writings, in Bowring's edition, occupy eleven stout volumes of close print, in double columns. But a very high proportion of this mass is taken up with the statement of small specific facts and with argument about them. To read it all would be a waste of time ; I have not attempted the task. But I must admit that I am not deeply enough read in eighteenth-century literature to be in a position to relate Bentham accurately to his antecedents. What I have to offer is an impression.

It is desirable always to avoid as far as possible what are called biographical details. But Jeremy Bentham's life was highly peculiar ; and its peculiarities are revealing, or at least suggestive. It was at once highly peculiar and very uneventful. Probably the most important and perhaps the most exciting events of his career were his first readings of Hume and Priestley and Beccaria. I do not exactly know when those events took place, but certainly before 1776, when, at the age of twenty-eight, he published his first book. Few men so active-minded as Bentham can ever have had interests so restricted. He reminds one of what Hazlitt wrote about Major Cartwright, the Radical Parliamentary reformer. "He has but one idea or subject of discourse, Parliamentary reform. Now, Parliamentary reform is, as far as I know, a very good thing, a very good idea, and a very good subject to talk about; but why should it be the only one?" Bentham's interests, however, were at least not so restricted as Cartwright's.

Even as a child Jeremy took the world very seriously, and had no inclination to play. He was extremely precocious.

At seven years old, he tells us, he found in the *Télémaque* of Fénelon "a model of perfect virtue." At the age of ten he was able to write letters in Greek as well as in Latin. It was, perhaps, a little later that he complained that he could find no "facts" in Molière. I note, also, that he was full of what eighteenth-century people called "sensibility." He informs us that he wept for hours over the epic fuss made by Clarissa Harlowe and Richardson, over what was, after all, nothing so very terrible. Still more remarkable is it, I think, that he should have been "happy in the happiness and uneasy in the uneasiness" of everybody in *Gil Blas*. This pleasurable sensibility of his seems to be correlated with the equally pleasurable and very conscious benevolence of his later years.

Jeremy's father, who was a solicitor and very well off, sent him to Oxford and then to the Bar, hoping to see him on the Woolsack one day. Jeremy did better than that; but he disappointed his father. The Oxford of those days, very unlike the Oxford of to-day, is said to have represented, chiefly, various half-dead but still pretentious orthodoxies. That, at all events, is how it looked to young Bentham. Far from being impressed, he reacted violently. Oxford appears to have done him grave harm: it biased him against the past; he learned there suspicion, dislike, even contempt, of everything traditional or even ancient in ideas and institutions.

As a law student he showed the same independence of mind. When in 1772 he was called to the Bar he seems to have felt, already, that he was called, not to practise in the courts, but to reconstruct the whole system. Boldness and independence of mind are certainly implied in such conclusions; and both are certainly characteristic of Bentham. But I think that in his case they resulted, partly at least, from his actual deficiencies. His contempt of the past was, as usual, comfortably based on an almost complete ignorance; and it is easy to be independent of what you do not understand. Lack of imagination is conspicuous in every phase of Bentham's thought; and inability to understand any temperament or point of view but one's own makes a man very independent, not to say impenetrable.

In 1785 Bentham was drawn abroad, not by any curiosity; and he remained on the Continent till 1788. He made a sort of circular tour of Europe, and saw something, as we say, of France and Italy, Constantinople, Russia and Poland, Germany and Holland. Actually he would seem to have seen nothing. His opinions were fully formed; he was not capable, apparently, of learning anything more. His belief in the average man—an attenuated being, rather like a mechanical doll, characterised by desire to obtain pleasure and avoid pain, by fear of his neighbours, and by a general reasonableness—survived his journeyings. Even Russia taught him nothing of the variousness of humanity; and the differences he hardly noticed could not well suggest to his mind that they must be rooted very deep in the past.

As early as 1776 he had already known what his life-work was to be. In that year he had published the *Fragment on Government*, which was his first book; and in that same year he was already at work on another, which, published in 1789 under the title *An Introduction to the Principles of Morals and Legislation*, expressed his matured philosophy. At once, after his return from Russia, he settled down to the interests and the labours that filled the rest of his life almost without a break. It was a life of constant intellectual activity, singularly purposive and consistent. It was also, it seems to me, a life singularly monotonous and dull to be the life of a man in a world so variously exciting as ours. There was no adventure in it, no struggle or doubt, or passion or agony. It seems that Bentham deliberately withdrew from the ordinary life of men, refusing all emotional experience and all intimate contacts, as though he feared them. It has been suggested to me that the bad dreams from which he is said to have suffered were Nature's revenge for that great refusal. It may possibly have been so: my impression is that it was not. I think, rather, that of any sort of passionate experience Bentham was really incapable.

From 1788 onwards he became more and more the hermit he liked to call himself; seeing few people except secretaries and disciples, working eight to ten hours a day, taking what he called his ante-jentacular and post-prandial constitutionals with a perfectly rational regularity; and always cheerfully conscious that he was working for the happiness of humanity. Even his intellectual life was very uneventful. He seems rarely, or never, to have felt doubt after he was thirty. Between 1800 and 1809, or thereabouts, his views underwent a certain development; but the change was superficial only; and though he lived till 1832, it was the last. He remained always serene, assured, confident that he held the key to the land of heart's desire. Nothing seems to have annoyed him except contradiction or depreciation. And he never understood how anyone could really disagree with him. He was apt to be very cross with anyone who did. He remained always, it seems to me, oddly and rather charmingly ignorant of the way of the world. Of men he knew very little, and of women, I should say, next to nothing at all. It was a little unfortunate that it was so, in view of the task he had set himself.

That task was nothing less than the exposition of the principles upon which all law-making, in all countries alike, ought to proceed; and the subsequent working out in detail of logically constructed and complete codes of law, ideally perfect for this people or for that. There is, I am pleased to find, a general agreement among scholars that Bentham was not primarily a moral philosopher or psychologist. Alike by intention and habit of mind he was a law-reformer. The main object of his lifelong effort was to bring about what he thought of as a rationalisation of law, in this and in other countries. The movement in that direction which issued in the Code Napoléon was already far advanced in France when Bentham wrote. The project might well have been suggested to him by Beccaria's treatise *On Crimes and Punishments*, published in 1764.

It seems to me that in Bentham's ideas there was little or nothing that was original or even highly distinctive. But the man himself certainly was what is called an 'original,' not to say a crank. His originality was a matter of temperament. It was compounded of an odd simplicity, an intellectualising temper, a lack alike of passion and of humour, and an amazing optimism. Many writers have noted his lack of passionate feeling as curious in a man of such consistent laboriousness. But Bentham was far from being free from passions of the intellect. He loved rationalisation for its own sake as much as William of Occam had loved it. That, I suppose, is why his writings are full of niggling criticism of other people's phraseology, of tediously elaborated dialectic and painful explanations of the obvious. He had, too, a passion for classification and tabulation ; which he seems to have regarded not merely as a form of summary statement, but rather as an instrument for arriving at truth.

It is, nevertheless, highly characteristic of Bentham that his vivid sense of mischievous defects, injustices, and abuses in law and in legal procedure, and even his undoubting conviction of the wickedness of people who obstructed the reforms he wanted, roused in him no fervour of indignation. This absence of passionate feeling may well be a disadvantage to a would-be practical reformer ; to a thinker it should always be favourable. But the absence of emotional disturbance, being merely negative, does not, of course, of itself produce tolerance of difference or an understanding of other people's points of view. For that imagination is needed; and Bentham had so little that he could not but be supremely dogmatic and intolerant. Like Calvin, he was certain that he was demonstrably right and that only persons of ill-will and moral perversity could disagree with him. He had no patience with such people. He described Dr Johnson as "a miserable and misery-propagating ascetic and instrument of despotism," and he spoke of Cobbett as a "vile rascal" and enemy of mankind.

His dogmatism must have been closely connected with his optimism. His certainty that he was demonstrably right assured him that all the world would finally be converted. Men, "let them but once clearly understand one another," he wrote, "will not be long ere they agree." [1] All that was needed for that understanding was a habit of thinking accurately and close definition of terms. It did not occur to him that the more clearly men understood each other the deeper might their disagreements appear. It must be remembered, too, that Bentham fully shared the delusion prevalent among eighteenth-century *philosophes* that man is a rational animal. Then, too, it must be remembered that to Bentham the past meant nothing. He had no sense or conception of the vast process of historic evolution. The past, to him, had all been a mere dark age, up to the time when Locke and Hume and

[1] *Fragment,* ed. Montague, p. 228.

Helvétius and Beccaria had begun to enlighten the world. In the preface to his *Fragment* he spoke of the "desolate and abject state of the human intellect" during all those earlier ages. "It is from the folly, not from the wisdom of our ancestors," he declared, "that we have so much to learn." Leslie Stephen remarked on this that Bentham himself has now become an ancestor, and may teach us by his errors. And surely, then, we in our turn shall teach by the errors we have learned? A fascinating vista is suggested: generation after generation learning fresh follies from the folly of its forbears.

All this, however, seems insufficient to account for an optimism so immense and undisturbed as Bentham's. Neither the French Revolution and what followed it nor his own frequent disappointments taught him anything. At different times he showed himself ready, and, in fact, eager, to provide complete codes of law for Spain, for Russia, and for Morocco. He even made a formal and public offer to construct a perfect code for any people in need of such a thing. He, quite truly, remarked that he could legislate for Hindustan as easily as for his own parish. He favoured the French Constituent with a plan for the reorganisation of the French judiciary. In 1811 he asked President Madison to authorise him to construct a code of law for the use of the United States. But perhaps his optimism reached its extreme limit in the hopes he attached to his Panopticon scheme. This was founded on the design of a building made by Jeremy's brother, Stephen. Jeremy published an account of it in 1791, pointing out how admirably it was adapted to the uses of a prison. In this wonderful structure, circular or polygonal in plan, the interior of every cell was to be visible from a room at the centre. Here was to sit the prison governor, with his eye on all the convicts, "begetting in them," says Bentham, "the sentiment of an invisible omniscience." A contractor was to undertake the maintenance of the unlucky prisoners at so much per head and make what profit he could out of their forced labour. He therefore, Bentham argued, would, in his own interest, teach the convicts useful trades and make over to them part of the profits in order to stimulate their industry. As a result of the application of this system to all prisons and workhouses, we should, Bentham declared, have "morals reformed, health preserved, industry invigorated, instruction diffused, public burdens lightened . . . the Gordian knot of the poor laws untied." He was eager to serve himself as the director and invisible omniscient of such a prison; whether in England or in France he did not mind.

Nothing came of it all, but he was not daunted. To the end of his life, with invincible hopefulness, he looked to the coming of that age of perfectly enlightened selfishness which was, for him, the reign of the saints. "He is said," records Leslie Stephen, "to have expressed the wish that he could awake once in a century to contemplate the prospect of a world gradually adopting his principles and so making steady progress in happiness and wisdom." [1] One is reminded of poor Enoch Soames in Mr Max Beerbohm's *Seven Men*.

Jeremy Bentham was not, I think, in any sense or degree an originator of ideas. He was a man of highly distinctive temperament, highly independent in thought, and of great mental activity. There was, indeed, a certain originality in the mere conception of a life devoted to the construction of perfect codes of law based on a few simple principles. But those principles were no discoveries of Bentham's; on the contrary, either they were assumptions common and fashionable among the educated at the time or they were such as Bentham had absorbed from Hume and Priestley and Helvétius. There was a great deal of moral philosophising in the eighteenth century. I fancy that the writings of Francis Hutcheson and Thomas Reid and Bishop Butler and Richard Price and Paley and Dugald Stewart are part of the background against which you ought to see Bentham. Not, of course, that Bentham reproduces the distinctive ideas of any of these. He agrees with them even less than they agreed with each other; and so far as I can ascertain he did not understand any of them. Yet there seems to have been a large amount of agreement among these thinkers. "That man's only possible end of action is happiness was a truism with the whole English school of moral philosophy," says Mr Montague. It was, it appears, equally axiomatic with them that happiness depends absolutely on a balance between pleasures and pains.

If you ask the question "Where is Bentham's philosophy

[1] *The English Utilitarians*, 1900 ed., i, 230.

to be found?" the answer seems to be, "In English moral philosophy of the eighteenth century generally, and in Hume and Helvétius in particular." Even the famous phrase which has come to seem to sum it up for most people is not Bentham's, even verbally. "That action is best," wrote Hutcheson in 1725, "which secures the greatest happiness of the greatest number." Beccaria had spoken of the "greatest happiness distributed among the larger number," and a French writer of 1767 had declared that the object of government is to secure "the greatest possible happiness to the largest possible population."

"The greatest happiness of the greatest number," wrote Bentham, sixty odd years after Hutcheson, "is the measure of right and wrong."[1] None of the conceptions that underlie these phrases were anything but part of quite ordinary mental furniture of the date. Bentham found them all ready-made. According to a statement of his own, the validity of the "principle of utility" was determined for his own mind by Priestley's *Essay on Government* of 1768. But he might just as well, or better, have acquired it from Hume. All one can say is that he assimilated it all so quickly and naturally that he soon came to think of it as unquestionable, and expected every one to be convinced by his explanations. What Bentham called the principle of utility belongs peculiarly to Bentham only because it is probable that he believed in it more thoroughly, clearly, and continuously than anyone else ever did. But I do not know whether you regard that as creditable to Bentham or not.

What does it all come to? The only rational end of action is happiness, and the only positive constituent of happiness is pleasure, happiness consisting in an excess of pleasure over pain. Not only so, but man being a rational animal the only actual end of all man's action is pleasure or happiness, as you like to put it. Every action of every human being is determined by his or her judgment of whether pain or pleasure is likely to result to himself, "whatsoever be the effect," says Bentham, "in relation to the happiness of other similar beings, any or all of them taken together."[2] "A thing is said to

---

[1] Preface to the *Fragment* Works, i, 227.
[2] *Constitutional Code*, Works, i, 5.

promote the interest . . . of an individual when it tends to add to the sum total of his pleasures or . . . to diminish the sum total of his pains." [1] All the individual need, or ought, to do is to calculate correctly. With respect to the community at large, an action may be said to be "conformable to the principle of utility . . . when the tendency it has to augment the happiness of the community is greater than any it has to diminish it." Actions thus conformable may be called good or right; actions not so conformable are wrong. "When thus interpreted," says Bentham, "the words ought and right and wrong . . . have a meaning; when otherwise they have none." [2]

Pleasure, then, is really the only good, and pain the only evil. The doctrine is at least as ancient as the philosophy of Carneades. For me the good is that which conduces on the whole to my pleasure; for the community it is, equally, what is conducive to the good of the community, though what that means is not so clear. But what is quite clear is that people in general will only call good and will only think of as good in others those kinds of action which they think will benefit themselves. When you generalise you must not think of the individual; you must think of the community or the happiness of the greatest number. For what you are really forming a judgment about is the question, What are the kinds of action in other people likely to benefit or likely to injure yourself? It is not, of course, that you care a jot about the community. It would be quite irrational to do that; and, in fact, according to Bentham quite impossible. Good is that which in my own interest I wish my neighbour to do. Bentham derived his doctrine from earlier eighteenth-century thought, and he regarded it as the supremely important discovery of the age of enlightenment that began with Locke. He would have been astonished, not to say shocked, had he been told that it was all in Machiavelli. He would never have believed it; but there it is.

It is perhaps needless to point out that to Bentham, as to Machiavelli, the moral quality of an action depends solely on its consequences. Motive and intention as such are neither good nor bad. All Bentham will admit is that certain kinds

---

[1] *An Introduction*, Works, i, 2.   [2] *Ibid.*, p. 2.

of motive are more likely than others to produce good conduct. I may remark in passing that a Benthamite motive appears to be an easily detachable, simple, and homogeneous affair, which automatically produces action. I have never myself experienced such a thing.

Before going farther it will be well to point to a rather obvious imperfection in the theory of morals thus presented. Pleasure or happiness is, Bentham says, the only rational end of action, and is for every individual the absolute measure of good and evil. To say that a man is under an obligation to do something merely means that he will suffer pain if he does not do it. I am, in fact, always justified in acting in any way that will increase the sum of my pleasures in proportion to my pains. And the same holds good of the community. The community, Bentham says, is the sum of its individuals, and its pleasures are the sum of theirs and its ends of their ends. So we get the greatest happiness formula, and so we reach the conclusion that goodness in action signifies simply a tendency to promote general welfare. Now let us grant Bentham all he asks for, even the validity of his quantitative measure of pleasures and pains. A serious difficulty remains unresolved. The trouble is that there is here no assigned relation between the good of the individual and the good of the community. Hume had taught that since men derive pleasure from the happiness of others they therefore ought to pursue the pleasure of others as well as of themselves. What does this "ought" mean? Bentham himself asks the necessary question in his own way. "What motives," he wrote, "can one man have to consult the happiness of another?"[1] And he goes on to declare that such motives are always present. "He has on all occasions the purely social motive of sympathy or benevolence . . . he has on most occasions . . . motives of love of amity and love of reputation." And he adds that the last two motives will be more or less powerful with a man "principally according to the strength of his intellectual powers"[2]—which is to me a very surprising assertion. But the motive he lays stress on most frequently is fear; fear of one's neighbours or fear of what Shakespeare once called "the blow of the law." I have sometimes been tempted to define

[1] *An Introduction*, Works, i, 143.   [2] *Ibid.*, p. 144.

JEREMY BENTHAM

a saint as a person absolutely without fear; but to Bentham fear was the main incentive to what he called goodness. In explaining why revenge does not pay he remarks that though the pain you inflict on your enemy gives you pleasure, this pleasant sensation is quickly succeeded by "fears of all kinds" —fear of retaliation, fear of the "public voice," religious fears, and "a secret remorse" awakened by "humanity." So "the pleasure is destroyed; internal reproach succeeds it," even if you escape the law. Bentham writes, sometimes, as though he believed that what he calls benevolence would always override self-regard in cases where the individual and the community clash. But if this be so I do not see how he squares it with his assertions about the radical selfishness of man. "Dream not," he says in one place, "that men will move their little fingers to serve you unless their advantage in so doing be obvious to them." [1] But I do not think that the inconsistencies of his language on this matter are of much account. Why should anyone worry about this vague thing, the happiness of this other vague thing, the community? Substantially Bentham's answer is simply that my happiness is bound up with that of the community. He was content with the truism that, in a general way and in the long run, the happiness of the community will contribute to mine. The answer, so far as it is one, seems to me as superficial as it is optimistic.

But I want to insist on one point. Bentham fully admits— indeed, asserts quite positively—that a man is under no obligation to consider in any way the welfare of others except as far as it involves his own. Indeed, there exists and can exist no sort of obligation except to oneself. A man is, you may put it, under no obligation to act rightly; but fear and benevolence will, as a rule, prevent him from acting wrongly. The view seems to me curiously simple and naïve. The fact appears to be that all Bentham wanted—though he did not realise this—was a practical rough-and-ready 'principle' of legislation. Yet his failure to examine the relation between utility from the individual's point of view and utility from the point of view of society is serious, even practically. He complains that the intuitionist practically allows that right and

[1] Works, ii, 133.

wrong, varying with the individual's sense of them, may be different for every man. This, Bentham argues, disables all legislation, because it renders the question What is the use of a thing? meaningless. But does not Bentham's own theory come to the same thing? If the measure of good for me is my own pleasure, the measure will vary with my tastes and desires. There are, perhaps, things that all men desire; but all men do not desire even those things in the same way or degree; and all men desire other and quite different things.

It may be my fault, but this is almost all I have found in Bentham that can be called philosophical. You will notice that only indirectly does it bear at all on the philosophy of politics. But it bears rather more directly on the structure of legal systems; and that it was intended to do. It all led up to a practical consideration of the law of England as it stood and how it could be improved. Bentham called that book of his of 1789 *An Introduction to the Principles of Morals and Legislation*. It was really an introduction to a revision of our criminal law.

The manner in which Bentham applied the principles laid down in that book to the reform of law was simple enough. Concerning any actual law or any proposed law, all you have to ask is this: Do, or will, its total effects produce more pleasure than pain on the whole, or *vice versa*? In the one case you scrap or you drop it; in the other you retain or adopt it. It sounds delightfully simple. But Bentham saw that it was not, after all, quite so simple as it looked. He saw that before you could be sure that the sum of the effects of an action or a measure would yield an excess of pleasure over pain you must find some way of weighing or measuring pain and pleasure, separately and together. No particular credit attaches to Bentham for perceiving this rather evident fact; what is characteristic of him, and almost peculiar to him, is that he was not the least daunted by it. Far from that, it seemed to him a not very difficult matter to provide the necessary calculus. He made a rather heroic, if rather ludicrous, attempt to do so. Chapters III and VI of his *Introduction* are devoted to the sources of pleasure and to the mode of its evaluation. Chapter IV is bravely headed "Value of a Lot of Pleasure or Pain, how to be measured." If, indeed, pleasures can be divided into definite lots, bits, or pieces, why should they not be weighed and measured? And of course a bit of pain of certain dimensions could be subtracted from a bit of pleasure. The value of a lot of pleasure depends, we are informed, on its intensity (there might be some trouble about this), its duration, its certainty, its propinquity, and its fecundity—that is, its tendency to produce other things. Bentham saw no real difficulty in measuring pleasure with at least approximate accuracy. And since pleasure can be measured, no ambiguity remains about the word ' happiness,' for happiness is constituted of pleasures. Personally I do not think any comment is needed on this.

Bentham, it has been said, is the philosopher of common sense; I should rather say that what I find in him is common sense masquerading as philosophy, with much tiresome and really useless apparatus and a dogmatic self-satisfaction that is apt to irritate. But I fully admit that when Bentham got to the discussion and criticism of actual law his common sense came into its own and, along with the acute closeness of his verbal analysis and his passion for exactness in phrase, enabled him to do excellent and very useful work in the planning of improvements in the tangled jungle that was English law. You can disregard all his crude, consequential, rather silly ethics and psychology when you reach his practical suggestions. You perceive, then, that most of his assumptions are only those that common sense habitually makes, and has to make, for its practical purposes. It all comes simply to this: that Bentham asks about everything, What is the use of it? That is what we all do, and always did, except when we are so sure that we feel no need to ask. Where we differ is as to the meaning of the word 'use.' Bentham thought that pleasure was the only thing of real use; others have thought that pleasure is a mere incident or accident of little or no importance. Our notion of what is of use depends upon our sense of values, and is, in fact, really the same thing. Our sense of values differs enormously. For all that, there are a number of things that we agree are useful, even though we do not agree about the degree of their utility. That agreement, just as far as it goes, forms a natural basis for law. So when

Bentham asked what was the use of a law or of an institution he was asking a quite relevant and practical question, and one that has to be asked, even though it be far harder to answer than Bentham perceived.

Of the practical value of Bentham's criticism of the law of his time and of his suggestions for its reform I am not in a position to judge. I am neither a lawyer nor an historian of law as such. Much of what he says strikes one as extremely obvious. But it may quite well be the case that tedious expositions of the obvious are of practical value.

But indeed there can be no doubt that Bentham's criticism of the law and the legal procedure of his day was on the whole acute, sensible, and sound. He was perfectly right in maintaining that our whole system of penal law and the whole system of procedure, including the law of evidence, needed a thorough reconstruction. He may be said to have proved his case in detail. More than that, he pointed out the lines on which reconstruction did actually proceed. He anticipated, ideally, the great change in penal law that was coming, the legal protection of lunatics, children, and animals, the establishment of civil marriage and divorce, and the great changes in procedure that came about, rather long after his death, between 1846 and 1875. But how far all this was due in any sense or degree to the actual influence of Bentham's writings on men's minds I do not know. I know only that it would be an extraordinarily hard question to answer.

I turn now to consideration of the more strictly political portion of Bentham's thinking. But there is, so far as I have discovered, very little to consider. It was not, apparently, till after the year 1800 that he began to be seriously dissatisfied with the constitution of government in England. He found fault in 1776 with Blackstone's praises of the British Constitution; but it was with the praises and not with the Constitution that he found fault. For long he seems to have seen no reason for constitutional change. "I supposed," he wrote, "they [the people in power] only wanted to know what was good in order to embrace it." His friendship with Shelburne and his acquaintance with other leading politicians he met at Shelburne's house may help to account for this belief. Apparently he thought that he had only to convert a few leading politicians to get a reasonable penal code and so on established by Parliament at once.

But nothing practical came of all his efforts, and by 1802 he was full of grievances against Ministers and against politicians in general. His disillusionment must have been pretty complete by that time, though his confidence in himself and his ideas was quite unaffected. He seems for a time to have been rather bewildered by his failure to convert the political and legal world. Long before 1802 he had, indeed, already come to the conclusion that the chaos into which English law had drifted was due to a sort of conspiracy among lawyers, whose interest lay in complicating procedure and multiplying suits. Soon after 1802 he began to ask why it was that the politicians also refused to be converted and take up his proposals. Why had there been since 1790 no alteration in the penal code, except in the wrong direction? How was it possible that men could fail to be convinced when principles undeniably sound were set lucidly before them? The only answer that seemed to Bentham possible was that the politicians and the ruling classes they represented did not really desire the greatest happiness of the greatest number. He had, indeed, given them no good reason why they should.

The result of these reflections was that he began to concern himself seriously with the organisation of power in the community. He had become convinced that the Government as constituted did not desire and would not pursue the greatest happiness of the greatest number. The question for him, therefore, became, What sort of Government can be trusted or expected to do so, and how must it be constituted?

Bentham's earliest and tentative answers to this question appeared in his *Catechism of Parliamentary Reform*, which was apparently written in 1809, though not published till 1817. His final and complete answer appears in his *Constitutional Code*, which was the work of the last years of his life.

Every man, he argued, desires always his own greatest happiness, and the right and proper end of government is the greatest happiness of the greatest possible number. But the actual end of every governing group is the greatest happiness of the group. In an absolute monarchy it will, of course, be the greatest happiness of the monarch; in any oligarchy of the oligarchs. Therefore if we put the government into the hands of all and establish the rule of numerical majorities, it is actually the greatest happiness of the greatest number that will be the end of the Government so constituted.

I am summarising, but I do not think unfairly. All I can say is that the reasoning strikes me as being as puerile as it certainly is old. And what Bentham adds to it makes the matter no better. "All government," says Bentham, "is in itself one vast evil." It is evil, he means, because it is based on and maintained by force and fear. It is mere organised coercion. But to secure the right use of the force of society all that is needed is to distribute among all the right to use it. Every one acting solely in his own interest, all can act only in the interest of all.

Bentham's optimism lifted him clear of all difficulties. The people—which apparently means a majority—can be trusted to form rational and usually accurate judgments concerning their own interests. They can be trusted to elect as their representatives men who will act on these judgments. They will naturally choose what Bentham calls "morally apt" agents; and men who wish to be chosen will desire to become morally apt. He actually asserts that all experience testifies that this will be the case. The electoral system, in fact, is bound to work as it is intended to work, because the homogeneous simplicity of human nature allows of no alternative.

And so Bentham reached his final, practical conclusions, in favour of manhood suffrage, annual Parliaments, vote by ballot, and the abolition of monarchy, the House of Lords, and the Established Church. His *Constitutional Code* provided, further, that members of the House of Commons are not to be immediately re-eligible; are simply deputies of constituencies; must attend the House regularly; and are to elect a Prime Minister to hold office four years. All officials are to be chosen by competitive examination, and as candidates are to be invited to send in tenders for doing the work at a reduced salary. Advocates are to be provided in all courts for the poor; and no barrister is ever to become a judge. Law, of course, is completely codified.

Whatever one may think of the practical value, then or now, of these proposals, nothing of all this can be taken very seriously as political philosophy. Even in relation merely to his own time Bentham's radicalism was a little belated; and he seems to have added nothing to the case for the changes he advocated. The fact that some of his proposals have since been adopted does not strike me as being of any special significance.

Some of the modern estimates of the extent and importance of Bentham's influence, I must admit, astonish me. In one place I read that as a result of Bentham's work "there is hardly an educated man who does not accept as too clear for argument truths which were invisible till Bentham pointed them out." I wish I could say what these truths are. Another writer informs me that "it has been said that before Bentham's days no one had ever dared to speak disrespectfully of English law or of the British Constitution." Unfortunately the author did not give the name of the ignoramus who made this assertion. He must have forgotten what happened to the British Constitution in the seventeenth century. And as to Bentham's disrespectful language about law and lawyers, in the seventeenth century it would not have stood out.

In a recent and good book I read that "every department of our public life, our political institutions, every portion of our civil and criminal jurisprudence, every part of our legal procedure, have been profoundly affected by his work."[1] Such a statement, if seriously intended as a statement of causation, I can only regard with scepticism. In support of such statements is given a long list of changes or reforms that were anticipated or suggested by Bentham. But much more than this is needed to prove anything to the purpose. All the reforms in the list were advocated by others besides Bentham, and in most cases had been long before he was born. A lot of positive evidence is required to justify the assertion that these developments would even have been retarded had Bentham never written. I do not, of course, mean to deny that Bentham was a factor in those developments. To do that would be to deny any appreciable influence to his distinguished disciples, to the Mills and to Grote and Ricardo and Romilly. But I think that the extent of his influence on the minds of these and of others needs to be carefully worked out before we have a right to say much about it.

[1] Coleman Phillipson, *Three Criminal Law Reformers* (1923), p. 229.

Except for the development of Radicalism in his later years and the very weak reasoning that accompanied it, there is little of strictly political philosophy to be found in Bentham's writings. Very early, in the *Fragment on Government*, he had criticised and repudiated the doctrine of original contract as he found it in Blackstone ; and he had discussed the conception of sovereignty as Blackstone had presented it. Blackstone's views on both these matters were completely conventional and quite perfunctorily expressed. They formed a very insufficient text for comment. Bentham's criticism of the doctrines of contract and of natural rights contains nothing that had not been said many times over in the seventeenth century, and is far less effective and complete than Filmer's. In his discussion of the idea of sovereignty there is little that does not refer merely to Blackstone's crudities. On the question of whether and when the sovereign may be resisted by force Bentham lays down that there can be no general rule for determining what he calls "the juncture for resistance." Each particular person must judge for himself "by his own internal persuasion of a balance of utility on the side of resistance." Just that view had been put forward by Philip Hunton in 1643.

Bentham solemnly objected to Blackstone's casual assertion that an unlimited authority must exist somewhere in all States whatever. That assertion had, of course, very frequently been made. What it means is that the existence of an unlimited authority is logically implied in the conception of a State and in the conception of law-making power, and that, therefore, it does, ideally, exist in every State, even though it be disembodied and unrecognised and even explicitly repudiated by law. Bentham simply did not understand what had been meant ; and neither, I suspect, did Blackstone. So Bentham irrelevantly amused himself by refuting the evidently absurd assertion of a recognition of absolute sovereignty in all political bodies ; an assertion that, had it ever been made, would not have been worth criticising.

Whatever one may think of Bentham's theory of morals, it was not originally or distinctively his ; his psychology seems little better than rubbish ; his Radicalism does not appear to me at all important or interesting. He made, in the course of his life, a very large number of good, practical suggestions.

JEREMY BENTHAM

Of their actual value in causation it is difficult to judge; and in any case such values are ephemeral. To my mind Bentham's value as a teacher, even for his own day, and certainly for us now, lies in his independence of outlook and in that passion for exactness in the use of words which so grievously wearies his readers and which finally ruined his style. At the close of the *Fragment on Government* he speaks of the objects with which he wrote that book. It was, he says,

> to do something to instruct, but more to undeceive, the timid and admiring student: to excite him to place more confidence in his own strength and less in the infallibility of great names: to help him to emancipate his judgment from the shackles of authority: . . . to teach him to distinguish between showy language and sound sense: to warn him not to pay himself with words.[1]

The passage might almost stand as a summary of the essential values of Bentham's work.

The spectacle of a mind freed from respect of persons, in revolt against orthodoxies, unhampered by any worldly or commercial considerations, desiring only to see and to express truth, is always stimulating and good for us, even though it may cause unpleasant sensations. A value even greater, and equally everlasting, attaches, in my view, to Bentham's constant and tiresome insistence on accuracy in the use of words. His meticulous and niggling criticism of other people's language, his careful explanations of the obvious, his attempts at definition, his relentless fullness of argumentative statement, all these dreary things were needed, and badly needed, and are always needed. Exactness in the use of words is the basis of all serious thinking. You will get nowhere without it. Words are clumsy tools, and it is very easy to cut one's fingers with them, and they need the closest attention in handling; but they are the only tools we have, and imagination itself cannot work without them. You must master the use of them or you will wander for ever guessing, at the mercy of mere impulse and unrecognised assumptions and arbitrary associations, carried away with every wind of doctrine. This, in my view, was the essence of Bentham's teaching; and it was never more needed than it is to-day.

J. W. Allen

[1] *Fragment*, ed. Montague, chapter v, p. 241.

BOOK LIST

BENTHAM, JEREMY: Works, 11 vols., ed. Bowring (1838–43). Especially important are the *Fragment on Government*, the *Introduction* of 1789, and the *Constitutional Code*. F. C. Montague's edition of *A Fragment on Government* (1891) has a valuable Introduction.

ALBEE, E.: *History of English Utilitarianism.* 1902.

DAVIDSON, W. L.: *From Bentham to J. S. Mill.* 1915.

PHILLIPSON, COLEMAN: *Three Criminal Law Reformers.* 1923.

STEPHEN, SIR LESLIE: *The English Utilitarians.* Vol. i. 1900.

VIII

THE SOCIALIST TRADITION IN THE FRENCH REVOLUTION

ALL revolutions centre round the relation of political authority to the distribution of economic power; for, as Madison long ago insisted, the only durable source of faction is property. Anyone who examines the history of French social thought in the eighteenth century realises at once that its very essence is a changing conception of the place of property in the State. In a sense, indeed, the main work of the Revolution was simply the translation of that change from the realm of ideas into the realm of fact. From Fénelon to the outbreak of catastrophe there were few thinkers who were not impressed by two things: the indefensible character of privilege, upon the one hand, and the immense disparity between rich and poor, with its attendant and inherent dangers, upon the other. Not merely the systematic philosopher and the professional pamphleteer, but the novelist, the playwright, even the theologian, find it difficult to defend the actual distribution of economic satisfactions. They seek consistently for a remedy for this condition. They are widely aware that its continuance must inevitably mean the disruption of the State.

The consequence is the presence throughout the eighteenth century of an attitude to the rights of property which is profoundly critical in character. In a sense it is even a socialist attitude, in that, not seldom, it is altogether sceptical of the *régime* in which individuals possess the means of production. But I hesitate to call it definitively socialist for three reasons. In the first place, it is a purely moral criticism; outside the Abbé Meslier there is no writer of repute who seriously considered the means of redressing the balance of social good. It is, moreover, hardly aware of the relationship of an economic system to the power of the State; even in Rousseau this defect is noteworthy. It is, in the third place, diagnostic rather than reconstructive; Mably and Morelly, Diderot and Rousseau, Sébastien Mercier and Rétif de la Bretonne, are all in an essential sense socialist; but, for all of them, the mechanism of transition to an egalitarian order is always by the conversion of men's hearts to better ways.

Rousseau and those I have named are, properly speaking, merely the extreme wing of a wider attack upon the notion that property can be a legal or moral right independently of the social consequences it involves. Attack upon the contemporary social order proceeded from the most various angles. Some of it came from a bitter revival of the sixteenth-century discussion of usury. Some of it was the outcome of that curious controversy over luxury of which Mandeville's too famous *Fable of the Bees* is, through Voltaire's *Mondain*, the real parent. Not a little can be traced to that grim defence of conservatism by Linguet, in which he anticipated so many of the theses of Karl Marx for almost antithetic ends. Part of it can be traced to the makers of imaginary Utopias where private property is unknown, or, related to this, to the reports of travellers of places like America, in which a Utopia of fact has come to birth. The creation, moreover, with Quesnay and the Physiocrats, of an economic philosophy upon something like scientific foundations was important. Administrative chaos, economic confusion, religious bankruptcy, all contributed their lesson to the torrent of criticism. When the States-General was summoned the mind of France had been widely prepared for large economic innovation.

II

I understand by socialism the deliberate intervention of the State in the process of production and distribution in order to secure an access to their benefits upon a consistently wider scale. From this angle it is clear that no theories are entitled to be regarded as socialist which are not distinguished by at least two features. They must admit the right and duty of the State to subordinate individual claim to social need not as an occasional incident of its operation, but as a permanent characteristic of its nature; and they must, in the second place, seek the deliberate and continuous reconstruction of social institutions to the end of satisfying social demand upon the largest possible scale. It is in terms of these definitions that I propose to approach the difficult and complex years from 1789 until the failure of Babeuf in 1796. I shall consider, first, how far a genuine socialism is discoverable in the *cahiers* and pamphlets which accompanied the summons of the States-General. Then I shall analyse the period until the advent of the Directory to see what of socialism there is in both the literature and the legislation of the time. I shall seek, above all, to show that the effort of Babeuf and his fellow-conspirators was the one genuine socialist movement in this epoch with a definite programme and an equally definite method of moving towards its realisation. Finally, I shall seek to estimate what of significance there was in the socialist experience of this epoch, and how far it has given any specific character to the socialist movement of a later time.

Let me begin with a simple affirmation. Neither in the *cahiers* nor in the pamphlets which resulted from the summons of the States-General is there any important or general socialist doctrine. That does not mean that it was non-existent; for, as Chassin has pointed out,[1] what we are dealing with here are the wants, at the most, of six million Frenchmen, and the needs of at least as many may have gone unexpressed. But when this type of literature is examined neither the grievance expressed nor the claims put forward are socialistic in any serious sense. There is bitterness, indignation, protest; but if these are the inevitable accompaniment of socialism, they are not of its inner substance. Taken as a whole, what do the *cahiers* demand? Fiscal reform, especially in the matter of equal taxation, judicial reform, administrative reorganisation. There is profound hostility to feudal rights. There is some criticism, not seldom urgent, of ecclesiastical property. There are occasional attacks on the greed of rich landowners. There is protest against the erosion, by aristocratic usurpation, of communal property. There is some demand for taxation in terms of ability to pay, a tendency to desire limitation of testamentary disposition. A careful search will discover scattered demands for the restriction of inheritance, occasional schemes

[1] *Le Génie de la Révolution* (1862), i, 334.

for public granaries, the fixation of prices, the limitation of usury. No one, I think, can honestly go through the *cahiers* upon any considerable scale without the impression that they represent not a theory of social reconstruction, but the keen expression of practical experience. They are what the solid merchant, the comfortable peasant, the thinking and social-minded *curé*, would naturally set down as the lessons of the *ancien régime*.

Nor is this all. Throughout the *cahiers* there is a universal sense of the respect that is due to private property. The main complaint, indeed, against the past age is that the capriciousness of its system prevented the wholesale expression of that respect. "The object of the laws," said the Third Estate of Paris, "is to secure liberty and property." That note is omnipresent. Men seem unable sufficiently to emphasise the fact that property is sacred and inviolable, that no one can be deprived of property save for public purposes and with adequate compensation. District after district emphasises the right of all property to respect, save where its possession entails abuse; and, to my own knowledge invariably, abuse only means the justly hated privileges of feudalism. There is no objection that I can discover to unequal property. There is dislike of luxury, a demand for special treatment of the needy and the orphan, a sense that the proletariat should be lightly taxed or even free from all imposts. One discovers suspicion of the financier, a claim that the poor man should be able as surely to live by his labour as the rich to be secure in his property. There is the well-known plea from Paris for the creation of public workshops. There are various suggestions for the more humane treatment of the poor and the mendicant and the improvement of hospitals. No one can look at demands like these and call them specifically socialist unless socialism is a mere synonym for humanitarianism. For the most part they are the obvious dictates of common sense; and they are far less radical in temper than much of the social criticism of the eighteenth-century *philosophes*. Those who drew up the *cahiers* of 1789 were entitled, like Clive, to be astounded at their own moderation.

The pamphlets of 1789 cannot, I think, be put upon quite the same footing as the *cahiers*; they announce certain principles which it is difficult not to describe as socialistic. But before I summarise some of their ideas I would venture upon a word of caution. It is necessary, I suggest, to distinguish between declamatory denunciation and definite plan. It is easy to find the first; it is difficult to find the second. We are no more entitled to call denunciations of inequality and misery socialistic than we can justifiably term Southey and Carlyle and Ruskin socialists because they were indignant with the horrors of factory civilisation. There are innumerable pamphlets which insist that the right to property is a social creation, which society can abolish as it pleases; there are literally hundreds which establish the principle of the right to work as inherent in the structure of the State. But most of the first groups insist equally on the immense danger of disturbing established expectation; and few, if any, of the second group leave the right as more than an empty declaration to which no concrete scheme is annexed. Even Marat, in his *Project of a Declaration of the Rights of Man*, while he begins by insisting that the law must prevent inequality of fortunes, and that a wise redistribution of wealth is necessary, ends by saying that the best thing that could have happened to France would have been for Montesquieu or Rousseau to have drawn up its constitution. But no one would have expected either to construct a socialist State.

We must, then, distinguish between declamation and positive plan. Of the first is abundance and to spare. There is passionate denunciation of those rich who " eat in a single meal what would suffice for ten families in a year "; [1] there is the warning that unless the people are fed and the right to work assured insurrection is certain and justified. There is the bitter plea of men like Devérité, that the worker is like an army mule who breaks beneath his burden; but the only remedy of which he can think is the suppression of machinery as the root cause of low wages. One writer, Dufourny de Villiers, points out with acuteness that the real poor are not represented in the States-General, and argues that they are entitled to compensation for the property they lack; but his cure for the evil he vividly depicts is merely " a new moral foundation for a better-organised society." Another writer,

[1] *La Colère du Père Duchêne.*

after a piteous description of the sufferings of the workers, is satisfied to urge that public workshops are the logical consequence of the right to work; yet he tells us nothing of how they are to be organised or what they are to produce.

We are nearer to socialistic ideas with Gosselin,[1] whose views are very akin to the agrarian socialists of the Cromwellian revolution. After a trenchant exposure of the injustice of the existing social order, and an emphatic note that conditions would justify such a socialisation of land as existed in Sparta, he agrees that the remedy would be worse than the disease. But he urges the desirability of four measures in order to obtain equality. Uncultivated land should be given to the poor as the Romans formerly settled soldiers on the soil. The clerical demesne should similarly be used, the recipients paying a small rent to the State and its former possessors; and, each year, the Government is to set aside a sum for buying up the estates of large landowners and distributing them in the same way. Finally, he suggests a progressive capital tax on private fortunes to extinguish the public debt. In a brief time, he thinks, these measures will establish a "happy equality," if the land so divided is declared indivisible and inalienable. The worst features of luxury will disappear; and the engagement of the vast majority of citizens in agricultural pursuits will make commercial fortunes of insignificant importance. Sufficiency will mean an instructed people. Population will increase; and emigrants will take this new model to happier climes. Gosselin has no doubt of the practicability of his scheme, and he offers it to the King with a simple faith of which no one can deny the charm.

Two other schemes of socialistic tendency deserve a word. Seven years before the Revolution Rétif de la Bretonne in his *Andrographe* had published a complete Utopia upon a rigorously communist foundation. But, like Plato with the *Republic*, he had realised that it was meat too strong for human digestion; only complete agreement could achieve it, and for this it was hopeless to look. In 1789, therefore, he published a revised version of his plan in the *Thesmographe* which might, he thought, be capable of realisation. While private property

---

[1] *Réflexions d'un citoyen* (1787). On Gosselin see A. Lichtenberger, *Le Socialisme utopique* (1898), p. 132.

is to remain, its possession is to be limited and difficult. Prices are to be controlled by local authorities and failure to cultivate as Government prescribes is to result in forfeiture. At the back of the whole scheme is the principle that private property is a mere legal convention made by the State, and subject at any moment to its power of eminent domain.

Rétif's ideas clearly have no more than a paper value, for he had no vision at all of how to bring them into being. If Babeuf's Utopia is not less visionary, it is more important, because it shows how constant was his devotion to the principle of equality. The son of a former tutor of Joseph II, after a grim and starved childhood he became an agent to a nobleman, and acquired there that practical acquaintance with feudal privileges which played so large a part in the shaping of his life. In 1787 he began to correspond with the secretary of a provincial academy, to whom he put questions which make evident his preoccupation with equality as the key to social good. It is to inequality that he traces the pride of the rich and the excessive humility of the poor; and he urges upon his friend that it is the cause of all the evils of our social condition. The correspondence reveals him as a man profoundly influenced by Rousseau, passionate, and bitterly antagonised by the inequities of the *ancien régime*.

In 1789, in conjunction with the mathematician Audiffred, he submitted his views to the National Assembly in something like coherent form. The *Cadastre perpétuel* does not yet envisage the need for revolution; but something at least of the spirit which, seven years later, was to take him to the scaffold is already there. No man, he says, who has sufficiency can be regarded as other than an exploiter if he seeks to obtain more than this. Men are by nature and right equal, and it is the business of the law to keep them so. Yet as the law works the very opposite is the case. The rich are the masters of society. The poor grow in numbers, and their wages continually decrease. This is an impossible position. The land, "the common mother of us all," must be divided equally, so that each citizen has an assured patrimony, which he cannot lose. Instruction must become general, lest the wise oppress the ignorant. Unless this is done the rich will cut the throats of the poor; and the latter are entitled to property as a ward may, when he attains his majority, recover his rights from a defaulting trustee. But the first step on the road to reform is education. Equality in knowledge is the keystone of the arch of social reconstruction.

Babeuf's plans, doubtless, did not reach more than a handful; the Assembly was occupied with more immediate questions. What I wish only to emphasise again is the presence of a socialist ideal among the pamphlets of 1789, while noting that it is extraordinarily rare. Where there is an attack on the existing order that is not socialism. It is nothing more than the final deposit of that sense of waste and injustice common, for instance, to all reformers of the age of Louis XIV. There is a good deal of Utopia-making, not a little violent paradox. But what there is of revolutionary destructiveness comes from sources which, as with Mably or Rousseau or Montesquieu, we cannot call genuinely socialist in the sense in which I have defined that term. Men feel vaguely that a new age has come, big with possibilities. There is a spirit of optimism abroad. But reform, and not revolution, is the essential tenor of men's minds in the first hours of the new dawn. What socialism there is is small in volume and insignificant in expression. It needed the realisation that civil equality and the reform of politics did not mean an end of suffering before a widespread change was possible.

III

By the early months of 1790 the ultimate character of the Revolution had been fixed. Feudal privileges had been abolished; the monarchy had been put in fetters; the Church had been overthrown. The Declaration of Rights contemplated a middle-class liberal State. If it was an exaggeration to say, with Loustalot, that "everything tends to substitute an aristocracy of wealth for an aristocracy of birth," the proletariat had not seriously benefited by the changes made. Phrases had been used in the Assembly, even by men so conservative as Mirabeau and Malouet, which implied a belief in equality, but the social legislation of the next few years showed clearly that they meant nothing. Already property was afraid; and the warnings of Edmund Burke had fallen upon ready ears. By 1790 the main preoccupation of the leaders was to stabilise and make effective the results of the first enthusiasm of the Revolution, while assuaging the sufferings of the common people. Few were able to see the effect of foreign war upon social policy, or to guess, as Burke so marvellously foresaw, that a successful general would emerge as the dictator of the State.

Anyone who analyses the literature and the legislation from 1790 until the fall of Robespierre has, above all, to be careful not to discover too much in what he reads. He must remember that he is dealing with a peasantry which was hungry for the indisputable possession of the land, and angrily suspicious of its former masters ; where, therefore, he sees peasant riots he must not assume that they are grounded in socialist principle. He must remember, too, that in these years bad harvests were general, and unemployment widespread. The problem of feeding the towns and finding work for the proletariat was a difficult one, intensified by the timidity of the rich and their anxiety to put a term to experiment in social policy. Every Revolutionary leader treads the edge of an abyss ; and in the effort to satisfy a hungry and indignant constituency he uses phrases and threatens measures which are meant as denunciation rather than argument. The period, therefore, is full of declamation which has a socialist character. Rights are asserted, pledges are made, which suggest much more than they in fact mean. The political figures of the time cannot, in my judgment, be called in any case socialist ; nor were they dealing with a public which, in any serious degree, expected socialist measures. What rather we are confronted with is a people full of misery, to whom attacks upon the wealthy as the source of their misfortune might be expected to appeal. The Girondins, certainly, had no sort of sympathy with socialism ; Danton, as I think, had no sort of social principles at all, and Brissot, differently from his earlier views, was the defender of the small proprietor rather than anything else. There is socialism among the Jacobins, as there is also among the *enragés* ; but I regard it less as a body of consistent and systematic principle than as a series of extraordinary ideas meant to cope with an extraordinary situation. It is not until the conspiracy of Babeuf that we meet with socialism in a serious and effective form. In a word, until Babeuf there are socialist ideas, but there is no socialism.

So to regard the character of this period is, I know, to run counter to a famous thesis of Taine. But I think his view is built upon a complete misunderstanding of the evidence. Undoubtedly there were attacks on property, hatred of the rich, revolutionary risings, a good deal of pillage and confiscation. But these are the inevitable accompaniments of any revolution, where there is a hungry mob, a bewildered Government, foreign and civil war. Socialism, as I have said, is theory of social reconstruction and a methodology; it is not an angry crowd attacking a speculator or burning the documents of its ancient servitude. It is not even a Jacobin deputy preaching the agrarian law, or Marat insisting that, in time of crisis, each commune can take measures without limit to help its poor; nor is it Robespierre arguing that excess of property is only justifiable where there is general sufficiency. Broadly speaking, the temper we confront is one which insists that in a period of scarcity the rich man who does not put his surplus at the disposal of the community is an enemy of society. It is a hatred of greed, of speculation, a suspicion that great wealth implies counter-revolutionary sentiment, that we meet almost everywhere. But this attitude cannot be described as socialism any more than its Russian analogue means an acceptance of the principles of Lenin.

The true approach lies, I believe, along quite different lines. The Revolution inherited from the *philosophes* a rigorous criticism of property as an absolute right, an ethical defence of communism, and a profound sense that, because the privileges of aristocracy are indefensible, that state might be made to serve the people creatively. These notions had to be applied in a time of crisis, without time to think either of their philosophic significance or their administrative possibility. They had to be applied when there was civil war at the centre of national life and foreign war at its circumference. Measures which are suitable to an extremity are rarely the expression of a considered philosophy. They represent merely the response to immediate exigency, and their very authors are, often enough, the first to deny that they have permanent significance. Certainly there could not have been any widespread socialism in a revolution which began in enthusiastic loyalty to Louis XVI and ended in a loyalty at least superficially enthusiastic to Napoleon; Girondins who anathematised the agrarian law, Jacobins who hissed the leading *enragés* out of the Paris clubs, do not sound like the apostles of socialist principle. Effectively, I should argue, there would have been no socialism at all if the economic condition had not been acute. What men were prepared for was the abrogation of what was restrictive in the *ancien régime*. Crisis drove many to heroic words and measures which they felt to be suited to an heroic time; but when the situation, after the death of Robespierre, became administratively manageable what emerges as stable is the *bourgeois* liberalism which drove Babeuf to revolt. And the very memory of how property had been in danger was so driven into men's minds that after 1796 it was in process of becoming the very absolute against which the eighteenth century had made its magistral protest.

This, at least, is how I read the evidence. It does not exclude the fact that there were socialist ideas; it does deny that there were either many to put forward or a wide public conscious of their meaning and anxious for their application. It is worth while to consider the expression of those ideas in some little detail, and to note their affiliations with orthodox Jacobinism on the one hand and the conspiracy of 1796 upon the other. I begin by noting one general point: all parties in the State agreed upon the undesirability of excessive differences of fortune. Mirabeau, Malouet, Vergniaud, Brissot, Condorcet, all spoke in this sense; and there was a fairly widespread tendency to approve the simple life and a progressive income-tax. These are, of course, views which the eloquence of Rousseau had made almost platitudes. They were things which every one had to say who did not wish to be regarded as reactionary. The first person worth mention who went at all far in a socialist direction was the Abbé Fauchet, who founded in 1790 a discussion circle, and was himself, later, a Girondin deputy. His views undoubtedly influenced a wide circle, though the fact that, as Camille Desmoulins tells us, he could be hissed in his own section for support of the agrarian law shows that men were rather interested in, than moved to accept, his ideas.

His views are obviously founded upon Rousseau. His journal—the *Bouche de Fer*—preaches the original goodness of man, and his right to an equal share of the earth. When he enters the State he surrenders all his rights which are then possessed by Government for the general welfare. By this is meant that all men have something, and no man has too much. What must be prevented is extreme poverty and wealth and, above all, social parasitism. He recommends the establishment of national factories, the limitation of land-holding, a rigorous control of inheritance, and such a regulation of the marriage laws as would prevent the union of large family fortunes. It is noteworthy that even these moderate views were bitterly attacked, not only by conservatives like Mallet du Pan, but also by radicals like Desmoulins. Fauchet himself continually softened whatever of rigour they may possess; and he put them forward rather as an ultimate, than as an immediate, programme. He was less a doctrinal socialist than a Christian mystic imbued with the importance of equality by his desire for a change in the heart of mankind.

Among the Girondins, I think, there was no one who was socialist in any real sense of the term. Brissot was an exponent of Jeffersonian democracy, Condorcet was a radical much of the school of Thomas Paine, Sébastien Mercier shares the horror which, as he tells us, Rousseau would have felt at the ideas of Babeuf; and Rétif abandoned his *Thesmographe*, being content, amid wild denunciation of Jacobin and sans-culottes, to insist that equality in land or in incomes below fifty thousand francs is both impossible and criminal. The only important Girondin who shows signs of more radical views is the one-time pastor Rabaut Saint-Étienne; though he may be said less to embrace socialism than to fringe its boundaries. Equality, he tells us, is the soul of a republic; unequal wealth divides classes and ruins equality in politics. But it cannot be established by force, and the best we can hope for is to reduce inequality by law. How this is to be done he does not tell us in detail. A maximum fortune can be fixed, the State taking the remainder, whether by gift or force, for foundations of public utility or unforeseen State expenditure. National workshops should be created, and inheritance and testamentary disposition should be controlled. But, even more, Rabaut Saint-Étienne would desire the State to encourage those moral habits in the people which are favourable to the atmosphere of equality.

These can hardly be called extreme views; though it is worth pointing out that they and their like excited the widest alarm among conservative thinkers. Equality and an agrarian law seemed to a charitable worker named Lambert "a violation of all the laws of nature." Men like La Harpe exhausted themselves in expressions of horror at the extreme and dangerous attacks upon the foundations of social order. Their very demand to have done with experiment naturally provoked the antithesis of their caution. To have accepted their attitude would have meant simple futility before the grave economic problems—how grave M. Mathiez has recently shown [1]—which confronted the State. The conservatism of the Right did not appeal to the Girondins. But the latter, to whom disorder was hateful, and whose fear of the proletariat was omnipresent, shrank from a policy which seemed to jeopardise the property of the middle classes. They were naturally overthrown by the Jacobins, whose policy of centralisation and experiment provided the only hope the masses could see for assuaging their misfortunes. Brissot might join hands with Mallet du Pan and Barruel, to accuse them of subverting the foundations of social order; to themselves, and, in general, I think, quite honestly, they merely appeared as men prepared to utilise the authority of the State for the preservation of the Revolution.

I do not mean to imply that there was not a definitely socialist background to Jacobin policy. Certainly there was; though to understand it we must remember that its sources are complex. Partly it was born of immediate necessity, partly of the fact that their leaders, Marat and Robespierre in particular, were deeply read in those earlier thinkers, especially Rousseau and Mably, who had insisted that the right to property is a social concept made by, and limited by, the will of the State. They never had a new theory of a different social order. For the most part, they were the *petite bourgeoisie* to whom Montesquieu and Rousseau were a gospel to which they were prepared to sacrifice much. And the

[1] *Robespierre et la vie chère* (Paris, 1927).

sacrifices they were prepared to make were such as the poorer classes welcomed, especially when these saw in hostility to the Jacobins the privileged of the old *régime* and the rich men of the new. What they said and did no more made them deliberately and consciously socialist than did the programme unfolded by Mr Lloyd George in 1909 make him a member of the socialist party. They would attack the rich, but they would not have the agrarian law. They would demand sacrifices—Mr Chamberlain's doctrine of 'ransom'—but they would do nothing to injure the idea of individual property itself. Danton, for example, was merely a democrat who wished that the rich should bear their full share of the common burden and that men should be recognised to have an equal right to happiness. Marat, as I have noted, was a moderate liberal in 1789. Experience made him more violent in declamation. But no journalist who merely thinks from one day to the next, especially if he is gambling for his head, has a considered philosophy. If he regarded economic equality as desirable, it was for some distant future he need not discuss. What he was above all concerned to maintain was the sovereign right of the State to take whatever measures it might think fit to prevent disaster. Reasonable wages, prices within the reach of the poor, local control of the food-supply—these were the things he emphasised day by day in the *Ami du Peuple*. But no one can read his articles without seeing that he is merely inventing remedies for a crisis. He has no thought of permanent principles.

With Robespierre it is different; from his writings and speeches one can, I think, piece together a coherent doctrine which has clearly socialist affinities. Property for him is simply a social institution; it is the citizen's right to enjoy as he will the goods guaranteed to him by the State. The latter can, therefore, limit its rights, punish speculators, and control inheritance. But absolute equality is a chimera impossible of realisation in civil society. To preach it is to invite a detestable anarchy. There is an excessive inequality which the State should control. It leads to the domination of the community by a few wealthy men, and their vices contaminate society. The State owes to the poor, the source of moderation and civic virtue, the right to work or maintenance; to procure

214

this for them is a more sacred task than to protect the wealth of the rich. Fixation of prices in their interest is essential, and no punishment is too strong for speculators in food. A severe and progressive income-tax is justified; in an ideal State no one would have more than an income of three thousand livres. All this, clearly enough, is the mind of a man nourished on Rousseau and Mably, the partisan of a simple and equal society, the enemy of the rich, whom he feels to stand in the way of its achievement. He speaks the language of bitterness and hate; for to him the rich are the enemies of the republic. But if Robespierre's ideal is anything it is that of the small-town radical rather than the socialist. It is the excess of wealth, not property itself, to which he takes objection.

Much the same might be said of Saint-Just, whose *Institutions républicaines* shows us pretty fully the direction of his mind. A nation of small farmers, general equality, a compulsion upon all to work, a rigorous control of inheritance to the direct line, a national system of education, and the endowment of young married couples are the chief proposals he makes. The Saint-Just of the Convention is less utopian and more bitter; but, loathing of the rich apart, there is nothing positively extreme in what he has to say. And this is, in general, the temper of his colleagues. The right of the poor to property, the danger of excessive wealth, the duty of the State to confiscate that excess for the general benefit—these are the themes of a thousand speeches. Violent class war is, of course, widely preached, especially by some of the representatives on mission. Lecomte Saint-Michel's phrase, that the rich are "the mortal enemies of the Republic," is typical of innumerable others. Billaud-Varenne calls them "the bane of ordered States"; but it is significant that he should add that property is "unfortunately the necessary foundation of civil society." But when, with them, or such journalists and pamphleteers as Prudhomme, Harmand, Desgiouas, we have exhausted the terminology of vituperation we come back inevitably to a positive theory on the lines of Robespierre's doctrine. When Boissy d'Anglas, in his exposition of the Constitution of the Year III, said that "un pays gouverné par les propriétaires est dans l'ordre social" he was not far from the Jacobin ideal; the owner must not be rich, and all must be owners. That is the distinguishing feature of Jacobin theory.

I would emphasise again the fact that all this is not socialistic innovation, but the inheritance of the criticism of property made by the eighteenth century. Political equality, it had taught, is nothing without economic equality; men like Turgot, Sieyès, and Condorcet had said so incessantly. "Equality, in fact," said Condorcet, "is the final aim of social technique, since inequality in riches, inequality of condition, and inequality of education are the main cause of all evils." And alongside this notion was the full realisation that a State composed of the two nations of rich and poor is bound to conflict. "There has never been, nor will there be," says a pamphlet of 1789, "any but two really distinct classes of citizens, the owners of property and those who have none; the first have everything, the second nothing." Jacobinism is simply these ideas applied to a critical period in which danger sharpened the antagonism between classes, and made the idea of equality and simplicity seem a definite measure of public safety. It was neither a theory nor a method of thoroughgoing social transformation. Rather was it a demand that the surplus of the rich be deliberately used by the State for the mitigation of popular suffering.

IV

Before I turn to Babeuf and his conspiracy it is worth while to spend a little time on one or two of his precursors. It is probable that ideas which may vaguely be termed communist began as early as 1789; for we are told by Bandot that the "acrimony and bitterness" of the Girondins was due to "fear of seeing the ideas of the Communists predominate." The sense continually grew that any society in which men, as Billaud-Varenne said, "existed upon a direct but not mutual dependence upon some other human being" was, in fact, in a condition of slavery. In 1793 and 1794 there were among the sections, and notably in the Club des Cordeliers, men to whom Jacobin doctrine seemed needlessly conservative. We get hints of secret societies, suggestions of plans like the credit schemes of Proudhon, demands that the profits of banking revert to the State. In men like Jacques Roux, Varlet, Dolivier, Boissel, Lange, there is a clear stream of doctrine looking toward a communist solution of social problems.

Thermidor destroyed whatever hopes and prospects these men may have cherished ; after it there came signs of what a police-spy, one hopes ironically, called "a profound and universal peace." But these men had their dreams, and it is worth while to note their substance. For they show how, even in the gravest moments of the Revolution, the incurable optimism of men was still prepared to make all things new. They had no clear idea of how their views could be realised ; and I think it probable that they had no sort of sympathy with the methods Babeuf was later to propose. They saw all the fallacies of *laissez-faire*, and their desire was to realise that equality of fact of which I have spoken. We know, alas, too little of most of them ; one would give much, for instance, for a detailed biography of Rose Lacombe, who must be very nearly the first woman communist. But what we do know suggests simple-minded and honest men, honoured by the masses for the high character of their ideals.

Among them, perhaps, Jacques Roux is worthy of particular mention. He had been a priest, and was, perhaps, one of those who had been freed by the Revolution from that burning indignation which still lives for us in the bitter pages of the Abbé Meslier. He was always poor, and we have a picture of a lonely figure, whose sole companion was a dog, preaching a simple communism to the working-class quarters of Paris. There is Chalier of Lyons, a mystic, whom Michelet has noted as an extraordinary man, and Lange, in some sort the precursor of Fourier. Important too is Varlet, a Parisian workman, about whom our ignorance is complete, and the *curé* of Mauchamp, Pierre Dolivier, whose book was published for him by his fellow-citizens of the commune of Anvers. All of them are typical of an outlook not without wide support in those days of agony. They desire the limitation of landholding, forced loans to feed the people, the confiscation of all property due to speculation, national workshops, and the public control of the food-supply. They differ from the Jacobins in that they do not pay regard to the rights of property. They consider the urgency of the position too great for measures of conciliation to be desirable. They see quite definitely in the rich and the comfortable the deliberate enemies of the poor, who will not hesitate to take advantage of public misery for private profit. They are mostly, again differently from the Jacobins, in favour of the agrarian law, though with definite leanings to a national control of its operation. Thermidor left them exasperated, largely because they saw, in the disappearance of Robespierre, the failure of their hope for drastic economic legislation. But they could not go so far as Babeuf, because they definitely respected a democratic system. "Dictatorship," said Roux, "is the annihilation of liberty"; and there is in most of them, especially in Dolivier, a marked trend toward anarchism.

Their ideas, on the whole, are seen most clearly in the pamphlet published in 1789 by Boissel, a Jacobin of the extreme Left, who was active throughout the Revolution.[1] Bitterly attacked in the Assembly, it seems to have exercised some influence, especially after 1793, and it is certainly an interesting link between ideas like those of Mably before 1789, and of Babeuf afterward. It begins with a passionate attack on organised society as the nurse of all evil. It examines and rejects property, marriage, and religion as the expressions of the worst impulses of men. Property is simply an instrument of oppression, and the root of a discord which the invention of money merely increases. The business of society is to respond to our true instincts, which are naturally good. This can be done if we recognise that God is the only true owner, and that we have the right to nothing save in terms of need. We must reform education, nationalise industry, and train men in the spirit of a collective ownership with a view to the introduction of complete communism. Here, clearly, his trust is in an educational system which will one day make men ready for the new order. By 1793 he was insisting to the Jacobins that the fruits of the earth belong to the poor by natural right, and may be taken by force, for property is a usurpation of the inalienable right of man to subsistence. But beyond that vague sense of the duty to use the law Boissel, like his fellows, has no clear notion of how the change he desires may be definitely effected. With him, as with Dolivier,[2] a

[1] *Le Catéchisme du genre humain.*   [2] *Essai sur la justice primitive.*

society can be reconstructed on the principles of a communism somewhat like that of the Russian *mir* and the right of each man to the whole produce of his labour. And much of their outlook is determined by the clear perception that the real result of the Revolution has been to establish the farmer and the merchant in the seat of power. They realise that the aristocrat has been dethroned in the interest of the middle classes. They insist that anything short of communism must mean of necessity the retention of a class-structure in society.

But they do not really know how communism is to be attained. I agree with Kropotkin that an analysis of this early philosophy anticipates much of the principles of 1848, that little of what was elaborated by Fourier and Owen and Proudhon cannot be found in pamphlets and speeches and local decrees of the period. They had an ideal, but not a method. The importance of Babeuf and his colleagues lies in the fact that not only did they envisage this ideal with some particularity, but they had quite definite notions of how to seize power for its attainment. It is probable enough that few of the two or three thousand people who seem definitely to have been influenced by the conspiracy knew or shared in their views with any precision; they may have known the battle-cries without thinking through the programme. That is not, I think, particularly important. All revolutions are the act of a minority; they depend for their success on sympathy for their general end rather than for their bill of particulars. Babeuf and his fellows knew how they proposed to proceed; and the strategy they invented has provided ever since the methodology of revolutionary socialism, at least in its large outline.

I have already noted that Babeuf was a communist from the outset of the Revolution; I need not here detail his later career. Though his *Système de dépopulation* shows that at one time he was both anti-terrorist and anti-egalitarian, he was one of those who saw in the fall of Robespierre the end of what was beneficent in the Revolution. Always in want, often in prison, rash, enthusiastic, self-confident, single-minded, he was just the man to lead a desperate attempt upon the conquest of power. The conspiracy seems to have been formed

219

during one of his terms in prison. A few fellow-prisoners were initiated into his ideas ; the group grew steadily, and became the Society of the Pantheon, which the Government did not fail to watch and proclaim. It had two wings : at the very centre were the real communists, and, closely affiliated, but remote from the heart of the affair, a number of ancient Jacobins to whom the abrogation of Robespierre's constitution was a bitter memory. The scheme was linked together by a secret committee of direction, to which its publications were almost certainly due. Among them were some extraordinary men—Darthe, Sylvain Maréchal, Germain, and Buonarroti, who was to survive them all and to be their historian. They had contacts with some former members of the Convention, with the army and the police, even with the underworld. I need not add that, from their early days, they were honeycombed with spies, one of whom was, unknown to them, introduced by Buonarroti and Darthe to the very heart of the affair. They never had any real chance of success. Their plans were known, almost from their inception, to the Directory ; it needed less honest and zealous men than they to elude the cold-blooded machinations of Barras. Every one, moreover, was tired of bloodshed and misery ; the police reports and the diplomatic correspondence show clearly that the Revolutionary spirit was exhausted. The leaders were arrested and tried by a special tribunal. Babeuf and Darthe, after a vain attempt at suicide, were executed ; other important conspirators, including Buonarroti, were imprisoned or deported. Those who lived on became the depositaries of a tradition which, after 1830, they found the new generation eager to cherish.

I shall discuss, first, the programme of Babeuf, and then his strategy. Neither is a very easy thing to do, partly because some of the evidence, being produced by spies at the trial, is suspect, and partly because not a little of what we have is clearly not in its final reaction. Yet the literature, checked by the narrative of Buonarroti, and, even more, by the invaluable discoveries of Advielle, enables us to see pretty clearly what was involved. And this can, I think, be put in a single sentence. There is no real innovation in doctrine, which is the eighteenth-century tradition clarified and made precise by the profound experience of seven Revolutionary years ; there is definite innovation in method, which opens an epoch of decisive importance in the history of socialism.

Let us start with two significant sentences used by Babeuf in his trial. " My companions and I," he told his judges, " have groaned over the unhappy results of the Revolution . . . it has merely replaced a band of ancient scoundrels by a band of new ones." For the object of society is the realisation of the common happiness. That is impossible without the rule of equality, which is the clear implication of natural law. This does not mean the agrarian law, which is not equality at all. All men have a permanent right to a continuous share in the social product. To recognise private property and differences of fortune is to admit theft to the heart of society. Heredity is unjust, respect for the superiority of talent is dangerous. All work has the same value, and all capacity shall be equally rewarded. Communism is the only way by which this can be realised. It means the common ownership of land. It means the socialisation of industry and universal and compulsory labour. Education too should be equal and common. The theory differs from what has gone before, in that earlier thinkers demanded relative equality. The Babouvistes insist that this is more difficult to achieve and to maintain than equality in the full sense of the term. Any society in which less than this exists is built upon civil war, and is bound to mean the exploitation of the poor, of, that is, the mass of the community. There can be no justice unless the only recognised differences in the State are those of age and sex. To put the whole wealth of society at the disposition of the people is to assure the maximum of virtue, justice, and happiness. Envy and hate disappear. Each can recognise that his well-being is intimately related to that of his neighbour. To serve society in such an order is to serve oneself. The reign of equality will be the last revolution necessary to the well-being of man.

This body of doctrine was developed in the most diverse and ingenious ways; in the art of literary propaganda the Babouvistes had certainly nothing to learn from their generation. Careful doctrinal analyses, as in the famous *Analyse de la doctrine de Babeuf*, a brilliant short programme, as in the *Manifeste des égaux* drawn up by Sylvain Maréchal, songs, poems, newspapers, special literature for the army and the police, placards, memoranda, slogans, invective, all the typical devices of modern publicity are there. It is easy to see how their eloquent denunciation of existing conditions would appeal to the unemployed, for they set out with simplicity the experience through which the working-classes had passed. It is even probable that their emphasis upon the failure of the Revolution, their attacks upon the rich, their hatred of the Directory, their impassioned defence of the honesty and greatness of Robespierre, commanded wide sympathy. The programme, clearly as Babeuf himself would have recognised, is simply a careful restatement of Rousseau and Mably, of Diderot and Morelly. It is both bolder and more precise than its predecessors. It has none of their faith in the possibility of changing men's hearts in an individualist society. It is much more bitter against the rich, much more insistent that they are "brigands" for whose destruction all patriots must hope. The Babouvistes are more optimistic than their predecessors in that they think the essential revolution is capable of immediate achievement. But in the general contour of their objective there is nothing essential to distinguish them from a half-score of thinkers in the pre-Revolutionary epoch.

That is not, as I have said, the case with their strategy, where there is genuine and important novelty. This can best be analysed in two ways. On the one hand there are the definite steps they took in the organisation of their conspiracy up to the time of their arrest; on the other there is the theory of what was to be its conduct after they had seized political power. At the head of affairs was the small central committee, with Babeuf at its head. This was the brains of the whole conspiracy. It met in secret, practically every night, always alone, and not seldom changing its headquarters to avoid any possible suspicion. It dealt with day-to-day business, the actual conditions under which the insurrection was to take place, the legislative measures to be taken on the morrow of the insurrection, and the future institutions of the new republic. It was responsible not only for the overt propaganda, but also for stimulating the activities of its local agents to these. The *personnel* of the committee remained unknown. Its individual members had relations with the agents, but rather as themselves officers of *liaison* than as chiefs. The agents, most of whom were chosen with great care, were of the essence of the plan. Tried revolutionaries, they were the contact between the central committee and the masses. They reported on the feeling of the population, its grievances and aspirations. They supplied, therefore, that knowledge upon which the leaders could build successful propaganda and action. Linked with them were local committees in the districts of Paris, who made their impress upon the workers, put up placards and distributed leaflets, addressed meetings in the workmen's clubs, talked in *cafés* and factories, and spread as widely as possible the volume of discontent, the hope that one final effort might make all things new. Women also played their part, and it was hoped, particularly, to employ the services of the *demi-monde* to neutralise any hostility in the army.

To the latter special attention was paid. The leaders had carefully chosen military agents to each of whom a definite task was allotted. General Fyon was in charge of the Invalides; Germain took care of the police; Massey controlled the detachments at Saint-Genès; Vanneck was given the task of infecting the remaining troops in Paris. Agents were obtained in each barracks to work on the minds of the soldiers; others, sometimes women, frequented their *cafés.* Sophie Lapierre, whose beauty was well known in Paris, declaimed the proclamations of the central committee and sang its songs. The evidence at the trial suggests that no mean success attended these efforts. They were paralleled by similar attention to the police. Information was also obtained about *agents provocateurs* from sympathisers in the force; and in several cases the head of a police section was in close contact with the conspirators.

Through these means every sort of step was taken which might injure the Government and create the expectation of some great impending event. Every rumour likely to injure the Directory was widely spread. Complaints were broadcast, meetings held, sympathisers from the provinces brought to Paris to create the illusion of a national movement, assemblies of street-mobs were organised. The Laws of the 27th and 28th Germinal, by which the Government took power to dissolve all political meetings, show that the importance of the movement was realised. Insubordination among the troops, the punishment of which revealed unrest in the police, is further proof that the danger was real. But the fact that Barras actually negotiated, probably dishonestly, an attempt at an alliance with Germain of the secret committee shows both that the Directory was alarmed and that it was, probably throughout, cognisant of the plan. When the committee, after discussions of military plans, was waiting for the critical moment the Directory swooped upon them. It was estimated at that time that, the masses apart, the insurrectionists could count upon 17,000 men, of whom 9500 were regular troops. These were to march upon the arsenals and the seat of Government, while others were to hold the streets of Paris and repulse all hostile attack. The plan was never put into action, as Barras was the first to strike his blow; but it is, I think, evidence of the hold the conspirators had obtained that some seven hundred men should have marched to Grenelle and sought to incite the troops there to revolt and rescue their leaders. They were only dispersed by military attack and numerous arrests. After that the conspiracy was at an end.

Clearly enough, as a piece of organisation, the plans of the Babouvistes were remarkably conceived. Not less interesting was their conception of the methods to be used in the event of success. Here their views were built upon the theory of the class war. Society for them was divided into rich and poor, and neither had any interest in common with the other. The rich depended for their position upon their power to keep the poor in subordination; the latter could conquer their rights only by the dethronement of the rich. In a society in which overt civil war was the main feature it was unthinkable that power could be conquered by the poor save by violent means, for the rich would never abandon their privileges without fighting for them. This, they felt, was the real lesson of 1789; it was the lesson of 1793; it was the lesson implicit in the experience of Thermidor. It meant that when the political State had been captured a period of rigorous dictatorship would be necessary as the prelude to communist democracy. Only in this way could the people be withdrawn from influences hostile to equality, and given that unity of will essential to the adoption of republican ideas. "It was evident," wrote Buonarroti thirty years later, "that the inherent necessity of things, even the success itself of our enterprise, meant an interval between the fall of aristocratic power and the final establishment of popular democracy." An assembly was impossible, since it left the success achieved to the hazard of a popular vote. The revolution had not been made merely to change the form of administration; its object was to change the nature of society itself. This could not be left to the people who had been trained to habits which ignored the natural order of things. The revolutionary Government must therefore act on behalf of the people. It must, as Buonarroti wrote, "snatch from the natural enemies of equality the means of deceit and fear and division." What was required was

> an extraordinary and necessary authority which would restore its liberty to the nation, despite the corruption which was the consequence of its ancient slavery, and despite the attacks of those enemies, within and without, sworn to its destruction.

It is the doctrine of permanent revolution by dictatorship in the name of the proletariat.

To seize power is, therefore, only the first step; it does not end the revolution. Parliamentarianism and democracy are impossible because they risk the whole purpose of the insurrection; the people are not yet fit to be entrusted with a power which counter-revolutionaries might seize from them again. "What was necessary," wrote Babeuf, "was men whose doctrines and manners, whose whole life, was in full harmony with the spirit of the institutions which they were called to create." Liberty must be denied at the outset lest it be lost for ever. What was to be done was in accord with natural law. It was what the people would itself desire when it came to understand the egalitarian State. The dictatorship was thus, in effect, the general will of the proletariat. It lost its freedom only the more fully to find it.

The institutions and measures this dictatorship would create are extraordinarily significant in the light of our recent experience. The central committee had at first considered the idea of appointing a single person as dictator; but this idea was rejected in favour of the government of the committee itself, advised by an assembly composed of one democrat chosen by each of the departments from a list of suitable persons submitted to them. This had, however, to be modified after discussion with their Jacobin allies; and the final form of assembly was to consist of some sixty former members of the Convention and a hundred other democrats nominated by the people from safe candidates. The committee retained the right to initiate legislation, together with full executive powers. Beneath it there were to be created commissars in each department, with great authority. Their business was to speed the successful revolution. They were to make propaganda for its ideas, create local societies for its completion, deal with counter-revolutionaries, and assist all active democrats in the provinces. Before appointment they were to declare their financial position, and a special tribunal was created to examine their accomplishment of their task. Further to strengthen the new order there was to be created a kind of revolutionary academy, a *séminaire normal*, "where citizens from each department would be sent, in a predetermined order, to learn the principles of the new revolution, and to be imbued with the spirit of the reformers." To complete the structure of the dictatorship the Babouvistes decided to re-create all local institutions, including the Revolutionary commissions, as they existed before the fall of Robespierre in Thermidor.

I cannot even attempt here to analyse in detail the actual measures by which the central committee proposed to accomplish its task. But it is, I think, worth while briefly to indicate the principles upon which those measures were based. All healthy persons were to work, and no idle person was to possess political rights. The homeless and the poor were to be housed in the houses of all who had conspired, or might conspire, against the revolution. The people were to be armed, and all "parasites" disarmed. The Press was to be controlled, to prevent the spread of false news or attack. Special taxes were to be levied on all not sympathetic to the new *régime*, with a right, at need, of complete confiscation. The old defenders of the Revolution and the unfortunate were to be given the use of new possessions. Anyone who had emigrated or rebelled was to lose his property; and confiscation was also visited upon the negligent farmer, the public servant enriched by the exercise of his office, and any who were judicially condemned. The sale of national property was suspended ; and, inheritance being abolished, all private estates, on death, were to revert to the State. Machinery was to be developed and uncultivated land brought into use ; to this end State shops were to be opened in each commune, and an economic council, representing the different professions, was to aid the local authorities in the provision and organisation of work. Education, with the necessary vocational bias, was to be common to all, and so developed that the average man might hope to play his full part in the life of the State. Foreign trade was to be a State monopoly, while money and wages were abolished for internal purposes. There was to be assistance for the old and free medical service for the sick ; and the treatment of criminals was to be entirely reformed. Whatever its weaknesses as a practical scheme, it is obvious that Babeuf and his colleagues had arrived at a clear perception of the programme they wished to achieve.

V

The modern theory of social revolution is naturally the outcome of a profounder study of historic conditions than it was open to Babeuf and his colleagues to make. Yet anyone who compares their analysis with the *Communist Manifesto* on the one hand, or the writings of Lenin and Trotsky upon the other, can hardly doubt the original source of their inspiration. The line of affiliation, indeed, is a direct one ; for Buonarroti was the master of that generation whose words and acts were the basis of Marxian strategy. The class war, the failure of reform, the necessity of dictatorship, the insistence on a social revolution, the ultimate significance of the economic question, the realisation that insurrection is an art, the careful preparation of the measures it is to entail, the insistence on the proletariat as the sole revolutionary class, the perception of the importance of education and propaganda, the sense that intellectual theories are born of the methods of economic production—all these the Babouvistes clearly understood. All these, also, became part of the essential socialist tradition of the nineteenth century. "It is nearly forty years since Babeuf died," wrote Charles Nodier in 1836, "and his party is still living . . . he recognised truths which no Government has deigned to accept, truths which can never die." Of the socialism of the Revolution, indeed, Babouvisme is the one element destined to permanent influence. Voyer d'Argenson, Teste, Raspail, Louis Blanc, Leroux, and Blanqui in France, Belhasse and Potter in Belgium, Bronterre O'Brien in England, have all borne testimony to the part it played in their lives through contact with Buonarroti. Weitling's work in the canton of Vaud brought him into direct contact with it also; and it is worth remembering the part that the League of the Just played as an instrument of early Marxism. And it is worth remembering, also, that one of the Communards of 1870 was the grandson of that Clemence who had sat with Babeuf in the central committee. It was with reason that Count Albert de Mun should, in 1896, in the Chamber of Deputies, have accused the French socialists of being the descendants of Babeuf. That is, in fact, their real and effective origin.

We must not, indeed, exaggerate their insight into the technique the modern Marxian has developed. They had practically no conception of socialism as an international force; it needed the impact of the Industrial Revolution to emphasise the limits of nationalism in revolutionary strategy. There was not enough realisation of successful revolution as grounded in a set of objective economic conditions, and not merely born of determined organisation at a premature moment. There were many of those elements in the theory of Babeuf which in 1847 Marx stigmatised as "utopian socialism"— the belief in an ultimate natural law, the conception of an original endowment of human impulse which was definitely good and merely obscured by evil institutions, something, at least, of the acceptance of insurrection for its own sake, upon the dangers of which Lenin has written so brilliantly. The latter's phrase, indeed, that "Babeuf was a Jacobin who leaned on the working classes" has a real truth in it; for he never sufficiently perceived the danger of the alliances he was prepared to make for the end he had in view. Nor did he realise at all how much in advance of effective possibility was his programme. A social revolution cannot be successful on the falling tide of a political revolution. Babouvisme was doomed to failure before it got under way.

Yet, it must be emphasised, the depth of its insight is remarkable. Anyone who reads its voluminous literature with attention, and compares the habits it postulates with the operations of Bolshevism, cannot help being impressed by the resemblance. Elsewhere I have pointed out [1] that the strength of communism lies in its effort to effect a complete transvaluation of values in terms of a great ideal passionately cherished. I have pointed out the strength given by faith in that ideal to its adherents, their profound sense of its exclusive truth, their willingness to sacrifice themselves to its principles, their insistence that the end is so great that the means adopted to it are, whatever their cost, justified. The detailed resemblances between the programme of Babeuf and that of the Russian Communist are remarkable enough; but even more remarkable is the similarity of ultimate temper which runs through the two movements. There is the same exhilaration of spirit, the same bitterly drawn distinction between friend and foe, the same urgency that all things be made new, the same power relentlessly to dissect the weaknesses of contemporary society, the same capacity for self-confident optimism, the same genius for propaganda and invective. Lenin, so to say, is the Babouvistes writ large; and the architect of the November Revolution was greatly indebted to men who, if they saw less clearly than he, envisaged a civilisation upon the same pattern he sought to build.

VI

What results from this analysis? The French Revolution, in a narrow perspective, must, I think, be regarded as primarily individualist in character; the real expression of its effective outcome is the Civil Code, in no sense a socialist document. Its real result was to transfer power from the aristocracy to the peasant and middle classes. The impress made upon them by the socialist tendencies of the period, especially by their extreme translation in the conspiracy of Babeuf, was to make the idea of private property more sacred and less susceptible to attack than it was held to be at any time in the eighteenth century. If it attacked the property of the old

[1] *Communism* (1927), p. 238 *et seq.*

régime, it consolidated that of the new upon a wider basis; and the era of change and confiscation only made men more eager to suppress the possibility that titles could be called into question. We must not forget that the abolition of feudal rights and corporate privilege was made in the name of the individual; that where confiscation took place it was done in the name of public safety, and could thus be regarded as essentially à transitory measure. Most of the attacks upon the rights of property which did take place were rather the inevitable accompaniment of civil war than an expression of any wide desire for social transformation. Given political liberty, a constitutional State, and equality before the law, and most men were content to abstain from speculative innovation. A State was created which lay at the service of the hard-working peasant and the active *entrepreneur*. No condition is more favourable to classes whose power is a function of the property they possess.

On a longer view, however, the French Revolution is a capital event in the history of socialism. It is so, I suggest, for four reasons. Before 1789 there was not, in the modern sense, any social problem. Men asked how the poor were to be relieved, not, as afterwards, what part they were to play in the State. The Revolution began that awakening of a social consciousness in the proletariat of which universal suffrage is merely a partial, and by no means the ultimate, consequence. Every radical party thenceforward has found that it must reckon with the wants, indistinct, indeed, and but half-formulated, of the poor; and every State has discovered that the growth of economic organisation sooner or later transforms the incoherent mass of the poor into a movement ultimately capable of organisation upon the classic lines of party conflict.

This birth of the social question has a special importance for another reason. Before 1789 socialist ideas were simply moral theories which lived in a vacuum, and had no chance of effective realisation. After 1789 they were in a different position. Men had seen the deliberate introduction of legislation the purpose of which was to legislate for equality. The fixation of maximum prices, the abolition of feudal privilege, the confiscation of Church property and the possessions of those hostile to the Revolution, the attempts at progressive taxation and the control of inheritance—these, as experiments, have an importance it is impossible to over-estimate. Doubtless they usually failed; doubtless, also, they were often suggested without conviction, and, more often still, applied without sincerity. This is less significant than the fact that men were accustomed to the perception that the State might be made the tactical instrument of those who possessed its machinery. It is less significant, also, than the fact that the Jacobins, not least their representatives on mission, schooled the masses to the understanding that distinctions of wealth are legislative creations, and that, where crisis demands it, egalitarian innovation may be deliberately attempted.

A third reason is outstanding in the impact it has made upon subsequent history. Before 1789 society was divided into privileged and unprivileged; since 1789 it has been divided into rich and poor. The distinction is a notable one. The pre-Revolutionary division was the expression of an age-long tradition rooted in the psychology of habit and custom; its landmarks were as mentally familiar to men as the house into which they were born. To the new division the sanction of tradition was no longer attached. Men could see change before their eyes. They could see that the attainment of riches meant food and shelter, clothing and security; they knew that its absence meant hunger and suffering. They learned not only that law could make and unmake the wealthy; they learned also that these opposed such changes in the law as involved sacrifice upon their part. They grew to think of the division as an antagonism of interest, a necessary hostility which could only be bridged by an attack upon the rights of property. From 1793 the life of the Republic was, until the execution of Babeuf, something not unlike a war against the rich in the interest of the poor. The Jacobins waged it, no doubt, for the preservation of the Republic. The poor who supported them did so, no doubt as well, because they were miserable and hungry, and not because they were socialists. But it was waged also with the idea in the background that equality is an idea, and that the rich are the enemies of equality. The notion permanently remains therefrom that great riches are always illegitimate; and with the class-conscious worker the more general view that the weaknesses of society are the outcome of class privilege. This feeling bit the more deeply because of wide disappointment with the results of the Revolution. After the fall of Robespierre the sense was widespread that the Revolution, which was to benefit the whole community, had, in fact, merely aided the *bourgeoisie* to the detriment of the worker. The latter's revolution, it was felt, was still to come; it was inherent in the nature of things. In this sense, as the principles of 1789 begin to impregnate the consequences of the factory system, revolutionary socialism became an inevitable part of nineteenth-century ideology.

The final outcome was the definition, with invincible clarity, of the problem of equality in all its aspects. Here I shall not venture to rely upon my own diagnosis, but attempt only to ask some questions. If a people seeks to improve its situation by the alteration of political institutions, and is dissatisfied either with the result itself or the slowness with which its benefits accumulate, will it be satisfied to remain inactive in the economic sphere? Will it not ask itself, as Tocqueville suggested, whether the privileges of property are not the main obstacle to equality among men, and assert that they are neither necessary nor desirable? If they ask the question will they not seek to experiment with the possibility of response? Will a new Napoleon be discovered to put a term to their inquiries? But to examine these possibilities would take me far beyond the boundaries of the French Revolution. It must suffice here to say that these questions have been raised and that the happiness of mankind depends upon the way in which we seek to meet the grave issues they involve.

HAROLD J. LASKI

BOOK LIST

ADVIELLE, V.: *Histoire de G. Babeuf.* 1884.
AULARD, A.: *Histoire politique de la Révolution française.* Edition of 1920.
AULARD, A.: *La Société des Jacobins.* 1889.
BUCHEZ ET ROUX: *Histoire parlementaire de la Révolution française.* 1834.
BUONARROTI, P.: *Histoire de la conspiration pour l'égalité.* 1828.
CHAMPION, E.: *La France d'après les cahiers de 1789.* 1897.
CHASSIN: *Le Génie de la Révolution.* 1862.
CHASSIN: *Les Élections et les cahiers de Paris.* 1888.

SOCIALISM IN THE FRENCH REVOLUTION

DEVILLE, G. : *Histoire socialiste.* Tome v, *Thermidor et Directoire.* 1905.

DONIOL, H. : *La Révolution française et la féodalité.* 1882.

ESPINAS, A. : *La Philosophie sociale du 18me siècle.* 1899.

JAURÈS, J. : *Histoire socialiste de la Révolution française.* Ed. Mathiez, 1922.

KROPOTKIN, PRINCE : *The Great French Revolution.*

LICHTENBERGER, A. : *Le Socialisme au 18me siècle.* 1895.

LICHTENBERGER, A. : *Le Socialisme utopique.* 1898.

LICHTENBERGER, A. : *Le Socialisme et la Révolution française.* 1899.

MARCEL, A. DE : *Types révolutionnaires.* 1873.

MARIN, V. : *Histoire littéraire de la Convention nationale.* 1866.

MATHIEZ, A. : *Autour de Robespierre.* 1925.

MATHIEZ, A. : *Robespierre et la vie chère.* 1927.

MATHIEZ, A. : *The French Revolution.* 1929.

ROBINET : *Danton, homme d'État.* 1889.

ROBIQUET, P. : *Buonarroti et la secte des égaux.* 1912.

SCHMIDT : *Paris pendant la Révolution.* 1885.

SENCIER, G. : *Le Babouvisme après Babeuf.* 1912.

IX

THE GERMAN THINKERS OF THE
REVOLUTIONARY ERA

THE theme proposed for the final article of this volume
—viz., the social and political ideas of the German
thinkers of the revolutionary era—is so vast that we
will attempt no more than to draw a broad picture of the
general trend of social and political thought in the great
period of German intellectual life. And as it can offer at
best but a bird's-eye view, the wider limits will be taken, and
it will treat of that whole movement, extending from Enlightenment through the Rousseauan Storm and Stress to the classical
period of German philosophy, which forms one single spiritual
organism.

The eighteenth century was a period of wonderful transformations in Germany. The change that came over the face
of the German world in the lifetime of a single man is brought
home to us very clearly when we see that representative man
of the age, Goethe, who himself lived to see the rise of modern
industrialism, depicted as a child in a well-known family group,
in all the whimsicality of the rococo fashion. The early
decades of the century were the age of baroque; a time of
etiquette and ceremony, of rank and precedence, of stiff
formality in life and art. The rococo, which followed it, and
which in France began to disappear by about the middle of
the century, lasted on in Germany for a couple of decades
more; and its light, fantastic elegance, its artificiality and mere
ornamentalism, had not died out when Rousseau's influence
surged over the land in the sixties. The different phases
crowded upon one another in rapidly shifting scenes, and so
rapidly did they follow that they tended to merge into one
another, and leave no very clear chronological demarcation.

The predominant philosophy of the early and middle century was that of the Enlightenment, based on the optimistic

idealism of Leibnitz, as systematised by Wolff, who himself gave it the name of *Aufklärung*, and popularised by a host of writers, of whom Moses Mendelssohn, the grandfather of the famous composer, was one of the best and most characteristic.

It was one of the hopeful ages, with an unbounded faith in the importance of man in the scheme of the universe, and in the power of his reason to solve all problems and remove all obstacles to his complete happiness and self-sufficiency. Its cosmology was anthropocentric; its criterion of all things their expediency and utility from the point of view of the human race. One of the favourite poets of the second quarter of the century was Barthold Heinrich Brockes of Hamburg, who, in the nine books of his *Irdisches Vergnügen in Gott*, justified the ways of God to man by demonstrating the serviceability of external nature and its adaptability to man's needs.

Reason was for the Enlightened a faculty common to all men, the *intelligence humaine* of Descartes, which remains invariable, to whatever diverse objects it may be applied. The faith in the power of reason was supreme. *Verstand* and *Vernunft* were ever on their lips, and the titles of their works and periodicals are variations of those terms. The names of most of Wolff's German works, and he wrote a large number both in German and Latin, begin with the words *Vernünftige Gedanken*. His best-known is called *Vernünftige Gedanken von Gott, der Welt und der Seele des Menschen, auch allen Dingen überhaupt*. Wolff was no original creative thinker, and on the whole his interpretation of the ideas of Leibnitz was a trivialisation of them; but he was clear and precise, and as men did not want profound or troublesome ideas, but reasonable and sensible ones, he voiced adequately the thought of his time. The lamp of reason was to shine into all the dark places, and banish all prejudice and superstition, all religious fanaticism and intolerance, all belief in wonders and miracles and incomprehensible dogmas. Men would become more and more alike, and in the end all differences between them merely a matter of externals.

This universalism and cosmopolitanism received its highest poetical expression in the *Nathan der Weise* of Lessing, who was himself the noblest representative and finest flower of the

Enlightenment. In that eloquent plea for religious tolerance and freedom of thought, the core of which is his version of the old and widespread Parable of the Three Rings, the doctrine is expounded that all religions may be proved true, or all proved false, by the use their disciples make of them, and that all men are potentially alike. Only a universal spread of reason was then needed to achieve the ideal, which may be described as a universal individualism, mankind as an aggregate of free individuals, each obeying the dictates of his own reason, which would function alike, independently of any difference of race or creed.

Of the State the men of the Enlightenment did not expect too much. In their individualism they regarded it as a necessary evil, which should interfere as little as possible with the cultural work of its individual citizens, and had itself no cultural functions or mission as such. They had no conception of it as an organic growth or human corporation. They did not attach much importance to any mere form of government, and of the absolute systems under which they lived they asked no more than that they should be guided by the lamp of reason. Enlightenment on the throne was a good enough ideal for them, and so we find many of them championing an enlightened absolutism as the best form of government.

A favourite literary device was to hold up the institutions of some imaginary country as a mirror to their own. One of the best-known of such works is Wieland's *Der goldene Spiegel oder die Könige von Scheschian*, which caused the Dowager Duchess, Anna Amalia, to invite the poet to Weimar as tutor of her two sons, and so was the indirect cause of the great Weimar tradition. A philosopher on the throne, with a poet-philosopher at his side, was a favourite dream which was realised more than once. It must have been very agreeable for a monarch to hear on the best of authority that he was the ideal thing in monarchs, especially as it did not always mean any inconvenient curtailment of sovereign power to be an Enlightened despot in those days! Wieland was followed to Weimar by Goethe, and the greatest poet of the age put himself in harness to the State. Klopstock had earlier been invited to Darmstadt, but his philosophy was too seraphic for practical consumption.

But whatever the triumphs of Enlightenment in the fields of philosophy and literature, its greatest victory was seen when it ascended the Prussian throne in the person of Frederick the Great. Frederick had already set the stamp of royal approval on the movement when shortly after his accession he recalled Wolff to Halle, whence he had been driven by the Pietists. What he did as the "First Servant of the State" is too well known to need recounting here. Other rulers too were inspired by the same ideals. The Emperor Joseph II was regarded by many as the ideal monarch, the enlightened benevolent despot on the throne. He was, in fact, the great hope of many of those who could not forgive Frederick his preference for French literature and philosophy and his indifference to the national aspirations in art and letters.

However, it is probably not in Prussia or Austria but in one of the smaller states that we can best study, as in a microcosm, the actual working of an Enlightened *régime*. The little state of Weimar, after the death of the Duke in 1757, was ruled for seventeen years by the Dowager Duchess, Anna Amalia, one of the best representatives of the Enlightened despotism, and inspired by the same ideals as her uncle, Frederick the Great. She could probably claim with justice that under her dispensation the people of Weimar enjoyed more happiness and prosperity than they had known for a very long time; while later, through Goethe's beneficent influence, much was done to further trade and commerce, and especially for the relief of the poorest classes. Yet, even there, the sharpest cleavage existed between the privileged and unprivileged, and the people took little part in the ideal culture of the Court. Goethe speaks in *Wilhelm Meister* of the favoured ones of this earth as placed from their birth in a ship, in which they float in pleasant security down the stream of life. "Hail to the great of this earth!" cries Meister. "Hail to all who are brought within their sphere, and can share in their advantages!" No one then questioned their right to a place in the vessel—neither those who, by their labour, made the careless voyage possible, nor the careless voyagers themselves.

This tiny state had to carry an enormous superstructure. The town itself had 6000 inhabitants, and the castle occupied about a third of its area. Yet the Duchy of Weimar maintained not only this big castle in the residence itself, but other more or less lordly pleasure-houses, north, south, east, and west, on the hills that look down upon the town. It was wonderful what such a little land could support in that way. It was more an estate than a state. Life for the favoured ones was a round of gaiety—ball and rout and masque and chase. Those last few years of unquestioning serenity have been preserved for us by Goethe in his calm and classic *Tasso*. There we have a beautifully harmonious picture of the halcyon days that were never to return; of an ideal Court that is, at the same time, in the transparency of its relation to Weimar, a monument to that Court, as Goethe half saw it and half would have it be. The crew do not exist; they are allowed to relieve the passengers of all material cares, that they may the more serenely tread the path of their high destiny.

Elsewhere, of course, things were often much worse. The most oppressive tyranny too was seen in some of the smaller states. Throughout the eighteenth century serfdom in various forms prevailed in Germany, and its oppression weighed heavily on the peasants. In 1771 Johann Michael von Loën writes: "To-day the peasant is the most wretched of all creatures; the farmers are slaves, and their servants are hardly to be distinguished from the beasts they tend." Modifications and alleviations were, it is true, granted, and in some states serfdom was abolished. Joseph II, for instance, suppressed it in most of his territories in 1781, though against the bitter opposition of the landowners, and it was restored by his successor, Leopold II, in 1790.

In Prussia the condition of the peasants varied greatly in the different provinces. Frederick the Great, who had the interest of his landed nobility above all at heart, and who believed that agriculture could not be carried on without forced labour, was content with regulating the conditions of compulsory service, and making life more endurable for the peasants, who formed the best material for his army. It needed the flames kindled by the French Revolution and the collapse of the Holy Roman Empire to put an end to the relics of this barbarous institution.

238

THE GERMAN THINKERS

It is strange to contemplate the complacency and optimism of the men of the Enlightenment in face of the conditions which actually prevailed, their belief that the millennium was just round the corner. They accepted the organisation of society as they found it, with king, aristocrat, philosopher, merchant, and peasant all in their various ranks. "All was for the best in the best of all possible worlds"—or could soon be made so, if only reason were allowed full play. Civilisation was for them the highest good, and the task of reason to extend its blessings uniformly over a uniform world.

To this world, with its ideals of clarity and tolerance, its belief in the perfectibility of mankind through the ordered advance of civilisation, there came a voice from beyond the Rhine which swept it all away with bitter scorn. Its ideals were those of the civilised townsman ; now there came one who opposed nature to their culture, the country to the town. Their very postulates were rejected ; to the question whether the progress of science and art had contributed to the elevation of morals Rousseau answered with a resounding "No!" The dignity of humanity was for him more important than any mere artificial distinctions of rank ; to be a man in itself the proudest title of all. The nearer to nature the better, and the humble, common man was more fortunate than a king. A prince was the victim of his rank and calling ; to a prince who consulted him Rousseau began his reply with the characteristic words, "Si j'avais eu le malheur d'être né prince." "Whoever lies in the arm of a friend," says Julius von Tarent in Leisewitz's play, "let him in his happiness not forget the unfortunate, and sometimes pay to good princes the tribute of a tear."

Mere book-learning was treated with contempt ; it was more important to read in the book of nature. Stress was laid above all on those deeper elements in human nature the lack of appreciation for which was the chief weakness of Enlightenment, on instinct and impulse. Heart and feeling became the new watchwords, before whose forum all things were brought, in place of being subjected to the cool scrutiny of reason. Many of these ideas had, to be sure, already been present in German minds, but it was Rousseau who first gave them their pregnant and effective expression.

THINKERS OF THE REVOLUTIONARY ERA

The story has often been told of the unheard-of event that occurred in Königsberg one day in the year 1762.

> Not the great clock of the cathedral [writes Heine] performed its daily round more regularly and dispassionately than its countryman, Immanuel Kant. Getting up, drinking coffee, writing, lecturing, eating, and walking, everything had its appointed time, and the neighbours knew for certain that it must be half-past three when Immanuel Kant, in his frock-coat, cane in hand, stepped from his door and walked to the little avenue of limes, which is still called after him the Philosopher's Walk. Eight times he paced up and down, whatever the season and whatever the weather.

One day, however, he was not to be seen on his daily walk; he was sitting at home reading Rousseau's *Émile*, with its passionate rejection of the whole hierarchy of his busy, contented world.

In the lectures of this *Privatdozent*, whose fame was all to come, there sat a pale, shy youth named Herder, who was introduced by him to Rousseau's world, and who was the critical founder of the Storm and Stress, even as his Strassburg pupil, Goethe, was its protagonist. When in 1774 Goethe's *Leiden des jungen Werther* appeared, and transplanted to German soil the world of feeling of Rousseau's *Nouvelle Héloïse*, it let loose the flood, and emotionalism for a time ran riot. Much has been written of the Werther fever in Germany and its excesses. Its outward and visible sign was the Werther uniform, itself a symbolic defiance of all the stiff ceremonial of that world which Rousseau despised. Not only young poets and dreamers were affected; we know that Napoleon was a great admirer of the work, which, as he told Goethe in their interview at Jena in 1806, he had taken with him to Egypt, and had read seven times. Karl August, as whose guest Goethe went to Weimar in 1775, himself wore the dress and shared in the extravagances, and the wildest stories spread of the doings of the monarch and his poet friend. The aristocrats and the dignitaries were enraged by the 'naturalness' of the relationship between prince and *bourgeois*. The Duke was so far inspired by the new ideas as to declare that people with dignity and fine manners were not worth the name of honest men, and that he could not endure people who had not something blunt and rough about them!

240

Rousseau's assumption of a primitive state of nature and innocence was historically unsound, and not even original, and he never arrived at any consistent conception of what he meant by nature. He was a man of genuine feelings and confused ideas, as Lamartine said, or, as others have put it, the first of the Romantics. But for all that he had a wonderful influence, not only in the world of thought, but in the domain of practical life. Men did try to find a more natural way of life and a more natural relationship to their fellow-men. They learnt to prize fresh air and cold water and country life. They tried to harden themselves, and Court dandies slept at night by a camp-fire in the forest, revelled in hard walking and hard riding, and in the dangers of the chase. Hermitages sprang up everywhere, like Goethe's *Gartenhaus* and Karl August's *Borckenhäuschen*, which faced one another across the Ilm in the Weimar park. Even if this nature-cult was sometimes rather an affectation, it did represent on the whole something genuine and beneficial. This teacher, who made such a mess of his own life, was accepted as a guide in the conduct of life by the fashionable people of the day; at his bidding the women of Society began to rear and nurse their own children again.

Above all in the field of education Rousseau had an immediate and lasting effect. His *Émile* awakened a lively and widespread interest. Basedow, who had already propounded views on a reform of the education of youth, was stirred to produce his *Elementarwerk* in 1774, and in the same year his *Philanthropin* was opened in Dessau. In 1781 Pestalozzi published his *Lienhard und Gertrud*, voicing the belief that moral education, the foundation of all culture, should start with the mother, and moral influence spread from the family to the community and the State. It was followed in 1807 by *Wie Gertrud ihre Kinder lehrt*, the recognised exposition of the Pestalozzian method. Pestalozzi's work was the culmination of the pedagogic movement of the eighteenth century, and we shall see shortly the part it played in the hands of Fichte in the regeneration of the State.

Many causes, no doubt, contributed, but to Rousseau's influence, more than to any one thing, was due that remarkable effervescence of German youth which is known as the Storm and Stress. Lenz, for instance, described *La Nouvelle Héloïse* as the best book that had ever been printed in French letters, while Klinger declared *Émile* to be "the first book of the new age." The men of the Storm and Stress were known at first as the *Original- und Kraftgenies*; originality, force, and genius were their great watchwords. Their cardinal doctrine was that no two men are alike, any more than any two roses are alike; that there are no such things as classes, but only individuals. The great interest taken in personality is seen in the popularity of the study of physiognomy, as exemplified by Lavater's famous work, the *Physiognomische Fragmente*, for which some of his most famous contemporaries not only furnished contributions, but stood themselves as models. Moreover, this individualistic conception applied also to nations. Herder above all emphasised the importance of building on the individual genius of a people, and that only through its own innate qualities, and not through the imitation of any other nation, however great, could a people achieve its destiny. We see the beginnings of that nationalism the morbid exaggeration of which was to prove one of the evils of a later time.

There was a fiery reaction against all the restrictions of organised society. "Law has never produced any great man," says Karl Moor in Schiller's *Räuber*, "but freedom breeds colossi and supermen." Learning and all settled ranks and professions were looked upon with scorn. The political element was, it is true, less marked than with Rousseau; the enthusiastic worship of freedom was of a somewhat vague and negative nature, being concerned rather with the rejection of restraint than with any constructive policy. Yet, for all the Enlightenment found in some states, there was tyranny enough to arouse genuine indignation. Some of the writers themselves suffered bitterly under the oppression of their rulers. The poet Schubart, for instance, was imprisoned by the Duke of Würtemberg for ten years in the Castle of Hohenasperg for the revolutionary tone of his writings. The note of revolt was most marked in the youthful plays of Schiller, who had suffered under the bullying and repression of the same ruler. *Die Räuber*, which appeared in 1781, bore on the second edition the motto "*In Tirannos.*" *Kabale und Liebe*, produced in 1784, reflects his personal acquaintance with the Court of Würtemberg, typical of the corruption of many such Courts, and a glaring light is thrown on two of the chief scandals of the time, the part played by princely mistresses, and the sale of soldiers for service in the American war.

As the century progresses through the seventies and eighties, and the storm drew on in France, it might well have been thought that Germany too was heading for a revolution. There were many similarities in the two countries, but at the same time there were great differences. In France the concentration of the State made possible an overthrow of the whole system in one great cataclysm. German *Kleinstaaterei*, the division into a large number of small states, made one great combined movement impossible, and the ruler was a much more ready and present terror and dealer of vengeance. Another and more profound difference was the absence of any truly revolutionary temper in the German character, as history has demonstrated over and over again.

So when at last the Revolution did break out in France, after a brief initial enthusiasm, in which men acclaimed with fervour the new dawn of humanity and envied the French for their glorious *rôle*, the more thoughtful turned away with horror at its excesses. The French Revolution drove Germany in upon itself, and the German revolution that actually befell was an inward and spiritual one.

The Germany upon which the flood-tide of the Revolution beat was a ramshackle empire, a relic from the lumber-room of the Middle Ages, the leadership of which, originally electoral and determined on the whole by merit, had passed into the hereditary keeping of one of the most effete and un-German of dynasties. Force failed, and the Prussia which had just lost its great philosopher-king went down no less than the Holy Roman Empire under Habsburg leadership, of which it formed a part. When Napoleon was beaten in the end it was by a Prussia reborn not in the spirit of the rationalist Frederick the Great, but in the spirit of that German idealism which will be ever associated with the great name of Kant.

We have already seen how Kant first came into contact

with Rousseau's world. If hitherto he had lived content, with modest pride in his place in the scheme of things, convinced that knowledge was the glory of mankind, Rousseau turned his thoughts to political problems, and made of him, in theory at least, a democrat. He too was at first thrilled by the mighty events in France, in which he thought he saw the inauguration of that reign of reason and universal liberty which had long been the utopian dream he shared with his fellow-thinkers. Yet before the crude realisation in fact of those pure ideals his hesitating practical nature and the innate conservatism of a subject of Frederick's firm-knit State revealed themselves. So he effects a compromise between the social contract and the absolutist State, and would separate the executive from the legislative functions. All laws must, it is true, be sanctioned by the popular will, but there must be no rebellion against the executive power, since that would lead to anarchy and destroy the foundations of the State. So he would harmonise freedom and obedience in the community, and combine a republican representative constitution with submission to the supreme authority. His famous treatise *Zum ewigen Frieden*, which appeared in 1795, was an attempt to place the relations of the various states to one another on the same foundations of law and reason as prevailed within the individual state.

More important than Kant's direct political doctrine was the tonic influence of his idealistic philosophy. The historic importance of his "Copernican Revolution" lies in the fact that it shook the absolutism of naturalistic philosophy and freed men's thoughts from the oppression of a belief in the necessity of natural law. It demonstrated the limitations of human reason, and placed the ideas of freedom, God, and immortality, which reason cannot prove, outside its jurisdiction, as necessary postulates of practical reason.

He begins his *Grundlegung der Metaphysik der Sitten* with the sentence: "There is nothing conceivable in the world, or outside it, which can be regarded as good without qualification, except only a good will." He knew, he said, nothing more sublime than the starry heavens above us and the moral law in man; and laid down unconditionally his categorical imperative: "Act as though you could will the maxim of your action to become a universal law." By the end of the century

Kant's philosophy had its representatives in most of the German universities, and above all in Jena. Nor was its influence confined to the professional philosophers, but directly, and perhaps even more indirectly, his teaching, abstruse though it was in form, had a far-reaching influence on the nation. For the German people as a whole, not Königsberg, where Kant lived and wrote, nor Jena, whence his philosophy was propounded to the world, stands as the symbol of the great flowering of German idealism, but Weimar, where the new ideals were incorporated in living figures of poetic creation.

Goethe and Schiller had already, before the outbreak of the French Revolution, turned away from the revolutionary ardour of their youth. With Goethe the revolt had been, even in the days of *Götz*, vague and romantic, and never a matter of political theory. The whole trend of his thought led him to a belief in ordered evolution, not revolution, and he had no faith in mass reform. Schiller was of a more genuinely reforming temperament, and he had more cause in his own life for protest and revolt. Yet he soon realised that physical freedom is unattainable in this world; that we cannot return to the postulated ' nature ' of primitive man. Not the sensuous natural man is truly free. Man is not born free, but must conquer his freedom for himself. It is not possible to control external circumstances, so man must rise above them—make himself captain of his soul and snatch moral victory from physical defeat. That is the lesson of all his last great plays, written in the years that preceded the battle of Jena. He had devoted three years to the study of Kant, and the influence of Kant's philosophy is plainly seen. He too accepted moral obligation as the highest law, as opposed to the expediency and utilitarianism, the comfortable eudæmonism of the Enlightenment. But he modifies the stern austerity of Kant; for him the highest type of man is he who does his duty with inclination, for whom duty and inclination are one, whose whole nature has attained to such harmony that moral action flows naturally from it.

In this Weimar idealism the one-sidedness of Enlightenment, in its reliance on the omnipotence of reason, and the one-sidedness of the Storm and Stress, in its undue emphasis of feeling and passion, are reconciled in a higher unity. From the dreary political and social conditions the Weimar idealists turned to seek salvation in an æsthetic and philosophic cultivation of the individual. Their ideal was the *Schöne Seele*, the "beautiful soul," in which moral action has become second nature, in which the good, the true, and the beautiful are fully harmonised. It was an attempt to realise Greek ideals in the modern world; an austere ideal, open, perhaps, to the reproof of being aristocratic and exclusive, and which aroused the contempt of the politically minded "Young Germans" of the thirties of the next century. It was self-culture, but not for selfish ends. Goethe undoubtedly felt that in the cultivation of his own powers he was performing his highest service to humanity; that only through the portals of self could he pass to the fullest service of his fellow-men.

If a charge of indifference is brought against the poets and thinkers of the age, it could with most justice be levelled against the leaders of the Romantic movement, especially in its earlier stages. They were the "German ideologists," who perhaps deserved some of Napoleon's scorn. In their indifference to the simple duties of the plain citizen and patriot they no doubt contributed to the disintegration of the German people, which laid it prostrate at the feet of the conqueror. In the pride of their unfettered personality they stood "ironically" above the world of reality. "Die Welt wird Traum, der Traum wird Welt." The fairy-story is their supreme literary type, and they lived, amid all the world-stirring events of the early years of the century, in a dream-world of their own. They looked down, with a more profound contempt even than the men of the Storm and Stress, on all commonplace *bourgeois* philistine service to the community, and upon all common *bourgeois* notions of morality. In contrast to the forward-looking optimism and belief in progress of Enlightenment, they looked backwards to the Middle Ages, an idealised Middle Ages, which lived only in their imagination, and had no relation to the historical reality. What attracted them in it above all was the æsthetic glamour of Catholicism and that unity of belief the destruction of which through the Enlightenment they held to be responsible for all the modern dissolution and decay. In its later phases, it is true, this glorification of

246

Germany's past took the form of an exaggerated national consciousness and a championship of the alliance of throne and altar which played into the hands of the reactionary forces, and was one of the contributory causes of the national rivalries which were to lead to such disastrous results.

But whatever its aberrations and incidental weaknesses, German idealism stored up a reserve of moral and spiritual power which needed only the harsh teachings of calamity to turn it into an irresistible force of national rejuvenation. The whole age was steeped in pedagogic interests, and the great national catastrophe found a crusader who could point in the darkest hour of all to an ideal education as the only hope of salvation, and give defeated Germany its soul and its pride again by proclaiming boldly its supremacy in the things of the spirit. Prussia lay apparently helpless at the feet of the conqueror when in the winter of 1807–8 Fichte delivered in Berlin, to the roll of French drums beneath his windows, his *Reden an die deutsche Nation*. There is no harking back here to past glories; no consolation from the wonders of the German past. He tells these defeated Germans that the world is looking to them and the world needs them; that without them the world will be lost. He seeks salvation in education —not of the few, but of all in the whole German fatherland of all the German states.

He has come now to a conception of the State very different from the cold acceptance of the Enlightenment or the calculated bargain of the social contract, or even his own earlier attitude. He had begun, in 1793, as an ardent champion of the ideas of the French Revolution, with an impassioned demand for freedom of thought and a fiery denunciation of tyranny and oppression. Three years later, in 1796, in his *Grundlage des Naturrechts*, he had advanced so far as to believe that a republic was suitable only for those long accustomed to order and justice, while for others a monarchical rule was necessary. In the following year appeared his treatise *Der geschlossene Handelsstaat*, in which he makes the State responsible for the material welfare of its citizens. It has to determine the work of each and see that such work secures its due reward. It must regulate the economic life,

247

and control export and import, production and distribution, and prices. Impracticable as many of its ideas were, it foreshadowed much of the socialistic thought of the coming years. If earlier the State was for him a "night-watchman," a police institution for the preservation and guardianship of life and property, within which the individual had his own inalienable rights, he is at this stage prepared to thrust upon it great responsibilities. Even before Jena his matured conception of the State is foreshadowed in a course of lectures delivered at Berlin, in 1804–5, on *Die Grundzüge des gegenwärtigen Zeitalters*, though his full conversion to the national faith was only completed by the great *débâcle*.

His conception of the State is the essential feature of the *Reden an die deutsche Nation*. We have a complete change from the old individualistic doctrine to one in which the State has the right to demand everything, even life itself, from its citizens. There can be no limits to the sacrifices it has the right to demand ; none shall say "thus far and no farther" when the supreme issues are at stake. The State is, in his own words, "the supreme arbiter of human affairs, and as the guardian of all who have not attained their majority, and responsible only to God and its own conscience, has a perfect right to compel them for their own good." It is to be no mechanistic form, but a living organism built up, from its foundation in the education of the child by its mother, through the education of the family, to the self-conscious and nationally educated State. He expounds a system of national education conceived, as he says, in the spirit of Pestalozzi. He would like to make this education compulsory for all, and holds that the State has a perfect right so to do, but would be prepared, as a concession, to grant some exemptions, such as had been granted from military service.

The *Reden* end with a fiery and eloquent peroration, in which he turns to men of all ages and ranks, telling them that now is the hour that will brook no delay, and that he calls upon them in the name not of Germany alone, but of the whole world. Fichte was one who looked reality in the face and called for deeds, not words, for clear resolves, not dreams. "Im Traum erringt man solche Dinge nicht," the tragic Romanticist Heinrich von Kleist told his fellow-Romantics

248

in his patriotic play, the *Prinz Friedrich von Homburg*, preaching the " Prussian State religion," the subordination of individual caprice to the necessity of the whole. Kleist's voice was not heard, and he left a world of which he despaired, but the voice of Fichte did not fall on deaf ears.

That reorganisation and rebirth of the Prussian State in the years after the battle of Jena which is associated with the names of Stein, Hardenberg, and Humboldt was inspired by the moral idealism of Kant as moulded to ideals of social service by Fichte. We meet everywhere with the same leading thought—that the nation must be roused to a sense of political responsibility and independence. From his experience Stein had gained the conviction that any reconstruction of the State must begin from below, and that mere constitutional forms are useless if not based on a sound and free administrative system. His great and outstanding reform was that effected by his *Edikt* of 1807—the Habeas Corpus Act of Prussia, as Schön calls it—by which serfdom was abolished for the great majority of the citizens of the State. At the same time it destroyed at one blow the old rigorous barriers between the estates, and freed labour no less than property, securing to all the right of entry to any trade or profession.

In calling the nation to active participation in public life he held it useless to begin with the recently and partially emancipated peasants. It was upon the towns that he staked his hopes. And so he effected that reform which he always expressly claimed as his own, however far his other reforms might be but the realisation of ideas that had long been in the air. By his *Städte-Ordnung* of 1808 the towns received the independent administration of their own finances, of their poor law and education, and might be required by the State to undertake responsibility for the police. They were even granted fiscal autonomy—a very doubtful blessing! With the abolition of the privileges of the guilds, all citizens were made equal and enjoyed equal rights. But at the same time— and this is the characteristic new note of the age—equal rights carried with them equal duties, and all citizens were bound to undertake all communal offices. And over all was

249

placed an elected magistracy, whose office was honorary, or virtually so.

It is difficult to over-estimate the importance of this measure, which put something new and vital in the place of the old and outlived system of caste distinctions and hampering monopolies, under which the German cities had languished for centuries. Under the guilds in the Middle Ages the towns had flourished and prospered; now there dawned for them a new era of prosperity. His *Städte-Ordnung* became the starting-point for German self-administration, and upon it were based all the new communal laws, which for two centuries, while Parliamentarianism was still immature and incomplete, formed the most reliable and assured feature of popular liberty in Germany.

Stein also planned a great fiscal reform : to break with the old domestic conception of budgeting, by which expenses depended on income, and introduce the modern method of high finance, by which revenue is dependent on expenditure; but this particular boon he was prevented by circumstances from conferring on his country! In 1809 he was forced to resign, and in his parting words to his officials reviewed the great innovations of this great year in a document which was long held in honour as the programme of the constitutional parties. In barely a twelvemonth he had effected changes which laid the foundations of Prussia's future greatness. Another achievement of the time in which Stein took a part was the introduction of universal military service—an idea that was implicit in much of the theory of the State at the time, and an essential feature of Fichte's programme in his *Reden*. The actual work stands mainly to the credit of Scharnhorst, who had round him a group of younger men fully in sympathy with the ideas of the age, and who looked upon the army, the "nation in arms," as one of the chief instruments for the education of the people.

The great educational work of this first decade of the century was crowned by the foundation in 1810 of the University of Berlin. When by the Peace of Tilsit Prussia lost some half of its territory, and in consequence, among other universities, that of Halle, the professors of Halle had begged for permission to transplant their university to Berlin.

The King, however, replied that he was going to establish a
new university in Berlin, adding the often-quoted words,
which might well stand as a motto for the Prussian idealists
of the time : "The State must make good in spiritual power
what it has lost in physical resources." Fichte was its first
Rector, while its inception was due above all to Wilhelm von
Humboldt, formerly an intimate friend of Schiller. Humboldt
was, from the spring of 1809, Prussian Minister of Education
for a little more than a year, and in that brief time did much
to foster the spirit of freedom in Prussian education. It was
intended from the first to be a university not for any one
province, but a royal Prussian university, and furthermore,
in the spirit of Fichte, a university for the whole greater
German fatherland. It was to have absolute freedom for both
teacher and taught, and as its prime purpose not professional
training, but the search for scientific truth. Among the band
of distinguished men who were summoned to occupy its chairs
were the bearers of such names as Fichte, Schleiermacher, and
Niebuhr ! This brilliant foundation of a brilliant university
in the capital of a vanquished State is a symbolic manifestation of the spirit of the age !

How this newly awakened sense of national unity fired the
imagination of Germany, and especially of her youth, and how
in the great uprising the yoke of foreign domination was
triumphantly shaken off, is an oft-told tale. All the succeeding
phases which have been here traced were ages of affirmation.
One hope succeeded another. The faith in reason was followed
by that in heart and feeling and the beneficence of nature.
In the pre-Revolutionary days there were, indeed, giants and
ogres in the path, but they only barred the way to a millennium!
Then when the French Revolution broke out hope soared
heaven-high. As in the flush of the Renaissance Ulrich von
Hutten could cry exultingly, " The sciences flourish, the arts
prosper. It is a joy to be alive," so men spoke now of this
new dawn of humanity. In Germany the very disillusionment
with the French Revolution was followed by one of the most
soaring flights of the human spirit—by the "great day" in
the life of the nation, as its own spokesmen have said.

And what happened in our own day, when at the end of
the Great War, in which Germany had not been spared the

greatest disillusion, after one of the mildest and most benevolent of revolutions, so characteristic of Germany, the country
again lay prostrate at the feet of a conqueror, as it had lain
a hundred years before ? Then the new German democracy
chose as the place for the meeting of its Constituent Assembly
not Berlin, or any other of the great towns, but, as Dr Gooch
says, "the German Athens, where Goethe counted for more
than Bismarck." It was not alone the convenience of its
central position ; not even the fact, if it had been considered,
that Weimar in 1816 was the first German state to receive
a constitution. Practical reasons no doubt counted for much ;
but if the first National Assembly met in Goethe's theatre,
before which stands Rietschel's famous statue of the two great
friends, it was above all because Weimar was a great symbol:
a symbol of that spiritual strength through which, when
equally powerless, Germany had once before raised itself from
material defeat.

And surely not Germany alone might still, even in this
twentieth century, find much to learn, and no mean inspiration, in that categorical affirmation of the moral law and that
mellowed conception of a harmonious development of the
totality of human character which were the great achievement
of the age of German idealism.

H. G. ATKINS

BOOK LIST

BOEHN, MAX VON : *Deutschland im 18. Jahrhundert.* Berlin, 1922.

FRANCKE, KUNO : *A History of German Literature as determined by Social Forces.*
New York, 1901.

GOOCH, G. P. : *Germany and the French Revolution.* London, 1920.

GOOCH, G. P. : *Germany.* London, 1926.

TREITSCHKE, HEINRICH VON : *Deutsche Geschichte im Neunzehnten Jahrhundert*
(Erstes Buch). Leipzig, 1879.

ZIEGLER, T. : *Die geistigen und socialen Strömungen des neunzehnten Jahr-
hunderts* (vol. i of *Das Neunzehnte Jahrhundert in Deutschlands Entwick-
lung*). Berlin, 1899.

DATE DUE

MAR 5 '74			
OC 30 '78			
FE 1 9 '80			
OC 14 '82			
GAYLORD			PRINTED IN U.S A.